An Explorers Club Book

House of Tears

WESTERNERS' ADVENTURES IN ISLAMIC LANDS

Edited and with an Introduction by Dr. John Hughes

THE LYONS PRESS
Guilford, Connecticut
AN IMPRINT OF THE GLOBE PEQUOT PRESS

The Lyons Press is an imprint of The Globe Pequot Press.

10 9 8 7 6 5 4 3 2 1

Printed in United States of America

"Lawrence the Train-Wrecker" from *With Lawrence in Arabia* by Lowell Thomas, Sr.,
copyright © 2005 by Lowell Thomas. Reprinted with permission.

ISBN 1-59228-799-9

Library of Congress Cataloging-in-Publication Data

House of tears : westerners adventures in Islamic lands / John Hughes.
     p. cm.
   Includes index.
   "An Explorers Club Book".
   ISBN 1-59228-799-9 (trade cloth)
  1. Islamic countries—Description and travel. 2. Adventure and adventurers. 3.
Travelers—Europe. 4. Travelers—United States. I. Hughes, John, 1960-
DS35.57.H68 2005
910'.917'67—dc22

                              2005022243

Contents

Acknowledgments

House of Tears is dedicated to my wife, Heidi, and son, Tristan. They bore the brunt of my working on this project.

My parents are due thanks for encouraging my love of history and supporting my educational and career goals.

Many others deserve gratitude. Novelist, journalist, playwright, and friend John MacLachlan Gray taught me how to write and is my guru in many other matters. Mystery buffs must read his Victorian whodunits. His countless hours of inspiring discussion made this book possible. His wife, Beverlee, was a supportive and wise friend. My colleague Verne Becott at St. George's School made it possible to teach and write at the same time. Headmaster Nigel Toy supported my interests; there is no better leader in the educational world. My former student Teddy Harrison, now a scholar of politics and history, helped me throughout this project. Other friends gave support: Marie Ingram, Boyd McClymont, and Christine Wessler in particular. I owe my students at St. George's School, Vancouver, British Columbia, Canada for their tolerance and special gift of reminding me how much fun and educational a good story can be. Michael Pixley of Eastern Approaches Books, Ireland, gave key advice. Ellen Scordato of Stone Song Press, New York, is a heaven-sent agent. Holly Rubino, my editor at The Lyons Press, turned a manuscript into a book. Fellow traveller, John Tyler, chair of History at Groton School, Massachusetts, indulged my visit to the House of Tears in 1994, which planted the seed for this collection and its title.

Introduction

My encounters with the Islamic world began with the taste of a warm glass of flat Coke. This drink was a gift from a café owner. It was 1971, and I was a twelve-year-old Canadian sitting at an outdoor grill café on a street in Segangane, Morocco.

Although the Coke tasted terrible, I did not want to refuse the hospitality. I sat at my table under a twig-and-pole canopy, drinking the Coke and smiling, watched by the local men. The air was scented with the heat of the dirt road, bundles of mint hanging in the café, and cigarettes. With me—as ever during my stay—was a semi-wild creature I had imaginatively named "Dog." My father said she and the pack she roamed with were hunting dogs left behind by Spanish colonists when Morocco gained independence. She was my constant companion. Whenever I walked from the compound where my family and those of the other foreign engineers lived, I leashed her up and strode confidently out of the gate, past the old watchman with his shoulder-slung rifle.

Accompanied by Dog, I had no fear. We developed a daily routine which included dropping by the café for sun-warmed Coke. My money was always refused. Without words or tension, or the sense of being an intruder—except that I was so gently and solemnly welcomed—I sat across from Berbers. My father had explained to me that the Berbers were the original inhabitants of North Africa before the interloping Punics, Romans, and Arabs had arrived. They were hardened men, resting there after a shift in the mines, or the mill that made pellets from iron ore. Although we didn't share a language, we managed pleasant interludes, Dog skulking behind my chair. I wondered— and I still wonder—what those men thought of me. I do know that in the weeks I visited with them, a kindness, even affection, was expressed. Although to them I must have been an absurd enigma laughably out of place, they never showed it.

My memories of Segangane range from imprecise to vivid. I cannot remember the layout of the settlement, but I can recall with clarity the hand of a prisoner shoved through the little barred hole in a solid-green cell door at a grotty gendarme post. Soiled fingers quivered a twist of paper—an appeal for a cigarette, I supposed. No one paid any notice, it seemed, except me, waiting there for my father to finish some business with the police. The man whispered too softly for me to hear his words.

Segangane was next to an iron mine called Setolazar. The mine's name was composed of letters plucked from the surnames of the Spanish partners who had founded it in 1906. Maps now show only a town called Segangane. My recollection of Setolazar is of a compound of villas and bungalows partially enclosed by a wall and green cactus hedges. Across from its main gate was the native town. The compound was formerly occupied by Spanish colonists until the mine was nationalized in 1968, fifteen years after Moroccan independence was achieved in 1953.

Colonists' homes were part Moorish, part Art Deco, resembling Mission architecture in the United States. Across from the compound, on the edge of the native settlement, was the closed-up Spanish church. To me, it was as exciting as living in an excavated African Pompeii. Artifacts abandoned by the colonists—both strange and ordinary—were so ubiquitous that it seemed to me they might come back and eject us squatters.

Our villa's cutlery was engraved with the Spanish company's initials. Over the kitchen door was a row of numbers that flipped up when a button was pressed in another room to summon a servant—we never used it, out of sheer distaste. My mother's housekeeper was a Berber woman we called Louisa, the Spanish name her old employers had foisted upon her. Jagged, miniature tattoos in the shapes of god's eyes, fish skeletons, and zigzags guarded her eyes and mouth against infestation by *jinn*—spirits. Once she held her face close to let me take a good look. Our house was near the clubhouse, where the unmarried engineers ate their meals. I would go there to listen to the BBC at night, and to enjoy the bonhomie inspired by whiskey and beer and funny stories about the day's travails.

I don't think my father and mother liked being in Setolazar. His company had sent him there to supervise the reopening of the mine on a contract with the Moroccan government. Successful experiences in mines around the world scarcely helped him there. At dinner he would describe that day's calamities: flawed machinery, untrained native workers, engineers who seemed prone to mishaps—so many problems, and all tied to the unrealistic schedule. Most of all, he worried that he simply could not—no matter how good a mining engineer he was—complete a project that was overpriced, instigated by corrupt officials, and simply not a sound economic proposition. He felt sorry for the local Berbers whose hopes for better times were fixed on a goliath miscalculation. The iron ore was of a quality too poor to support the expensive new mine and processing mill.

It was clear where things were headed. Ruined Spanish mine works provided both backdrop and prophecy. A gigantic crater bottom held jade-colored sludge and rusted machinery. Ancient steam shovels and heavy equipment rotted on the edge of the Berber town. A rampart of brick chimneys and old furnaces, half shattered and crooked, crumbled near the railroad tracks. My father knew his efforts were adding to a landscape already scarred by false optimism.

I first saw a Muslim at prayer on the abandoned tennis courts in the center of the Setolazar compound. I watched from outside the fence as the compound's watchman leaned his rifle on the court wall and knelt to perform midday prayers. After he was gone, I went to where his prayers had made impressions and scuffs in the pale red clay. I felt as if I had seen something forbidden. I had no understanding of Islam, or of Muslim or Moroccan culture; the idea that hundreds of millions of people all over the world did precisely what the watchman had done did not even occur to me.

It has taken me most of my lifetime to understand how that man's solitary devotion was connected to a vast complex world called Islam—and no less time to understand how symbolic it was for me to witness his prayers taking place in derelict tennis courts originally built to serve European colonists.

No journey, either back to Morocco or to any other destination, has ever had the profound impact on me of that first stay in Setolazar. It started me asking questions and reading about Westerners in the Islamic world. As a teenager I was drawn to reading travel and adventure books like Geoffrey Moorhouse's *The Fearful Void*, about an Englishman attempting to cross the Sahara by camel. I read T. E. Lawrence's *Seven Pillars of Wisdom* several times. But it was not until much later, before a trip to Morocco in 1994, that I realized how much literature had been written by Westerners recounting their amazing experiences in Muslim countries.

While visiting the Boston Athenaeum, that magnificent private library on Beacon Hill, I had the chance to explore one of the best collections of vintage travel and adventure I have ever seen. Unlike in many libraries, these books were readily accessible on the shelves. Seeing these books (many of them rare) up close, as opposed to on a catalog list, made me realize how many adventurers had brought back their experiences to Western readers. I wanted to know how these stories fit into the history of the relationship between the West and Islam. It led to me writing this book, which is a collection of Westerners' adventures in the Islamic world from the eighteenth to the early twentieth century. I hope that these excerpts will entice readers to explore the books in their entirety.

A constant feature of these journeys is the intimate collaboration between Muslims and Westerners. Virtually all the pilgrims in this book succeeded because their ventures were guided by Muslims who shared both their adversity and their success. There is a message in this: If we do not understand Islam, it is not because it has been closed to the West. On the contrary; what these stories show us is that Westerners have developed a vast understanding of some of the most inaccessible regions of the Muslim world, with the help of Muslims.

The chronological layout of this book is deliberate. During the mid-eighteenth century, Europeans controlled little of the Islamic world. Extensive regions of Eastern Europe, the Middle East, and North Africa were ruled by the Ottoman Empire. By the end of this book, in the year 1922, we find that the Ottoman Empire has collapsed, and Western influence has penetrated—and weakened—the entire Muslim world. The adventures in this collection reveal how Westerners have perceived the Islamic world during the two centuries of decline immediately prior to the period in which we live.

Some readers might object to the terms *the West* or *Westerner*. Admittedly, they are archaic and extremely imprecise. For the purposes of this book, these terms refer to North America and Europe. While millions of Muslims now live in these parts of the world, this was not the case when these adventures took place.

Equally difficult is the task of defining the Islamic world. Muslims enrich the culture of every inhabited region on earth. I use *Islamic world* to signify the regions and countries where Muslims predominate. But it is important to keep in mind that the Muslim world then and now was not in any sense homogeneous. Few Westerners appreciate how diverse the Muslim world is. Many of the stories in this collection give indications of the varieties of ethnic, cultural, and religious beliefs within Islam that existed in the past and are no less significant today.

Why were these writers and stories selected?

Writers in this collection were not bystanders; they took risks. They not only saw the Muslim world—they had to survive it. Adventure intensifies encounters. It sharpens the conclusions drawn about other people because so much is at stake. Most of these stories involve journeys; many Westerners traveled through the Islamic world not to study Muslims but to get to places within that world. Reaching Timbuktu, for example, was a kind of Grail quest for nineteenth-century Saharan explorers. And crossing the Sahara did not require hostility from the natives to make it dangerous.

I had other criteria in mind, as well; I wanted variety. These adventurers are of several nationalities: Hungarian, German, French, Venezuelan, British, and American. But I also wanted their books to be available to readers. All of these titles can be found in English, which explains the prevalence of British writers. Four of the writers are women with experiences that shatter stereotypes. Several of these books have not been reprinted, and some are less-well-known works by major writers—lost or nearly forgotten treasures. Thus, American journalist John Reed, best known for *Ten Days that Shook the World*—his book about the Russian Revolution—is included, but his excerpt is from *The War in Eastern Europe*, a title unfamiliar to many. Author T. E. Lawrence is not included; he is available and well known. But Lowell Thomas's book about Lawrence of Arabia is in the collection because it is so important to how the West imagined, and still imagines, the Middle East. More people should read it than do. Lawrence is the archetype of the "liberating" Westerner who supposedly led Arabs to freedom and nationhood. Lawrence's adventures came to the world's attention through Thomas, and the consequences of that myth-making still haunt events in the Middle East today.

Each adventure has a short introduction to explain the journey and its historical context. A common feature in these stories is that they resonate with readers today, making us consider how the legacy of interaction between the West and Islam in the past connects to current events. One example especially shows how troubling this resonance can be.

In 1921, Zetton Buchanan and her family went to Iraq to develop an irrigation system at Shahraban to help local farmers. The British were rebuilding Iraq after liberating it from the Ottoman Empire, thanks to T. E. Lawrence. Insurgents killed her husband and made her a hostage until British troops freed her. Buchanan's bitterness and reproach against her own government for underestimating the hostility of some tribes to British occupation, and her own harrowing imprisonment, sounds all too familiar. Her writing is not just an adventure—it's a chance to ponder why things have come around to this, yet again. In 2003 I read a report that Hans Blix sent teams inspecting for weapons of mass destruction to Shahraban and found nothing but damaged agricultural equipment warehouses. Two years later, U.S. troops garrisoned the town, skirmishing with the new insurgents.

Thirty-three years ago I drank sun-warmed Coke in a place named Segangane, Morocco. Above the town was a ruined Spanish Foreign Legion post that once guarded the mine and colony against Berber rebels. That started me wondering what the distance between past and present really is; surely part of the answer is that without knowing the past, we have no means of gauging if we have crossed into new realms of experience, or are merely replaying old ones.

While I was considering a title for this book, the palace of the Moroccan warlord Ahmed el Raisuni, came to my mind. Raisuni built his palace in 1909 using forced labor and paid for it with ransom money extracted from the United States government in exchange for the life of Ion Perdicaris, a Greek-American (whose story appears later in this collection). Besides being a *sherif* (a descendent of the Prophet), Raisuni's staggering capacity for violence and audacious crimes made him both heroic and terrifying to his people. The resentful townspeople of Asilah, whom Raisuni coerced into labor, named the palace the "House of Tears." The name stuck and is still used in guidebooks to this day. Raisuni kidnapped three prominent Westerners, and his exploits were celebrated in the writings of Western adventurers, including two of his former captives. Interestingly, all his Western hostages became his friends. Even Walter B. Harris, the *London Times* correspondent Raisuni had kidnapped in 1903, was a regular visitor to the House of Tears. On one occasion Harris felt comfortable enough to bring two young English ladies. During luncheon, Raisuni "with the sweetest of smiles, and in the most successful endeavour to interest his young lady guests" told of throwing a prisoner out the window to the sea rocks below the chamber where he entertained them.

The House of Tears is a setting where allegorical collisions of friendship and conflict, fascination and horror, real events and half-truths give insights to the Islamic-Western relationship as experienced by the adventurers in this book. The collection that follows contains only fragments of a long list of encounters and only from the relatively recent past. But it is a start whereby we may begin to understand today's events and the journeys that led here.

—John Hughes

Adventures of Thomas Pellow

T H O M A S   P E L L O W

from *The Adventures of Thomas Pellow, of Penyn, Mariner,* 1890

Morocco: 1720. Thousands of ears, hacked from severed heads, are rotting on the walls of Meknes. Recently unpacked from barrels of salt, the ears were war trophies sent to the capital. An imperial army had destroyed the rebel town of Guzlan and massacred all the defenders—after they had surrendered.

Sultan Moulay Ishmael was disappointed by these prizes; he had expected thousands of heads. Apologetically, the victorious general explained that the reek of so many heads was unbearable, so he had salted the ears and stowed them in barrels to be transported north to Meknes. At first Moulay Ishmael considered storing the ears, to be sent as warnings to tribal leaders when necessary, but decided instead to festoon his ramparts with them.

Thomas Pellow, an English slave in the sultan's army, witnessed the slaughter at Guzlan, and the sultan's muted pleasure when the ears were presented at court. Pellow was an eleven-year-old crew member on his uncle's ship when he was captured in 1715 by pirates from Sale in Morocco. *Xebecs* (fast pirate ships) from this city raided as far north as Ireland. Pellow was nearly killed on the way back; at the entrance to Sale's harbor, a British ship attacked and sank the xebecs carrying the English prisoners. Pellow survived by swimming to shore but was soon captured.

After being held in *metamores* (underground slave pens), Pellow and hundreds of English and American colonials were marched inland to Meknes, Moulay Ishmael's new capital. Moulay Ishmael (1672–1727) was a contemporary of Louis XIV. (Gilded clocks sent by the French Sun King still decorate the sultan's magnificent tomb.) Like the absolutist ruler of France, the sultan worked hard to establish his new capital city, on a scale as grand as that of Versailles. Thirty thousand European slaves, mostly Spanish—but also large numbers of Portuguese, French, Italians, and hundreds of British and Americans—labored under horrific conditions. The scale of the building projects in Meknes, which included palaces, mosques, gardens, fortifications, avenues, and a water system, dazzled European diplomats.

Originally, Pellow was selected to clean weapons in the Koubbat el Khayyatin, the imperial armory. He was noticed by the sultan and given to one of his sons, Moulay es Sfa. The prince decided that Pellow must convert to Islam. For months he tortured him, often personally, using his favorite tool, the *bastinado*. This entailed clamping Pellow's feet in stocks and beating his soles to a pulp with a wooden or metal bar. The boy renounced Christianity after months of such beatings.

Pellow's first break came in 1717, when the sultan gave him to his wife, Halima el Aziza. Now thirteen years old, Pellow was made porter in the palace quarter containing the imperial harem. Eventually, he was rewarded with a promotion—from palace slave to "Renegade," a European soldier-slave in the sultan's army—and a wife. In 1720, he took his first command (300 European troops) and his pregnant wife from Meknes to Kasbah Temsna. For the next seventeen years, he witnessed military campaigns and court intrigues, sweeping majesty and fearful brutality.

Moulay Ishmael died in 1727, and Pellow's wife and daughter died a year or so later of disease. Although the chronology is confused, in 1728–29 he made two escape attempts which are included in this excerpt. Years later, he made another attempt during a campaign on the Senegal River, which also failed. Finally, in 1737, he escaped, surviving desert travel, a vicious wound, and the pursuit of a posse to reach the coast at Wallada. There he boarded an Irish merchant ship, eventually returning home to his family in Cornwall.

Pellow's book, not published until 1890, is important because it provides personal and credible insights into the last Islamic state in North Africa vibrant and powerful enough to expand against the West. His narrative balances the usual picture of an Islam declining in the face of Western ascendancy.

—J. H.

After some time, I was taken out of the armoury, and given by the Emperor to Muley Spha, one of his favourite sons (a sad villain), born of his wife Allaobenabiz, by whom he had in all ten children, viz., seven sons and three daughters. My business now, for some time, was to run from morning to night after his horse's heels; during which he often prompted me to turn Moor, and told me, if I would, I should have a very fine horse to ride on, and I should live like one of his best esteemed friends. To which I used to reply, that as that was the only command wherein I could not readily gratify him, I humbly hoped that he would be pleased, of his great goodness, to suspend all future thoughts that way, for that I was thoroughly resolved not to renounce my Christian faith, be the consequence what it would. Then said he, in a most furious and haughty manner, "Prepare yourself for such torture as shall be inflicted on you, and the nature of your obstinacy deserves." When I humbly entreating him, on my knees, not to let loose his rage on a poor, helpless, innocent creature; he, without making any further reply, committed me prisoner to one of his own rooms, keeping me there several months in irons, and every day most severely bastinading me, and furiously screaming in the Moorish language, "Shehed, Shehed! Cunmoora, Cunmoora!" in English, "Turn Moor! turn Moor!" by holding up your finger. Of which cruelty my uncle hearing, he came one day, and with him one John Phillips, to see if it might be in their power to give me any relief; and which indeed was not, although they very heartily endeavoured it, gaining nothing by their so very kind and Christian-like intention, but many severe blows on themselves, and on me a more frequent repetition of them than before.

And now is my accursed master still more and more enraged, and my tortures daily increasing; insomuch, that had not my uncle, and some other good Christians through his means, notwithstanding his so late ill usage and repulse (even to the extreme hazard of their lives), privately conveyed me some few refreshments, I must have inevitably perished, my prison allowance being nothing but bread and water; so that I was, through my severe scourging, and such hard fare, every day in expectation of its being my last; and happy, no doubt, had I been, had it so happened: I should certainly then have dy'd a martyr, and probably thereby gained a glorious crown in the kingdom of heaven; but the Almighty did not then see it fit. My tortures were now exceedingly increased, burning my flesh off my bones by fire; which the tyrant did, by frequent repetitions, after a most cruel manner; insomuch, that through my so very acute pains, I was at last constrained to submit, calling upon God to forgive me, who knows that I never gave the consent of the heart, though I seemingly yielded, by holding up my finger; and that I always abominated them, and their accursed principle of Mahometism, my only trust and confidence being firmly fixed on Him, and in the all-sufficient merits of His only Son Jesus Christ, my Saviour.

I was kept forty days longer in prison, on my refusing to put on the Moorish habit; but I at length reflected, that to refuse this any longer was a very foolish obstinacy, since it was a thing indifferent in its own nature, seeing I had already been compelled to give my assent to Mahometism. Therefore, rather than undergo fresh torments, I also complied with it, appearing like a Mahometan; and I make no doubt but some ill-natured people think me so even to this day. I pray God to forgive them, and that it may never be their mishap to undergo the like trails; and which, if it should, that they may maintain their Christian faith no worse than I did mine.

I was now delivered once more from my prison and chains; and, at the command of the Emperor, put to school, to learn the Moorish language, and to write Arabick; and in the latter I should have certainly been a tolerable proficient, had not my master's insolence, and violent death by the Emperor's orders, prevented it; for after being with him about three months, during which he had often called me Christian dog, and most severely beat me, it coming to the Emperor's ears, he was by his order instantly despatched, by tossing him up, and so breaking his neck.

After this, I was put no more to school to learn the language, but immediately into the hands of Emhamenet Sageer, whose business was to train up and instruct youth how they should speak and behave before the Emperor, and in the war; he having for such purposes under his care about six hundred boys; and with whom I had not been above a fortnight, before I had the charge of eighty of them committed to me, I being made their Alcayde, or captain, to see they kept clean the walks (during all intervals from exercise) in the Emperor's garden, where he and his favourite Queen Hellema Hazzezas (in English the beloved) were used to walk. In this station I had not been but a very little time, when the Queen coming one day into the walks, before I had the power to hide myself in a little house set there for that purpose (and which, at her approach, we were commanded always to do), happened to see me, and the next day begged me of the Emperor, which he readily granting, ordered us immediately out one by one, till she should see the same person; and after the first, second, and third were presented, and turned back again, he ordered their captain to appear, when I instantly appeared, and the Queen saying I was the same she would have, I was forthwith given her, and by her again to her favourite son Muly Zidan, a youth of about eight years of age, and then resident with his mother in the palace of Sherrers; where she, with thirty-eight of the Emperor's concubines, and several eunuchs, were closely shut up, and to which I was made chief porter of the innermost door, that is to say, of the door next without that of the entrance into the galleries leading to the several apartments, and where none could gain admittance, but through me; as indeed none were to be admitted, the Emperor only excepted, nor him neither, in case he should offer to come, without giving notice, at an unseasonable hour; as once indeed he did, and though he had gained admittance in at the several outer doors, yet was he by me denied; for how could I tell it was him, when he was on the one side, and I on the other, of a thick door close shut; and allowing, as by his being let in at the several outer doors, and his usual way of knocking, I might have very little reason to doubt it, and which might likewise have induced me to open it, yet, what did that signify to me, when I had positive orders before (as no doubt had all the rest) to admit none after such an hour, without being before advised of it, and of some certain signs to be given accordingly on the outside of the door; and further, my orders were, that in case any one should attempt to enter at such an unseasonable hour, and not immediately depart after his first and second knocking, and denials of entrance, but should presume to knock a third time without giving the signs as aforesaid, I should then fire through the door—as indeed I had now an occasion to do.

The Emperor being admitted, as aforementioned, in at the several outer doors, and knocking at mine, I demanded aloud, "Who was there?" to which I was answered, "Muly Smine"; and which, indeed, by his voice and usual way of knocking, I was pretty well assured it was. However, I told him that I very much doubted it; for that I had never known His Excellency to come at such an unseasonable hour, without my being pre-advised thereof; and which, as I then was not, he should at his peril be gone, or I would present him with half a dozen bullets through the door, which he prayed me not to do, for that it was actually himself, and that if I would not let him in, he would certainly chop off my head the next day, knocking again louder than before; but, on the contrary, if I would admit him, he would give me such a fine horse (calling him by his name), with all the rich furniture belonging to him, and would make me a great man. I told him I would not do it if he would give me all the horses and furniture in the empire; for that as I was entrusted and commanded by the renowned Muly Smine or Ishmael, the most glorious Emperor in the world, to keep that post inviolable against all impostors and intruders whomsoever, and as I had but too much reason to believe him such, I would not on any terms open the door, be the consequence what it would, being thoroughly resolved not to betray my trust; therefore it was in vain for him any longer to persist. When he changing his note from rewards to threats, and knocking again, I fired all the bullets which I had ready by me in a blunderbuss, quite through the door, which indeed (he keeping himself close on one side, as I before imagined) could in nowise hurt him; and on his seeing my so resolute resistance, and no likelihood of his admittance, he returned as he came, highly threatening me for keeping him out, and as much commending those at the several outer doors for their so readily letting him in, assuring us that we should on neither side lose our reward; and indeed we did not, being very early in the morning all ordered out, and all those who gave him admittance had some their heads cut off, others cruelly used; and myself, after being highly commended for my fidelity, rewarded with a much finer horse than that he offered to give me in case I would betray my trust.

This palace of Sherrers is a very large spacious building (as indeed are all the Emperor's houses), and certainly prodigious strong, the walls twelve feet thick, and five stories high, built only of fine earth and hot lime, mixed and well incorporated by a vast number of slaves kept for that purpose; for it is thrown, as I may say, into a mould, being first boarded up on each side, so that being very well rammed together, it becomes, in a very little time, harder and more durable than stone. It is covered on the top with blue tiles, ceiled in the inside, and finely painted, and hath in it several hundred separate apartments for his concubines and eunuchs, besides those set apart for his favourite queen and her retinue. All his other wives (in number no less than four thousand) being closely shut up in several other sumptuous houses allotted for them; though all, as I may say adjacent, and all within the same enclosure.

My lodging was between the inner door before mentioned and that of the entrance into the galleries, leading to the several apartments; my companions six boys, and two young lions about half grown, being reared up there from whelps; but becoming unruly, their removal was desired, and complied with.

Now am I, after my hard keeping, again become in pretty good plight, being allowed very good eatables, as beef, mutton, and cuscassoo (of the nature of which I shall speak by and by), I having in a manner now nothing else to do than to eat my meat, and be careful of my young master's and the Queen's motions, and especially those of the latter, who I found was about to cut me out some new work; so that I was obliged to walk like one walking on the brink of a dangerous precipice, whence, should he happen to make but the least wry step, he is sure to tumble down and break his neck. The Queen, in short, being extremely amorous, and the Emperor no less jealous of her, which really made my condition very dangerous, and might through some unforeseen accident (let my behaviour be never so innocent), happen to prove of very bad consequence to me, therefore I thought it highly prudent to keep a very strict guard upon all my actions.

I now was strictly charged by the Emperor, on pain of losing my life, to visit my uncle every day, he saying to me, in a loud and vehement tone, "Cossam billa illamattim Shea Culsbah Occulashea bus ede Ameck Woolastan cuttarossick," that is, "If you don't go every day, morning and evening, to kiss your uncle's hand, by Allah I'll cut your head off. For if he were a brute," says he, "you are by nature obliged so to do."

This, any one may suppose, as being the only command my present inclinations could be best gratified with, did not at all terrify me, and therefore I forthwith most cheerfully put it in practice; but, alas! that pleasure was of a very short duration, he being, poor man, in a few weeks after taken off by a violent flux, as were a little before him Briant Clark, Thomas Crimes, and John Dunnal, three of our unhappy men; and I shall never forget my uncle's tender behaviour at the interment of the latter, where I and a great many other Englishmen happened to be. The corpse being brought to the grave, and no particular person appointed to read the Christian ceremony of burial, my uncle took it upon him, but indeed he was not able (through the abundance of tears flowing) to go through it, his speech being thereby to that degree obstructed, that he could only now and then utter a word imperfectly; insomuch, that he was obliged to deliver over the book to another; and never did I see such a mournful meeting, every one catching the contagion, and all standing for a considerable time in a dead silence, quite overwhelmed with grief.

I am now to expect no further comfort by way of my poor uncle; and though, indeed, I might not probably stand in so much need of him as formerly I had done, yet was it the sorest affliction I ever met with, and I could never put the remembrance of him out of my thoughts.

Now it is my chief business and greatest concern to study how to oblige the Emperor, his dear Hellema, and my young master; but the latter I confess I did not mind, though he was by nature cruel enough, and I had seen him, even in the seventeenth year of his age, kill his favourite black with his own hand, by stabbing him into the belly with a knife, and only for coming very accidentally where he was feeding a pair of pigeons, and their flying away for a few minutes. Yet, I say, I did not much mind him, as having much higher objects to observe, the Queen being in a particular manner kind, and often recommending me to the Emperor's good liking as a careful and diligent servant, as indeed I really was, so far as I thought might be consistent with my advantage and safety. But I thinking this service very precarious, and that I was every moment exposed, and in danger of her poison, or his sword, I humbly intreated her to desire the Emperor to find out for me some other employment, wherein I might be less suspected, and not altogether out of the way of obliging her; which she readily complied with, I being directly ordered by the Emperor to quit this dangerous office, and to wait on him at his palace for such future commands as should be by him enjoined me. A sudden and pleasing alteration indeed; and though my new business might be attended with more masculine exercises, yet was I well satisfied that it could not be with more danger and uneasiness, of which I was very soon confirmed, I being strictly charged to be observant of the Emperor's commands only, and to wait on him on all occasions; and when he pleased to ride out, I was generally mounted on the fine horse he gave me for my fidelity in maintaining my post at the door, always carrying at my girdle a club of about three feet long, of Brazil wood, with which he used, on any slight occasion, to knock his people on the head, as I had several times the pleasure of beholding. For, in short (although I did not know how soon it might have been my own fate), I did not care how soon they were all dead; and indeed he was of so fickle, cruel, and sanguine a nature, that none could be even for one hour secure of life. He had many despatched, by having their heads cut off, or by being strangled, others by tossing, for which he had several very dexterous executioners always ready at hand; but scarce would he on those occasions afford a verbal command, he thinking that too mean, and his words of more value than the life of the best of them, generally giving it by signs or motions of his head and hand; as, for instance, when he would have any person's head cut off, by drawing or shrinking his own as close as he could to his shoulders, and then with a very quick or sudden motion extending it; and when he would have any strangled, by the quick turn of his arm-wrist, his eye being fixed on the victims. The punishment of "tossing" is a very particular one, and peculiar to the Moors.

The person whom the Emperor orders to be thus punished, is seized upon by three or four strong negroes, who, taking hold of his hams, throw him up with all their strength, and at the same time turning him round, pitch him down head foremost; at which they are so dexterous by long use, that they can either break his neck the first toss, dislocate his shoulder, or let him fall with less hurt. They continue doing this as often as the Emperor has ordered, so that many times they are killed upon the spot; sometimes they come off with only being severely bruised; and the person that is tossed must not stir a limb, if he is able, while the Emperor is in sight, under penalty of being tossed again, but is forced to lie as if he was dead; which, if he should really be, nobody dares bury the body till the Emperor has given orders for it.

The Emperor's wrath is terrible, which the Christians have often felt. One day passing by a high wall on which they were at work, and being affronted that they did not keep time in their strokes, as he expects they should, he made his guards go up and throw them all off the wall, breaking their legs and arms, knocking them on the head in a miserable manner. Another time he ordered them to bury a man alive, and beat him down along with the mortar in the wall.

Nor is the Emperor less cruel to the Moors, whom he'll frequently command to be burnt, crucified, sawed in two, or dragged at a mule's tail through the streets, till they are torn all to pieces.

The most favourable death to die is by his hand, for then they only lose their heads, have their brains knocked out, or are run through the body, for which purpose he always has his lances ready, and is very dexterous at using them, seldom letting his hand go out for want of practice.

In the year 1721, during the time that Commodore Stewart was in Morocco as ambassador from England, the Emperor despatched, in the most cruel manner, Larbe Shott, a man of one of the best families in Barbary, being descended from the old Andalusian Moors, and deserved the esteem both of his own countrymen and of us, with whom he had lived till the time of his imprisonment; for he had been a considerable time in Gibraltar, as a pledge from the Bashaw to an English merchant, for the payment of money due for goods he had supplied the Bashaw with. Part of the crime laid to his charge was for going out of his country, and living in Christendom a considerable time, without the Emperor's knowledge, and having been friendly himself with Christian women, and often been in liquor. He was also accused of being an unbeliever, and one of those who have invited the Spaniards to invade Barbary.

These things being insinuated to the Emperor, after the usual manner of that court (where everybody has it in their power to do harm, but few to do good), brought this poor man to his end; for early one morning he was carried before the Emperor, who (not allowing him any other trial, but giving way to his accusers, who said, "He was an unbeliever, and not fit to live") commanded him to be sawed in two; upon which he was immediately carried to the place of execution, which is at one of the gates of the town, and there tied between two boards and sawed in two, beginning at the head and going downwards, till his body fell asunder, which must have remained to have been eaten by the dogs, if the Emperor had not pardoned him;—an extravagant custom, to pardon a man after he is dead; but unless he does so, nobody dares bury the body.

It was reported the next day after, that the Emperor dreamt Shott had appeared to him, and asked him, "What he had done to deserve such usage?" telling him, "There would be a time when God would judge between them both;" which gave the Emperor so much concern, that he sent to the place of his execution for some of the dust his blood was spilt on, with which he rubbed himself all over as an atonement for his crime."

The Horde of the Wela'D Slima'N

HEINRICH BARTH

from *Travels and Discoveries in North and Central Africa*, 1860

The names of vanished Saharan empires—Mali, Songhai, Bornu, Fulani—are some of the most beautiful in history. On antique European maps, they covered expanses almost as unknown to Westerners as the deep ocean floor. Early-nineteenth-century European expeditions, marked by appalling death rates, explored patches of the Sahara (its Arabic form is closer to Zahara, meaning "the great desert"). European adventurers tackled mapping the Sahara in the same way that Arctic explorers of the same period went seeking the Northwest Passage. The great desert, just across the Mediterranean from Europe, offered trade, missionary, and conquest routes to southern Africa.

Between 1850 and 1855, Heinrich Barth, a German linguist employed by the British government, mapped and explored the Sahara on an unprecedented scale. His partners, Richardson and Overweg, died in the desert. High casualty rates had characterized Saharan expeditions before Barth's, and his proved to be no exception. By the time Heinrich Barth and his doomed partners set out from Tripoli in 1850, trans-Saharan exploration was motivated by complex European interests. Knowledge of the Sahara was required if Europe's influence was to spread in Africa.

The Barth expedition tellingly included Overweg, a geologist, and Richardson, who was keen to study the slave trade so it could be eradicated. Barth wanted to map trade routes, study resources, make contact with native governments, and do reconnaissance for the destruction of the slave trade. In his introduction to *Travels and Discoveries in Northern and Central Africa*, he wrote that hopefully his example would "give a fresh impulse to the endeavors to open the fertile regions and Central Africa to European commerce and civilization."

Barth survived several scrapes with death: He was lost in the desert, attacked in Timbuktu, and participated in a dangerous slave raid. To enter Timbuktu, he had to travel in disguise, or the Tuaregs—desert tribesmen infamous in European folklore about the Sahara—would have killed him. Twice, he was morally affronted by what he called the "wanton manners" of local women, which he found deeply unsettling.

The world he explored was in turmoil. The Bornu Empire—having once stretched to Nigeria, and now centered on Lake Chad—was shrinking. Timbuktu was in decline, and the Fulani Empire was unstable. Barth observed the last of the great Saharan states before European expansion became more aggressive.

Fifty years later, the names of those independent states were gone from the maps, now merely territories in European empires. Barth's expedition did not start an avalanche of European expansion. Enticing as his reports were, climate, terrain, and native resistance stalled European empires on the coasts of West and North Africa. It was not until 1893 that a French column occupied Timbuktu.

—J. H.

⸺◆●◆⸺

The dust raised by the horsemen having subsided a little, and the country being clearer of wood, we now saw before us the whole cavalry of the Welád Slimán drawn up in a line in their best attire, their chief Ghét, the son of Séf el Nasr ben Ghét, and his uncle 'Omár, the son of Ghét, and brother of 'Abd el Jelíl, in the midst of them. This stately reception, not having been anticipated by Overweg and myself, made a great impression upon us; but we were not left to gaze long, but were desired by our Arab companions to ride in advance of the line in compliment to the chiefs. We accordingly put our steeds into a gallop, and, riding straight up to our new friends, saluted them with our pistols. Having answered our compliments, and bidding us welcome to their wild abode, the young Ghét galloping along at the head of his squadrons, his sword drawn, and with the continuous cry "yá riyáb, yá riyáb," they led us to the encampment, and we had a place shown to us where we might pitch our tents.

We had now joined our fate with that of this band of robbers, who, in consequence of their reckless habits, having been driven from their original dwelling-places in the Syrtis, after a great variety of events, have at length established themselves in this border region between the desert and the fertile regions of Negroland, under the guidance of Mohammed, the son of 'Abd el Jelíl, on the ruins of the old kingdom of Kánem.

The Vizier of Bórnu had taken this young man, to whom very little power and property were left, under his special protection, entering with him and the remaining part of the tribe into a contract to the effect that he would furnish them with horses and muskets, as far as they should stand in need of them, on condition of their delivering to him a certain share of their booty in every expedition. Of course, such a troop of swift horsemen, armed with muskets, if kept in strict subjection and subordination, might have proved exceedingly useful on the northern borders of Bórnu, on the one side as a check upon the Tawárek, on the other upon Wádáy. But the great difficulty, which the vizier appears not to have overcome, was to subject the predatory excursions of such a set of people to some sort of political rule.

With this view, he sent the young chief, who was scarcely more than twenty years of age, to Kánem, with all that were left of the Welád Slimán, keeping back in Kúkawa, as hostages for his proceedings, his mother, and the wives and little children of some of the principal men. But from the beginning there was a strong party against the young chief, who had not yet achieved any exploit, and whose sole merit consisted in his being the nearest relation of 'Abd el Jelíl. 'Omár, his uncle, who from his youth had given himself up to a life of devotion, and was called a Merábet, had a considerable party; and there were, besides, several men who thought themselves of as much importance as their chief.

This was the horde with which, in order to carry out the objects of our mission to the utmost of our power, Mr. Overweg and I were obliged to associate our fate; but, unfortunately, we were unprovided with that most essential article for exciting a more than common interest in ourselves personally, or the objects of our mission, namely, valuable presents.

While our people pitched our tents, Mr. Overweg and I went to pay our compliments to Sheikh Ghét and 'Omár, and to have a friendly talk with them before we proceeded to more serious business. They seemed to expect this compliment, having lain down in the shade of a tree at a short distance from our place of encampment. Ghét, who was smoking a long pipe, was a tolerably handsome young man; but his pronunciation was very defective, and he had nothing very commanding in his manner. Having exchanged a few compliments and asked some general questions, we withdrew, and soon after received a present of dates and milk.

When the heat of the day had a little abated, we prepared the small present we had to give to Sheikh Ghét, and which consisted of a red cloth bernús of good workmanship, a pound of cloves, a pound of jáwi or benzoin, and a razor. We were well aware that is was rather a trifling gift, considering the assistance we required from these people to carry out our object; but we knew also that it was rather a favor bestowed upon us by the Vizier of Bórnu, who regarded these people as in his service. Referring, therefore, to the friendship which existed of old between their tribe, when still in their old settlements in the Syrtis, and the English consul in Tripoli, and delivering a letter from Mr. Frederick Warrington, who was personally well known to the chief men, we openly professed that the object of our coming was to try, with their assistance, to visit the eastern shore of the lake, and especially the Bahar el Ghazál, which had formed a remarkable object of curiosity in our country for some time. But Sheikh Ghét, without hesitation, declared it was impossible for them to take us to that place, the most dangerous locality in all these quarters, on account of the many predatory expeditions which were made to that spot from different quarters, and by tribes hostile to them. After some commonplace talk about the English, we left him, and went to his uncle with a present of precisely the same kind, and began here to urge the distinct object of our coming in a more positive way. I expressed the opinion that, as they would render acceptable service to the British government if they were to enable us to investigate the connection between the Bahar el Ghazál and the lake, so, on the other hand, a great portion of the blame, if we should not be able to carry out our design, would certainly fall upon them, inasmuch as they had always professed to be under great obligations toward the English. 'Omár ben Ghét ben Séf e' Nasr acknowledged all this; but he doubted very much if the band, in its present reduced state, would be able to carry us to those quarters, which were entirely under the sway of Wádáy.

We then took our leave of 'Omár and returned to our tents. The place of the encampment was a fine, open, sandy, undulating level, commanding the vale, where are the wells Yongo or Bú-Halíma, covered with verdure, and richly adorned with scattered mimosas. The tents and sheds of the Arabs were spread over a great space, and no precaution was taken to obtain some degree of security by means of fences and stockades. The sun having set, I lay down outside my tent to enjoy the coolness and tranquillity of the evening after a hot and troublesome day.

All seemed calm and tranquil, when suddenly a terrible screaming and crying arose from the women in the west part of the encampment. We hurried to our arms, thinking that an enemy had entered the place. The cry, " 'Alá e' dhahar! 'alá e' dhahar!" (mount! mount!)—properly speaking, "in the saddle! in the saddle!"—sounded from all sides, and the horsemen hurried past us; but it was only a small party of freebooters, who, in the twilight of the evening, had made an attack upon the camels, and, after having put to flight two or three men and killed a horseman, had driven off a part of the herd. Our friends pursued the robbers at full speed and soon overtook them, when they retreated into the thicket and gave up their booty.

In this way we had a specimen of the character of our present expedition the very first day we had joined this little horde; and the lamentations of the females on account of the man who had been slain sounded woefully through the night, and brought before our minds the fate which, in a very short time, might befall ourselves. Late in the night, when the alarm had subsided, Sheikh Ghét sent us a heifer as a present.

[Dr. Barth and Dr. Overweg continued to accompany the Arab free-booters, and witness their plundering skirmishes. Their rapid marches occasioned much inconvenience to the travellers. The following record in Dr. Barth's journal of October 19th, affords a fair specimen of the kind of life he led among the Arabs.]

The Arabs had not made a very considerable booty, the Woghda having received intelligence of their approach and saved what they could. The whole result of the expedition was fifteen camels, a little more than three hundred head of cattle, and about fifteen hundred sheep and goats. The Arabs were for some time in great anxiety about Ghét, and a party of horsemen who had gone with him to a greater distance; but he joined us here, driving before him a large flock of sheep. We were busy watering our horses, and providing ourselves with this necessary element. But there was not much leisure; for scarcely had we begun to draw water, when the alarm was given that the Woghda were attacking us, and three bodies of horsemen were formed in order to protect the train and the booty. The main body rushed out of the valley on the southeast side, and drove the enemy back to a considerable distance; but the intention of encamping on the slope near this well was given up as too dangerous, and it was decided to go to a greater distance, though the intention of penetrating to M'awó seemed not as yet entirely to be abandoned. It took us a considerable time to get out of this wooded valley, the Arabs being afraid of being attacked and losing their booty.

At length, the cattle and flocks having been driven in advance, we started, and, leaving the vale, ascended elevated rocky ground, from which, following a southwesterly direction, we descended, a little before two o'clock in the afternoon, into the narrower eastern part of a deep and beautiful valley, which here is adorned by a pretty grove of date-trees, while its western part expands into fine cultivated ground. Here we made a halt of about half an hour, in order to water the animals and replenish our skins; for not even here was it thought advisable to encamp, as it is regarded as a very inauspicious place, this being the spot where, in 1850, the Kél-owí fell upon the Welád Slimán and almost exterminated them. After so short a halt we again pursued our march. I was now so totally exhausted that I was obliged to dismount at short intervals and lie down for a moment; and once, when left alone, it was only with the utmost exertion that I was able to mount my horse again; but nevertheless I managed to drag myself along. At length, about sunset, we chose a place for our encampment on the brow of the slope descending into a deep valley. Having now been thirty-four hours on horseback with only short and insufficient intervals, I fell senseless to the ground, and was considered by Mr. Overweg and our people as about to breathe my last. But after an hour's repose I recovered a little, and, having had a good night's rest, felt myself much stronger on the following morning, so that I could even undergo some exertion which was not exactly necessary.

Monday, October 20th. Descended with our people into the valley when they went to fetch water. It is called A'láli A 'dia, or Jerád, from a small hamlet lying on the highest ground, and called A'láli. The well was very rich and plentiful; but no traces of cultivation appeared at the foot of the date-trees. The slope was rather steep, and about 130 feet high. The Arabs, who had contracted their encampment or "dowar" within the smallest possible compass, barricading it with their baggage, as all the empty bags which they had taken with them on the expedition were now full of corn from the magazines of the enemy, were not at all at their ease, and seemed not to know exactly what course to take, whether to penetrate further in advance or to return. Several Fugábú and people belonging to Hallúf came to pay their respects to Sheikh Ghét; and a person of considerable authority, called Keghámma, or rather Keghámma-futébe (Seraskier of the West), the very man of whom we before had heard so much talk, came also and paid me a visit in my tent; for, being in a weak state, I had been obliged, when the sun became oppressive, to pitch my tent, as there was no shade. There being no other tent in the encampment, I received visits from several parties who wished to breakfast a little at their ease, and among others from a man called Kédel Batrám, Hallúf's brother. Keghámma stated that he was certainly able to bring us to Kárká; but this was a mere pretence, and he himself retracted his promise shortly afterward before the sheikh. Our cherished object lay still before us, at a considerable distance;

but our friend Ghét thought that he had brought us already far enough to deserve some more presents, and plainly intimated as much to us through 'Abd-Allah. Fortunately, I had a handsome yellow cloth caftan with me, embroidered with gold, and toward evening, when I had recovered from a severe fit of fever, which had suddenly attacked me in the afternoon, we went to pay our compliments to the chief, and begged him to accept of it; at the same time we told him we should be satisfied if we were enabled to visit the district belonging to the keghámma. But the situation of the Arabs soon became more dangerous, and nothing was thought of but to retrace our steps westward with the greatest possible expedition.

I was lying sleepless in my tent, in a rather weak state, having scarcely tasted any kind of food for the last few days on account of my feverish state, when, in the latter part of the night, a great alarm was raised in the camp, and I heard the Arabs mount their horses and ride about in several detachments, raising their usual war-cry, "yá riyáb, yá riyáb;" but I remained quietly on my mat, and was not even roused from my lethargical state when I received the intelligence that a numerous hostile army, consisting of the Woghda, the Médelé, the Shíri, and the people of the Eastern Keghámma, was advancing against the camp. I received this news with that indifference with which a sick and exhausted man regards even the most important events. Neither did I stir when, with the first dawn of day on the 21st, the enemy having actually arrived within a short distance, our friends left the camp in order to offer battle. I heard about ten shots fired, but did not thinks that the Arabs would be beaten. Suddenly Overweg, who had saddled his horse at the very beginning of the alarm, called out anxiously to me that our friends were defeated, and, mounting his horse, started off at a gallop. My mounted servant, Bú-Zéd, had long taken to his heels; and thus, while Mohammed was hastily saddling my horse, I flung my bernús over me, and grasping my pistols and gun, and throwing my double sack over the saddle, I mounted and started off toward the west, ordering Mohammed to cling fast to my horse's tail. It was the very last moment, for at the same time the enemy began to attack the east side of the camp. All the people had fled, and I saw only the chief slave of Ghét, who, with great anxiety, entreated me to take his master's state sword with me, that it might not fall into the hands of the enemy.

But I had not gone a great distance when I heard firing close behind me, and, turning round, saw the Arab horsemen rallying, and with the cry "He keléb, keléb," turn round against the enemy, who had dispersed in order to collect the spoil. I went on in order to inform Mr. Overweg, who, together with the Arabs who were mounted on camels, and even several horsemen, had fled to some distance and posted themselves on a hill. Assuring him that the danger was over, I returned with him to the camp, where we were rather surprised to find that not only all our luggage was gone, but that not even a vestige of my tent was left.

The enemy, attracted only by the English tent and Sheikh Ghét's baggage, had scarcely touched the effects of the other people, but considered my tent as a fair prize and ran away with it. But the Arabs pursuing them, we got back most of our things. A leathern English bag of mine, which contained some articles of value, had been cut open, just, as it seemed, at the moment when our friends came up with the enemy. Our chief loss consisted in our cooking utensils and provisions; I also much regretted the loss of an English prayer-book which had belonged to Mr. Richardson. Four of the Arabs had been killed, and thirty-four of the enemy. Mr. Overweg was busily employed in dressing some severe wounds inflicted on our friends. The Arabs were furious at the insolence, as they called it, of the enemy, who had dared to attack them in their own encampment, and they swore they would now go and burn down all their hamlets and their corn. The horsemen actually left, but returned in the course of the afternoon rather silently, with a sullen face and unfavorable tidings, and before sunset they were once more obliged to defend their own encampment against another attack of the energetic natives; they, however, succeeded in beating them off. Hallúf distinguished himself greatly by his valor, killing three or four of the enemy with his own hand.

But, notwithstanding this little victory, the forebodings for the night were very unfavorable, and our friends would certainly have decamped immediately if they had not been afraid that in the darkness of the night the greater part might take to their heels, and that a shameful flight would be followed by great loss of life and property. Accordingly, they determined to remain till the next morning. But an anxious and restless night it was; for they had received authentic news that a body of from thirty to forty Wádáy horsemen were to join their enemies that night, and to make a joint and last attack upon them, and they were well aware that the enemy had only been beaten from want of horses. All the horses remained saddled, and the whole night they sounded the watch-cry.

From Al-Suwayrkiyah to Meccah

SIR RICHARD BURTON

from *Personal Narrative of a Pilgrimage to El Medinah and Meccah*, 1906

Posing as a hajji, a Muslim pilgrim, Sir Richard Burton made the pilgrimage to Mecca and Medina in 1853. This stunt, and his explorations of Arabia, made him the most audacious Victorian explorer of the Islamic world.

Burton was not the first European to enter Islam's most holy cities. Jacob Ludwig Burkhardt, a Swiss explorer in disguise, had reached Mecca in 1815. Burton's ambitions and achievements, however, exceeded Burkhardt's. The Royal Geographical Society sponsored his plan to investigate what Burton called the "huge white blob," or the Empty Quarter of central Arabia. His *Personal Narrative of a Pilgrimage to El Medinah and Meccah* is important because it provided detailed information about regions and religious sites barred to non-Muslims.

Burton's life was driven by nonconformity, restlessness, and passion — not typical ingredients for respectability in Victorian Britain. He studied Arabic at Oxford before being thrown out of university for attending a horse race in 1842. Drawn to adventure, he joined the British Army in India. He became an adept student of Indian cultures and languages and was initiated into Sufism, a mystical branch of Islam. Armed with a depth of knowledge, perhaps unprecedented in a British officer or any other European, he served as an undercover intelligence officer. These experiences inspired him to take a pilgrimage to Mecca, the heart of Islam in 1853.

Burton began his pilgrimage with a stay in Cairo, where he disguised himself as a physician. Attaching himself to a Bedouin caravan, he went first to Suez, then by ship to the Arabian port of Yambo. From Yambo he went overland to Medina, the site of the Prophet's Tomb, then on to Mecca, the holiest of Moslem cities.

Burton's feat was not without controversy. Although his reputation rested more on his exploits in Africa, his name was tarnished when he locked horns with William Palgrave, another Arabia explorer. Palgrave's *Narrative of a Year's Journey Through Central and Eastern Arabia* was not published until 1865. Burton questioned the story's authenticity, as did others. Inconsistencies in Palgrave's account suggest he exaggerated the ground he covered in Arabia. Neither man's reputation was helped by their slashing exchanges.

Teamed with John Hanning Speke, in 1855 and from 1857 to 1859, he pursued the source of the Nile. Although Burton remained an explorer and adventurer his entire life, these African explorations overshadowed all of his other accomplishments—even his 1853 *hajj* in disguise. As Britain's most famous living explorer and Orientalist scholar, he was given diplomatic postings in West Africa, Brazil, Syria, and finally Trieste. His career went sideways, when in characteristically maverick fashion, he upset his Foreign Office superiors by trying to protect locals from the oppressive pasha of Damascus. He was removed to Trieste, which was something of a rebuke, but he continued to publish until his death in 1890.

Soldier, explorer, writer, diplomat—Burton's many achievements make him one of the most studied of the great Victorian adventurers. He wrote over forty books, on topics ranging from sword fighting to exquisite translations of *A Thousand and One Nights* and *The Hindu Art of Love*. None of his other works come close to the incredible novelty of his *Personal Narrative of a Pilgrimage to El Medinah and Meccah*. After 1,300 years, this book finally exposed Islam's heart to Western readers.

—J. H.

S haykh Abdullah, who acted as director of our consciences, bade us be good pilgrims, avoiding quarrels, immorality, bad language, and light conversation. We must so reverence life that we should avoid killing game, causing an animal to fly, and even pointing it out for destruction; nor should we scratch ourselves, save with the open palm, lest vermin be destroyed, or a hair uprooted by the nail. We were to respect the sanctuary by sparing the trees, and not to pluck a single blade of grass. As regards personal considerations, we were to abstain from all oils, perfumes, and unguents; from washing the head with mallow or with lote leaves; from dyeing, shaving, cutting, or vellicating a single pile or hair; and though we might take advantage of shade, and even form it with upraised hands, we must by no means cover our sconces. For each infraction of these ordinances we must sacrifice a sheep; and it is commonly said by Moslems that none but the Prophet could be perfect in the intricacies of pilgrimage. Old Ali began with an irregularity; he declared that age prevented his assuming the garb, but that, arrived at Meccah, he would clear himself by an offering.

The wife and daughters of a Turkish pilgrim of our party assumed the Ihram at the same time as ourselves. They appeared dressed in white garments; and they had exchanged the Lisam, that coquettish fold of muslin which veils without concealing the lower part of the face, for a hideous mask, made of split, dried, and plaited palm-leaves, with two "bulls'-eyes" for light. I could not help laughing when these strange figures met my sight, and, to judge from the shaking of their shoulders, they were not less susceptible to the merriment which they had caused.

At three P.M. we left Al-Zaribah, travelling towards the South-West, and a wondrously picturesque scene met the eye. Crowds hurried along, habited in the pilgrim-garb, whose whiteness contrasted strangely with their black skins; their newly shaven heads glistening in the sun, and their long black hair streaming in the wind. The rocks rang with shouts of *Labbayk! Labbayk!* At a pass we fell in with the Wahhabis, accompanying the Baghdad Caravan, screaming "Here am I"; and, guided by a large loud kettle-drum, they followed in double file the camel of a standard-bearer, whose green flag bore in huge

white letters the formula of the Moslem creed. They were wild-looking mountaineers, dark and fierce, with hair twisted into thin Dalik or plaits: each was
armed with a long spear, a matchlock, or a dagger. They were seated upon
coarse wooden saddles, without cushions or stirrups, a fine saddle-cloth alone
denoting a chief. The women emulated the men; they either guided their own
dromedaries, or, sitting in pillion, they clung to their husbands; veils they dis-
dained, and their countenances certainly belonged not to a "soft sex." These
Wahhabis were by no means pleasant companions. Most of them were followed by spare dromedaries, either unladen or carrying water-skins, fodder,
fuel, and other necessaries for the march. The beasts delighted in dashing furiously through our file, which being lashed together, head and tail, was
thrown each time into the greatest confusion. And whenever we were observed smoking, we were cursed aloud for Infidels and Idolaters.

Looking back at Al-Zaribah, soon after our departure, I saw a heavy nim-
bus settle upon the hill-tops, a sheet of rain being stretched between it and
the plain. The low grumbling of thunder sounded joyfully in our ears. We
hoped for a shower, but were disappointed by a dust-storm, which ended with
a few heavy drops. There arose a report that the Badawin had attacked a party
of Meccans with stones, and the news caused men to look exceeding grave.

At five P.M. we entered the wide bed of the Fiumara, down which we
were to travel all night. Here the country falls rapidly towards the sea, as the
increasing heat of the air, the direction of the watercourses, and signs of violence in the torrent-bed show. The Fiumara varies in breadth from a hundred
and fifty feet to three-quarters of a mile; its course, I was told, is towards the
South-West, and it enters the sea near Jeddah. The channel is a coarse sand,
with here and there masses of sheet rock and patches of thin vegetation.

At about half-past five P.M. we entered a suspicious-looking place. On the
right was a stony buttress, along whose base the stream, when there is one,
swings; and to this depression was our road limited by the rocks and thorn
trees which filled the other half of the channel. The left side was a precipice,
grim and barren, but no so abrupt as its brother. Opposite us the way seemed
barred by piles of hills, crest rising above crest into the far blue distance. Day

still smiled upon the upper peaks, but the lower slopes and the Fiumara bed were already curtained with grey sombre shade.

A damp seemed to fall upon our spirits as we approached this Valley Perilous. I remarked that the voices of the women and children sank into silence, and the loud Labbayk of the pilgrims were gradually stilled. Whilst still speculating upon the cause of this phenomenon, it became apparent. A small curl of the smoke, like a lady's ringlet, on the summit of the right-hand precipice, caught my eye; and simultaneous with the echoing crack of the matchlock, a high-trotting dromedary in front of me rolled over upon the sands,—a bullet had split its heart,—throwing the rider a goodly somersault of five or six yards.

Ensued terrible confusion; women screamed, children cried, and men vociferated, each one striving with might and main to urge his animal out of the place of death. But the road being narrow, they only managed to jam the vehicles in a solid immovable mass. At every matchlock shot, a shudder ran through the huge body, as when the surgeon's scalpel touches some more sensitive nerve. The Irregular horsemen, perfectly useless, galloped up and down over the stones, shouting to and ordering one another. The Pasha of the army had his carpet spread at the foot of the left-hand precipice, and debated over his pipe with the officers what ought to be done. No good genius whispered "Crown the heights."

Then it was that the conduct of the Wahhabis found favour in my eyes. They came up, galloping their camels,—

"Torrents less rapid, and less rash,—"

with their elf-locks tossing in the wind, and their flaring matches casting a strange lurid light over their features. Taking up a position, one body began to fire upon the Utaybah robbers, whilst two or three hundred, dismounting, swarmed up the hill under the guidance of the Sharif Zayd. I had remarked this nobleman at Al-Madinah as a model specimen of the pure Arab. Like all Sharifs, he is celebrated for bravery, and has killed many with his own hand. When urged at Al-Zaribah to ride into Meccah, he swore that he would not leave the Caravan till in sight of the walls; and, fortunately for the pilgrims, he kept his word. Presently the firing was heard far in our rear, the robbers having fled. The head of the column advanced, and the dense body of pilgrims opened out. Our forced halt was now exchanged for a flight. It required much management to steer our Desert-craft clear of danger; but Shaykh Mas'ud was equal to the occasion. That many were not, was evident by the boxes and baggage that strewed the shingles. I had no means of ascertaining the number of men killed and wounded: reports were contradictory, and exaggeration unanimous. The robbers were said to be a hundred and fifty in number; their object was plunder, and they would eat the shot camels. But their principal ambition was the boast, "We, the Utaybah, on such and such a night, stopped the Sultan's Mahmil one whole hour in the Pass."

At the beginning of the skirmish I had primed my pistols, and sat with them ready for use. But soon seeing that there was nothing to be done, and wishing to make an impression,—nowhere does Bobadil now "go down" so well as in the East,—I called aloud for my supper. Shaykh Nur, exanimate with fear, could not move. The boy Mohammed ejaculated only an "Oh, sir!" and the people around exclaimed in disgust, "By Allah, he eats!" Shaykh Abdullah, the Meccan, being a man of spirit, was amused by the spectacle. "Are these Afghan manners, Effendim?" he enquired from the Shugduf behind me. "Yes," I replied aloud, "in my country we always dine before an attack of robbers, because that gentry is in the habit of sending men to bed supperless." The Shaykh laughed aloud, but those around him looked offended. I thought the bravado this time *mal placé*; but a little event which took place on my way to Jeddah proved that it was not quite a failure.

As we advanced, our escort took care to fire every large dry Asclepias, to disperse the shades which buried us. Again the scene became wondrous wild:—

> "*Full many a waste I've wander'd o'er,*
> *Clomb many a crag, cross'd many a shore,*
> *But, by my halidome,*
> *A scene so rude, so wild as this,*

Yet so sublime in barrenness,
Ne'er did my wandering footsteps press,
   Where'er I chanced to roam."

On either side were ribbed precipices, dark, angry, and towering above, till their summits mingled with the glooms of night; and between them formidable looked the chasm, down which our host hurried with shouts and discharges of matchlocks. The torch-smoke and the night-fires of flaming Asclepias formed a canopy, sable above and livid red below; it hung over our heads like a sheet, and divided the cliffs into two equal parts. Here the fire flashed fiercely from a tall thorn, that crackled and shot up showers of sparks into the air; there it died away in lurid gleams, which lit up a truly Stygian scene. As usual, however, the picturesque had its inconveniences. There was no path. Rocks, stone-banks, and trees obstructed our passage. The camels, now blind in darkness, then dazzled by a flood of light, stumbled frequently; in some places slipping down a steep descent, in others sliding over a sheet of mud. There were furious quarrels and fierce language between camel-men and their hirers, and threats to fellow-travellers; in fact, we were united in discord. I passed that night crying, "Hai! Hai!" switching the camel, and fruitlessly endeavouring to fustigate Mas'ud's nephew, who resolutely slept upon the water-bags. During the hours of darkness we made four or five halts, when we boiled coffee and smoked pipes; but man and beasts were beginning to suffer from a deadly fatigue.

The Desert of Devils

ARMIN VAMBERY

From *Arminius Vambery: His Life and Adventures*, 1884

Armin Vambery lived a double life as a respected Hungarian academic and a British spy during the nineteenth-century Great Game, Britain's cold war with Russia in the Middle East and Asia. He gathered intelligence that had a profound influence on British strategy. On one mission, he was able to interview the Ottoman sultan and send secret reports on the conversations back to London. His reputation peaked in 1885. By then he was well known at the British Court, corresponded regularly with the prime minister, and was a friend of Bram Stoker, who used folklore Vambery provided to create his version of Dracula. Although he was a subject of the Austro-Hungarian Empire, Vambery believed Britain was the most progressive and civilized European power, and therefore the best protector of Muslim countries from Russian expansion.

His reputation in Britain as an expert on Muslim Asia began after his 1862–64 adventures, recounted in the fascinating book, *Arminius Vambery: His Life and Adventures*, excerpted here. Posing as a Sunni Muslim holy man-beggar (a dervish), he traveled through Persia into Afghanistan. He risked visits to Khiva, Bokhara, and Herat, all hostile to *ferangi* (foreigners). On several occasions he was accused of being a Christian, but his knowledge of the culture and language was impeccable and stood him in good stead. Once, the suspicious emir of Samarkand interviewed him for half an hour; at the end of their session, the emir was so pleased by Vambery's piety that he rewarded him with gifts.

When Vambery returned to Budapest, his exploits caught the attention of British diplomats. He went to London and spoke at the Royal Geographical Society. At the height of the Great Game he was a celebrity among interested circles in Britain, even though his academic post was at the University of Budapest. His views on Central Asia and the Russian threat found an appreciative audience in the British government. London's strategy was to use the Ottoman Empire and other Muslim states as a buffer between Russia and British possessions, especially India. Vambery provided vital information used against the Russians for more than thirty years.

—J. H.

⸺⸺⸺⸺⸺◆◆◆⸺⸺⸺⸺⸺

I left Teheran on the 2nd of September, 1862, by the gate of *Shah Abdul-Azim*, dressed in the costume of a Sunnite dervish from Bagdad, my *entari* (nether garment) reaching down to my heels, a red girdle round my waist, a striped black *mashlak* (a waterproof coat) on my back, and on my head a neat *keffie*, both useful and ornamental. As it was usual to close the gates of Teheran after sunset, our little caravan had fixed upon a caravansary outside the town for our place of meeting. The travellers composing the caravan, became, for the most part, first acquainted with each other there. The caravan consisted of about thirty laden mules, a couple of horsemen, mollahs, pilgrims returning from Meshed, merchants, mechanics and my insignificant self. It was two hours after midnight when we started and proceeded along the wide path leading to Shah Abdul-Azim, a place which is held in high esteem by the Teheran people as a resort for pilgrims. I walked there frequently during my stay in Teheran. The place is full of life and noise during the day, especially in the afternoon hours. There can be seen at all times a troop of gaudily dressed women of the better classes, sitting on horseback man fashion, prominent mirzahs and khans with numerous followers, and now and then a European coach, used generally by the court only. Of course at the time of night that we passed through it a dead silence was brooding over it. The moon shed an almost day-like light upon the mountain range stretching to the left and upon the gilded cupola beneath which the earthly remains of Shah Abdul-Azim reposed. After we had been riding in silence for two hours, some of the members of our caravan began to thaw into a social mood, and interrupted the monotony of our march by conversation and lively sallies.

I selected for my companion a young Seid from Bagdad, who was about to make a starring tour, as a *rawzekhan* (singer of sacred songs), through Southern Persia. Properly speaking only such persons are called rawzekhans who sing Tazies, *i.e.*, elegies in honour of Hussein, of great renown in Persia. These men are the most fanatic Shi-ites, and it may cause some surprise that we became more intimately acquainted. But the Seid, as an inhabitant of Bagdad, and a subject of the Sublime Porte, was willing enough to cultivate the acquaintance of an Effendi. He introduced me to the other members of the caravan, and being a jovial fellow, who would easily pass from his funeral songs to a livelier and more worldly tune, he very soon became a favourite with the whole company, and I, too, indirectly, profited by his popularity.

I at first scrupulously avoided all religious discussions, as I wished to ingratiate myself with my fellow-travellers, although it was by no means easy to do so; the Persians being very fond of arguing, and willingly entering into a discussion with Christians, Ghebers, and especially with Sunnites. The night was a magnificent one, and in Persia these moonlit nights are simply entrancing. The clear, transparent air, the graceful outline of the mountains, the darkling ruins, the spectre-like shadows of the advancing caravan, and, above all, the wonders of the starry vault above us, do not fail to produce an unutterable impression upon the imagination of a traveller coming from the far West to the East. Our road, however, was the worst imaginable; we had to make our way over fragments and boulders of rock, and cross ditches, ravines and the beds of rivers run dry. The difficulties of the road affected me but little; I abandoned myself entirely to the safe gait of my trusty asinine quadruped, and watched with intense interest every movement of the Seid, who contemplated the star-covered sky, and had some story to tell about each star. Every star had a legend of its own, an influence good or baneful, and I listened to his wonderful accounts with a soul full of faith. The constellation of the Great Bear was already inclining towards the margin of the western sky when we reached the height of *Karizek*, upon whose downward slopes

Kenaregird, the village which was to be our first station, was lying. I cast one more glance at the beautiful moonlit landscape before descending, and as we went down on the other side of the mountain, the soft light of the moon slowly paled at the approach of the dawning day. As soon as the morning star appears to the eye it is the custom, for the whole caravan, to hail the coming day. The most zealous person in the company engages in the recital of the Ezan, a task which quite naturally fell this time to the lot of our Seid. The ablutions are performed in the twilight of the dawn of morning, and before the first rays of the sun touch the crest of the mountains, the caravan stops and morning prayers are engaged in.

The animals stand quietly with their heads bent low, whilst the men, with their faces turned towards the East, are kneeling, in a line, side by side, with such a penitent and remorseful expression on their countenances, as may be witnessed only with Mohammedans. When the rays of the sun reach the devout faithful, they lift up their voices and chant the melodious prayer beginning with the words Allah Ekber (*i.e.*, God is the greatest). After sunrise it is customary for the caravan to march on for a longer or shorter space of time, according as it happens to start earlier or later the night before, or as the next station is nearer or farther off. When we turned into our station the rays of the sun shot down mercilessly on our heads. We put up at the spacious caravansary, near the village of Kenaregird. The meaning of its name is, "Border of Sand," for to the east of it extends the salt desert of *Deshti-Kuvir*. This desert must be an awful place, for during all my wanderings through Persia I never met with a native who had travelled over that portion of it lying between Kenaregird and *Tebbes*. A Persian talking about the desert of Deshti-Kuvir is always ready to frighten his listeners with a batch of tales of horror, in each of which devils and evil spirits conspicuously figure. The favourite legend which is most often repeated, is the story of *Shamr*, Hussein's murderer and the mortal enemy of every Shi-ite Persian, to whom the desolation of this region is attributed. Flying from his own remorse, he took refuge here, and the once flourishing country suddenly became a sterile desert. The salt lakes and the bottomless morasses are caused by the drops of sweat rolling down his body in the agony of his sufferings. The most dreadful place of all is *Kebir Kuh*, where Shamr is dwelling to this day. Woe to the poor traveller who allows himself to be lured to this region by the deceptive light of the ignis fatuus! Such and similar stories I was regaled with by my fellow-travellers in connection with the salt desert of Persia. As soon as we arrived at the caravansary every one of us hastened to seek a shelter in the shade, and we were all of us soon comfortably settled. In a few instants the city of travellers presented the appearance of a lively and stirring settlement. Whilst the animals were crunching their dry barley straw, the Persians looked to the preparation of their meals. Those who were better off got their servants to rub their backs and shoulders and to pull their limbs until they cracked, this somewhat singular pastime being evidently intended to restore elasticity to the body. After a short rest we breakfasted, and then immediately retired to rest again. The caravan recuperates from the fatigues of the journey during the heat of the day, and continues its way at the dusk of evening. The animals follow the example of their masters. Towards evening men and cattle are on their feet again, and whilst the animals are being scrubbed and attended to, the men prepare their *pilar* (a dish composed of meat and rice). The supper is eaten about an hour before starting. The dervish fares better than any one else, for no sooner does the caravan arrive than he, without a care, seeks his rest, and when the savory steam of the kettle announces the approach of the evening meal, he seizes his *keshkul* (a vessel made of the shell of the cocoa-nut), and goes the rounds of the various groups, shouting out lustily "Ya hu, Ya hakk!" He gets a few slices from every one, mixes the heterogeneous contributions, and swallows it all with a good appetite. "He carries with him nothing," say the people of the East; "he does not cook, yet he eats; his kitchen is provided by God."

We had to cross the desert in its entire length to get to our next station. The silence of the night becomes, in this wilderness, doubly oppressive, and as far as the eye of the traveller can reach he will find no spot to repose it upon. Only here and there may be seen piled up columns of sand, driven about by the wind, and gliding from place to place like so many dark spectres. I did not wonder that these shifting shadows were taken by timid and credulous souls for evil spirits pursued by furies. My companion seemed to belong to the superstitious class, for wrapping his cloak tightly round him, he kept close to the densest part of the caravan, and would not, for the world, so much as glance at the wilderness stretching to the east.

It was about midnight when we heard the sound of bells, and upon my inquiry as to the meaning of this, I was told that a larger caravan, which had left an hour earlier than we did, was in front of us. We accelerated our march in order to overtake it, but had hardly come within a hundred paces from it when an intolerable stench, as if of dead bodies, filled the air. The Persians were aware of the cause of this poisonous stench and hurried silently on; but it went on increasing the further we advanced. I could not restrain my curiosity any longer, but turning to my nearest neighbour, I asked again what this meant, but he curtly replied, betraying, however, great anxiety: "Hurry up, hurry up! this is the caravan of the dead." This information was sufficient to make me urge my wearied beast forward to greater speed, and after a while I reached, together with my companions, the caravan. It consisted of about forty animals, horses and mules, under the leadership of three Arabs. The backs of the animals were laden with coffins, and we made every effort to avoid the dread procession. In passing near one of the horsemen who had charge of the caravan I caught sight of a face, which was frightful to look at; the eyes and nose were concealed by some wraps, and the rest of his lividly pale face looked ghastly by the light of the moon. Undaunted by the sickening atmosphere, I rode up to his side and inquired about the particulars of his errand. The Arab informed me that he had been now ten days on the way, and that twenty more would pass in taking the dead bodies to Kerbela, the place where, out of devotion for Hussein, the pious wish to sleep their eternal sleep. This custom prevails all over Persia; and every person who can afford it, even if he live in distant Khorassan, makes arrangements to have his remains carried to Kerbela, in order that they may be interred in the soil wherein the beloved Imam Hussein is reposing. It takes sometimes two months before the dead body can reach its place of destination. One mule is frequently laden with four coffins, and whilst their conveyance during the winter is comparatively harmless, it is of deadly effect, to beast and man alike, in the heat of July in Persia.

At some distance from the caravan of the dead, I glanced back at the strange funeral procession. The animals with their sad burden of coffins hung their heads, seemingly trying to bury their nostrils in their breasts, whilst the horsemen keeping at a good distance from them, were urging them on with loud cries to greater speed. It was a spectacle which seen anywhere could not fail to produce a profound impression of terror, but seen in the very centre of the desert, at the dead hour of the night, in the ghastly illumination of the moon, it could not fail to strike the most intrepid soul with awe and terror.

The members of the little caravan had now been travelling together for three days, and this short time was amply sufficient to establish the friendliest feelings of good fellowship amongst them. Of course, no one entertained the faintest suspicion of my being one of those Europeans, the barest touch of whom renders a Shi-ite unclean, and with whom to eat out of the same plate is a capital sin. In their eyes I was the Effendi from Constantinople, the guest of the Turkish Embassy, who instigated by a desire to travel was about to visit imperial Isfahan and Shiraz, the paradise-like. I rapidly made friends with most of the company, although some of the most obdurate Shi-ites could not refrain, at times, from casting in my teeth, the manifold wrong-doings of the Sunnites. One man in particular, a shoemaker, whose tall green turban denoted his descent from Ali, annoyed me with his everlasting reiterations of the sinful usurpations of the three Caliphs. The quieter members of the company would try to soothe his ruffled spirits on such occasions, and turn the conversation into calmer channels; but my man very soon came back to the charge, and waxing warm with his favourite topic, he would take hold of the horse's bridle and talk with as much animation about the case of succession mooted a trifle of twelve hundred years ago, as though the whole affair had happened but yesterday.

Kum, with its green cupolas, loomed up before our eyes on the fourth day of our march. It is the sacred city of the Persian female world, for here, in the company of 444 saints, repose in eternal sleep the remains of Fatima, a sister to Imam (Saint) Riza, who, longing to see her brother, undertook for that purpose a journey from Bagdad to Meshed, but, on her way, was attacked by sickness in Kum, and died there. Kum, like Kerbela, is a favourite place of burial for Persian women, who cause their remains to be brought to this place from all parts of the country. But the town of Kum enjoys the less enviable distinction of being known as the abode of numerous evil-doers, owing to its having the privilege of sanctuary; and he who is lucky enough to escape the hands of the executioner, and to find a refuge within its sacred walls, is safe from all molestation.

Every member of our caravan was eager to visit Kum, some wanting to take part in the penitential processions as pilgrims, others to make purchases and to attend to their affairs. At a considerable distance from Kum, the environs, like those of all places of resort for pilgrims, are dotted by small heaps of stones, which are raised by the hands of pious pilgrims, amidst the chanting of sacred psalms. Here and there a bush can be seen, too, decorated with the gaudiest kind of rags which are hanging on it. Every one is anxious to leave some mark of his devotion in the neighbourhood; according to their inclinations, some resort to stones, others to rags in the accomplishment of their devotional duties. It is said that in former times another custom prevailed by which travellers might pay their tribute of respect — every passer-by would drive a nail into some tree on the road. I, too, dismounted and hung upon a bush a red silk tassel from my keffie. What a wonderful collection of fabrics from all parts of the world! On these bushes are represented the costly handiwork of India and Cashmere, the manufactures of England and America, and the humble frieze and coarse linen of the nomadic Turkoman, Arab Kurdistan tribes. Now and then the eye is caught by a magnificent shawl suspended on the branches of a bush, exciting no doubt the cupidity of more than one pious pilgrim passing by; but it is perfectly safe, as no one would dare to touch it, it being considered the blackest act of sacrilege to remove any of these tokens of piety.

Before reaching the town we had to pass a cemetery of extraordinary dimensions, almost two English miles in length. My fellow-travellers, however, perceiving my astonishment at the extent of the burial ground, assured me that in point of size it could not be compared to that of Kerbek. We were in Kum at last; our caravan put up at the caravansary in the centre of the bazaar, and I learned with pleasure that we were to take a two days' rest here.

As pious pilgrims we allowed ourselves but little time for rest, and shortly after our arrival, having washed and brushed our clothes, we repaired to the holy tomb. No European before me ever saw the interior of this sanctuary, for there is no power on earth to procure admission to it for a Frengi.

Innumerable Seids, entrusted with the custody of the tomb of their "first ancestress," are camping in the outer courtyard, planted with trees. A chapel with a richly gilded cupola rises in the centre of the inner court. Twelve marble steps lead up to the door. The pilgrims remove their shoes at the first of these steps; their arms or sticks are taken away from them, and not until they have kissed the marble threshold are they permitted to enter. The beholder is struck with the extraordinary splendour of the interior of the chapel. The coffin, enclosed by a strong trellised bar of solid silver, remains always covered with a costly carpet. From the enclosure are suspended tablets containing prayers, which the faithful either read themselves, or have read to them by one of the numerous Seids who are loitering about. Any amount of shouting, singing, weeping, and moaning, and vociferous begging of the Seids is going on in the chapel; but this infernal din does not interfere with the devotions of a great number of pious pilgrims, who, leaning their foreheads against the cold bars of the enclosure, gaze with fixed eyes upon the coffin, and mutter their silent prayers. I particularly admired the many valuable and precious objects, ornaments of pearls and diamonds, arms inlaid with gold, which were laid down upon the tomb of St. Fatima as sacrificial gift-offerings. My Bagdad costume offended the eye of many a person in the fanatic Shi-ite crowd, but, thanks to the kindness of my fellow-travellers, I experienced no annoyance whatever. From the tomb of Fatima the pilgrims frequently go to the tombs of some of the great ones of the earth; and I followed my companions to the tomb of Feth Ali Shah and his two sons, who for some reason or other stood in particularly high favour with the devout. The tomb was of the purest alabaster, and the portraits of the departed ones were very cleverly carved into it on the outside. After having thus accomplished our pious devotions, we felt at liberty to wander back to the town and look at its remarkable sights.

Here, as elsewhere, the first thing to look at was the bazaar. We were just then in the season of ripe fruit, and the whole bazaar was filled with the water-melons, which are so celebrated throughout all Persia. The water-melon is, during the autumnal months, the almost exclusive food of one portion of the people of Iran, and its juice is frequently used in case of sickness for its medicinal properties. The Kum bazaar is remarkable not only for the abundance and delicacy of its water-melons, but also for its earthenware, one variety of which in particular, a long-necked pitcher, manufactured from potter's clay taken from the soil of the sacred city, is highly valued in trade. As I was making my rounds in the bazaar, examining everything, I happened to stop before a muslin dyer's shop. The Persian tradesman was industriously engaged in stamping and printing the rude stuff spread out before him, by means of stencils, which had been previously dipped in a blue dye, pressing them down with all his strength; and as he observed me looking at his doings, he turned upon me angrily, and evidently taking me for a Frengi, exclaimed: "We shall get rid of your expensive cotton fabrics, and will by and by know all your tricks of trade; and when the Persians will be able to do without Frengistan manufacture, I know you will all come begging to us."

We left Kum on the third day after our arrival there, and passing through several smaller places, where nothing worthy of note could be seen, we came to *Kashan*, after a fatiguing march of two days. My Persian fellow-travellers, long before we arrived in Kashan, were praising up, in the most extravagant style, as usual, the beauty and attractions of that town. For my part, the only thing of note I saw there was the bazaar of the braziers, where the celebrated kettles of Kashan are being manufactured. About eight braziers' shops are standing close to each other in a line, and in each of them muscular arms are hammering away the whole blessed day. The brass wares manufactured here are considered to be without rivals in point of solid workmanship and elegance. Those highly polished bricks, which retain the brilliancy of their shining colours for centuries, are said to have been invented in this town. Formerly they were called bricks of Kashan, but now they are known only by the name of Kashi, and serve as the chief ornaments in all architectural monuments throughout Central Asia. The inhabitants had also a great deal to tell about a dangerous species of scorpion, which made Kashan their home, but from motives of hospitality never hurt a stranger. I never came across any of these scorpions, but I had a great deal to suffer from a no less annoying tribe of animals, the *lutis* (strolling comedians), who attack every stranger coming to Kashan, and from whose clutches nothing can save you except a ransom in the shape of some gift. About ten of them stood there looking out for me as I was entering the caravansary, and immediately made a rush upon me, some producing hideous ear-splitting music with their fifes, drums and trumpets, others showing off a dancing bear; and one of them, seating himself opposite to me, engaged in a declamation, at the top of his voice, of a panegyrical poem, in my honour, in which, to my utter astonishment, I heard my name mentioned. Of course, he had managed to ferret out my name from my companions. I bore the infliction for a little while patiently enough, listening to this charivari of sounds, but finally retired. But it was not an easy thing, by any means, to effect my retreat, for I was followed, on the spot, by one of the artists, evidently the chief of the strolling company, insisting upon some remuneration; and although I argued with him that I was but a beggar myself, he would not listen to reason, but bravely stood his place until I had given him something.

Leaving Kashan we had to proceed along a narrow mountain pass, flanked by gigantic rocks and mountains of strange and fantastic shapes. The moon shed a light almost as clear as that of the day, and the wonderful tints in which the landscape before me was clothed seemed to vary and change at every step we took. When we arrived beneath the great Bend, as is called the large water-basin cut by Shah Abbas the Great into the solid rock, in order to convey the waters produced by the snow melting on the mountains to the sterile plain not far off, the scene before us was startling in its rare and exceeding beauty. Although it was late in autumn, the oval-shaped basin,

formed by the enclosed valley, was brimful of water, and the waterfall rushing down the rocky wall from a height of fifty feet looked in the moonlit
night, to borrow a Persian phrase, like a river of diamonds. The deep roar of
the waterfall is heard far off in the stilly night, and the tired traveller coming
from the desert and quenching his thirst at the limpid waters of the basin,
would not exchange the refreshing and crystal-like fluid for all the costly
wines in the world.

The road from *Kuhrud* goes uphill for a time, and then inclines with a
rather abrupt slope towards the plain lying on the other side of the mountain,
where our next station was to be. The mornings had grown rather chilly and
the travellers used to dismount on the way and pick up stray sticks of *buta*, a
species of gumwood growing in bushes, which burns very well in its green
state, but blazes with a loud crackling sound when dry. It is usual to raise a
large pile of these sticks and then kindle it; the travellers range themselves
round the blazing fire and afterwards resume their journey. We were standing
for the second time, on the same morning, around this sort of fire when we
were suddenly startled by the sound of voices, in the rear, mingling with savage exclamations, as if people were quarrelling, and upon listening attentively
we heard two reports from firearms, and the loud yelling of some person badly
hurt. The whole caravan was thoroughly alarmed, and, running in the direction whence the report of the firearm had proceeded, found there lying on the
ground one of our companions, with a shattered arm. The affray had happened in this way. Several horsemen who were conveying the annual taxes
from Shiraz to Teheran had come up with a couple of Jewish shopkeepers,
whom they first insulted, and afterwards, passing from insult to injury, were
about to lay violent hands upon. One of our company, a Persian, happening
to be present, had pity on the poor Jews, stood up in their defence and took
the impudent fellows from Shiraz rather roughly to task for their unbecoming
conduct. One of the horsemen, a hotheaded young fellow, became so enraged
at this interference, that he lifted his rifle and shot at the Jews. He afterwards
pretended that the whole thing had been a joke, that he intended only to
frighten one of the Jews by sending a bullet through his tall fur cap, but that

unluckily he missed his aim and hit, instead, the Persian's arm. The incident so exasperated the whole caravan that our men at once started in pursuit of the culprit, who had meanwhile turned his horse's head and galloped away for his life, at a break-neck speed, but he was finally overtaken, dreadfully beaten, spit at amid loud curses, securely tied and brought back to the caravansary. Both the Shiraz man, who was bruised all over, and our wounded companion being unable to proceed either on foot or on horseback, they were placed side by side each in a basket, upon the back of a mule, and in the course of half an hour they were chatting away in the friendliest manner. They tied up each other's wounds, consoled one another, and went so far in their newborn friendship as to kiss each other; for according to the Eastern way of thinking neither of them was to be held responsible for what had happened. Fate had willed it so, and in its decrees every one must acquiesce.

In a village, called *Murtchekhar*, the judge of that place, evidently desirous of currying favour with the governor of Shiraz, attempted to liberate him, but the caravan stoutly refused to give him up, and only delivered him over, later, into the hands of justice, at Isfahan.

On the 13th of September I saw Isfahan, the former capital of Shah Abbas, through the thin mist of the morning. Whenever a Persian, and, especially a native of Isfahan, sets his eyes, after an absence of some time, upon his native town he is sure to exclaim: "Isfahan is half the world, but for Lahore," meaning thereby that Isfahan is, after Lahore, the largest city in the world. The citizens determine the extent of their city, by stating, with Oriental exaggeration, that it would take the boldest horseman two full days to make the circuit of its walls. And indeed the appearance of the city, with its extensive gardens, avenues of trees, and cupolas is really an imposing one. But in the East things look beautiful only on the surface, and shine only at a distance, and I was therefore but little disappointed when upon entering the town I met with the same labyrinth of crooked, narrow streets, the same miserable huts, dirt and extensive mud puddles in the roads, that I had before occasion to observe in Teheran and other towns of Persia.

Abou Do's Blade Tastes Blood

SIR SAMUEL BAKER

From *The Nile Tributaries of Abyssinia and the Sword Hunters of the Hamran Arabs*, 1868

Sir Samuel Baker's greatest contribution to Western understanding of the Islamic world was his book, *The Nile Tributaries of Abyssinia*. It recounts the first year of his maiden African expedition to find the Nile's source. Even though Baker failed to discover the source of the Nile, he wrote an intelligent and exciting account of the Muslim peoples he encountered during his journey. Hamran Arab aggageers—skilled horsemen who used swords to hunt elephants—impressed him the most:

> Never were there more complete centaurs than these Hamran
> Arabs: horse and man appeared to be one animal, of the most elastic nature, that could twist and turn with the suppleness of a snake.

Baker is less well known today than Richard Burton and John Speke, famous Nile explorers and contemporaries. He set off down the Nile in 1861 with two missions sponsored by the Royal Geographical Society: to locate the source of the Nile and also to find the Speke-Grant expedition, thought to be near Lake Victoria. When he met up with these fellow British explorers in 1862, they claimed to have already found the Nile's source. Deflated, he was nevertheless determined to make a discovery of his own. Using information given to him by Speke and Grant, he reached and named Lake Albert for the British Prince Consort, west of Lake Victoria. Lake Albert was not the source of the Nile, but reaching it earned Baker the Royal Geographical Society's gold medal in 1865.

Baker's encore made him a wealthy man. In 1870, he was hired by the Khedive of Egypt to be governor of Sudan and to destroy the slave trade. Slavery appalled him. His talent was to write about such things without being sententious, even with some self-effacing humor. He described the purchase of a Sudanese slave he intended to free and make the expedition's cook—and his embarrassment when she gratefully embraced him in front of his wife, Florence. It would be interesting to know what his wife thought about the matter; Baker had purchased Florence, a Hungarian slave, at a Turkish slave market, freeing and later marrying her.

Baker did not idealize Arabs or Muslim culture, and his vignettes often reveal his generous humanity. His compulsion to hunt elephants and other big game is less understandable for most modern readers. Big-game hunting went almost hand in hand with nineteenth-century African exploration—partly for sport, and partly for specimen collection. Baker had an impressive arsenal that included an elephant-killer rifle he called "Baby," which fired a half-pound exploding shell.

Baker's respect for the Muslim people infused his writing with positive impressions of a culture only a handful of Europeans had ever experienced, but thanks to his book, many more had the chance to read about.

—J. H.

❖

Early on the following morning the lions were still roaring, apparently within a hundred yards of the camp. I accordingly took a Reilly No. 10, double rifle, and accompanied by my wife, who was anxious to see these glorious animals, and who carried my little Fletcher No. 24, I skirted the outside of the jungle on the high bank, on the narrow arm of the river. We were not long in finding traces of the lions. A broad track in the sandy bed of the dried stream showed where the buffalo had been dragged across to the thick and impervious green bushes, exactly beneath us on the margin of the river. A hind quarter of the buffalo, much gnawed, lay within seven or eight paces of us, among the bushes that had been trampled down, and the dung of numerous lions lay upon the open ground near the place of their concealment. We had two Tokrooris with us, carrying spare rifles, and I felt sure that the lions were within the bushes of dense nabbuk, which concealed them as perfectly as though behind a closed curtain. We approached within three or four yards of this effective screen, when suddenly we heard the cracking of bones, as the lions feasted in their den close to us; they would not show themselves, nor was there any possibility of obtaining a shot; therefore, after ascending the high bank, and waiting for some time in the hope that one might emerge to drag away the exposed portion of the buffalo, we returned to camp.

The aggageers had already returned from a reconnaisance of the country, as they had started before daybreak in search of elephants; they reported the fresh tracks of a herd, and they begged me to lose no time in accompanying them, as the elephants might retreat to a great distance. There was no need for this advice; in a few minutes my horse Tétel was saddled, and my six Tokrooris and Bacheet, with spare rifles, were in attendance. Bacheet, who had so ingloriously failed in his first essay at Wat el Négur, had been so laughed at by the girls of the village for his want of pluck, that he had declared himself ready to face the devil rather than the ridicule of the fair sex; and, to do him justice, he subsequently became a first-rate lad in moments of danger.

The aggageers were quickly mounted. It was a sight most grateful to a sportsman to witness the start of these superb hunters, who with the sabres slung from the saddle-bow, as though upon an everyday occasion, now left the camp with these simple weapons, to meet the mightiest animal of the creation in hand-to-hand conflict. The horses' hoofs clattered as we descended the shingly beach, and forded the river shoulder-deep, through the rapid current, while those on foot clung to the manes of the horses, and to the stirrup-leathers, to steady themselves over the loose stones beneath.

Shortly after our arrival upon the opposite side, we came upon numerous antelopes of the nellut (*A. Strepsiceros*) and tétel (*A. Bubalis*). I would not fire at these tempting animals as we were seeking nobler game.

Tracking was very difficult; as there was a total absence of rain, it was next to impossible to distinguish the tracks of two days' date from those most

recent upon the hard and parched soil; the only positive clue was the fresh
dung of the elephants, and this being deposited at long intervals rendered
the search extremely tedious. The greater part of the day passed in useless
toil, and, after fording the river backwards and forwards several times, we at
length arrived at a large area of sand in the bend of the stream, that was evidently overflowed when the river was full; this surface of many acres was
backed by a forest of large trees. Upon arrival at this spot, the aggageers, who
appeared to know every inch of the country, declared that, unless the elephants had gone far away, they must be close at hand, within the forest. We
were speculating upon the direction of the wind, when we were surprised by
the sudden trumpet of an elephant, that proceeded from the forest already
declared to be the covert of the herd. In a few minutes later, a fine bull elephant marched majestically from the jungle upon the large area of sand,
and proudly stalked direct towards the river.

At that time we were stationed under cover of a high bank of sand that
had been left by the retiring river in sweeping round an angle; we immediately dismounted, and remained well concealed. The question of attack was
quickly settled; the elephant was quietly stalking towards the water, which
was about three hundred paces distant from the jungle: this intervening space
was heavy dry sand, that had been thrown up by the stream in the sudden
bend of the river, which, turning from this point at a right angle, swept beneath a perpendicular cliff of conglomerate rock formed of rounded pebbles
cemented together.

I proposed that we should endeavour to stalk the elephant, by creeping
along the edge of the river, under cover of a sand-bank about three feet
high, and that, should the rifles fail, the aggageers should come on at full
gallop, and cut off his retreat from the jungle; we should then have a
chance for the swords.

Accordingly, I led the way, followed by Hadji Ali, my head Tokroori, with
a rifle, while I carried the "Baby." Florian accompanied us. Having the wind
fair, we advanced quickly for about half the distance, at which time we were
within a hundred and fifty yards of the elephant, who had just arrived at the

water, and had commenced drinking. We now crept cautiously towards him; the sand-bank had decreased to a height of about two feet, and afforded very little shelter. Not a tree nor bush grew upon the surface of the barren sand, which was so deep that we sank nearly to the ankles at every footstep. Still we crept forward, as the elephant alternately drank, and then spouted the water in a shower over his colossal form; but just as we had arrived within about fifty yards, he happened to turn his head in our direction, and immediately perceived us. He cocked his enormous ears, gave a short trumpet, and for an instant he wavered in his determination whether to attack or fly; but as I rushed towards him with a shout, he turned towards the jungle, and I immediately fired a steady shot at the shoulder with the "Baby." As usual, the fearful recoil of the rifle, with a half-pound shell and twelve drachms of powder, nearly threw me backwards; but I saw the mark upon the elephant's shoulder in an excellent line, although rather high. The only effect of the shot was to send him off at great speed towards the jungle; but at the same moment the three aggageers came galloping across the sand like greyhounds in a course, and, judiciously keeping parallel with the jungle, they cut off his retreat, and, turning towards the elephant, they confronted him, sword in hand. At once the furious beast charged straight at the enemy; but now came the very gallant, but foolish, part of the hunt. Instead of leading the elephant by the flight of one man and horse, according to their usual method, all the aggageers at the same moment sprang from their saddles, and upon foot in the heavy sand they attacked the elephant with their swords.

In the way of sport, I never saw anything so magnificent, or so absurdly dangerous. No gladiatorial exhibition in the Roman arena could have surpassed this fight. The elephant was mad with rage, and nevertheless he seemed to know that the object of the hunters was to get behind him. This he avoided with great dexterity, turning as it were upon a pivot with extreme quickness, and charging headlong, first at one, and then at another of his assailants, while he blew clouds of sand in the air with his trunk, and screamed with fury. Nimble as monkeys, nevertheless the aggageers could not get behind him. In the folly of excitement they had forsaken their horses, who had escaped from the spot. The depth of the loose sand was in favour of the elephant, and was so much against the men that they avoided his charges with extreme difficulty. It was only by the determined pluck of all three, that they alternately saved each other, as two invariably dashed in at the flanks when the elephant charged the third, upon which the wary animal immediately relinquished the chase, and turned round upon his pursuers. During this time, I had been labouring through the heavy sand, and shortly after I arrived at the fight, the elephant charged directly through the aggageers, receiving a shoulder shot from one of my Reilly No. 10 rifles, and at the same time a slash from the sword of Abou Do, who, with great dexterity and speed, had closed in behind him, just in time to reach the leg. Unfortunately, he could not deliver the cut in the right place, as the elephant, with increased speed, completely distanced the aggageers; he charged across the deep sand, and reached the jungle. We were shortly upon his tracks, and after running about a quarter of a mile, he fell dead in a dry watercourse. His tusks were, like the generality of Abyssinian elephants, exceedingly short, but of good thickness.

Some of our men, who had followed the runaway horses, shortly returned, and reported that, during our fight with the bull, they had heard other elephants trumpeting in the dense nabbuk jungle near the river. A portion of thick forest of about two hundred acres, upon this side of the river, was a tempting covert for elephants, and the aggageers, who were perfectly cognisant with the habits of the animals, positively declared that the herd must be within this jungle. Accordingly, we proposed to skirt the margin of the river, which, as it made a bend at right angles, commanded two sides of a square. Upon reaching the jungle by the river side, we again heard the trumpet of an elephant, and about a quarter of a mile distant we observed a herd of twelve of these animals shoulder-deep in the river, which were in the act of crossing to the opposite side, to secure themselves in an almost impenetrable jungle of thorny nabbuk. The aggageers advised that we should return to the ford that we had already crossed, and, by repassing the river, we should most probably meet the elephants, as they would not leave the thick jungle until the night. Having implicit confidence in their knowledge of the country, I followed their directions, and we shortly recrossed the ford, and arrived upon a dry portion of the river's bed, banked by a dense thicket of nabbuk.

Jali now took the management of affairs. We all dismounted, and sent the horses to a considerable distance lest they should by some noise disturb the elephants. We shortly heard a cracking in the jungle on our right, and Jali assured us, that, as he had expected, the elephants were slowly advancing along the jungle on the bank of the river, and, they would pass exactly before us. We waited patiently in the bed of the river, and the cracking in the jungle sounded closer as the herd evidently approached. The strip of thick thorny covert that fringed the margin was in no place wider than half a mile—beyond that, the country was open and park-like, but at this season it was covered with parched grass from eight to ten feet high; the elephants would, therefore, most probably remain in the jungle until driven out.

In about a quarter of an hour, we heard by the noise in the jungle, about a hundred yards from the river, that the elephants were directly opposite to us. I accordingly instructed Jali to creep quietly by himself into the bush and to bring me information of their position: to this he at once agreed.

In three or four minutes he returned; he declared it impossible to use the sword, as the jungle was so dense that it would check the blow, but that I could use the rifle, as the elephants were close to us—he had seen three standing together, between us and the main body of the herd. I told Jali to lead me direct to the spot, and, followed by Florian and the aggageers, with my gun-bearers, I kept within a foot of my dependable little guide, who crept gently into the jungle; this was intensely thick, and quite impenetrable, except in such places where elephants and other heavy animals had trodden numerous alleys. Along one of these narrow passages we stealthily advanced, until Jali stepped quietly on one side, and pointed with his finger: I immediately observed two elephants looming through the thick bushes about eight paces from me. One offered a temple shot, which I quickly took with a Reilly No. 10, and floored it on the spot. The smoke hung so thickly, that I could not see sufficiently distinctly to fire my second barrel before the remaining elephant had turned; but Florian, with a three-ounce steel-tipped bullet, by a curious shot at the hind quarters, injured the hip joint to such an extent that we could more than equal the elephant in speed. In a few moments we found ourselves in a small open glade in the middle of the jungle, close to the stern of the elephant we were following. I had taken a fresh rifle, with both barrels loaded, and hardly had I made the exchange, when the elephant turned suddenly, and charged. Determined to try fairly the forehead shot, I kept my ground, and fired a Reilly No. 10, quicksilver and lead bullet, exactly in the centre, when certainly within four yards. The only effect was to make her stagger backwards, when, in another moment, with her immense ears thrown forward, she again rushed on. This was touch-and-go; but I fired my remaining barrel a little lower than the first shot. Checked in her rush, she backed towards the dense jungle, throwing her trunk about and trumpeting with rage. Snatching the Ceylon No. 10 from one of my trusty Tokrooris (Hassan), I ran straight at her, took a most deliberate aim at the forehead, and once more fired. The only effect was a decisive charge; but before I fired my last barrel, Jali rushed in, and, with one blow of his sharp sword, severed the back sinew. She was utterly helpless in the same instant. Bravo Jali! I had fired three beautifully correct shots with No. 10 bullets, and seven drachms of powder in each charge; these were so nearly together that they occupied a space in her forehead of about three inches, and all had failed to kill! There could no longer by any doubt that the forehead shot at an African elephant could not be relied upon, although so fatal to the Indian species: this increased the danger tenfold, as in Ceylon I had generally made certain of an elephant by steadily waiting until it was close upon me.

I now reloaded my rifles, and the aggageers quitted the jungle to remount their horses, as they expected the herd had broken cover on the other side of the jungle; in which case they intended to give chase, and, if possible, to turn them back into the covert, and drive them towards the guns. We accordingly took our stand in the small open glade, and I lent Florian one of my double rifles, as he was only provided with one single-barrelled elephant gun. I did not wish to destroy the prestige of the rifles, by hinting to the aggageers that it would be rather awkward for us to receive the charge of the infuriated herd, as the foreheads were invulnerable; but inwardly I rather hoped that they would not come so direct upon our position as the aggageers wished.

About a quarter of an hour passed in suspense, when we suddenly heard a chorus of wild cries of excitement on the other side of the jungle, raised by the aggageers who had headed the herd, and were driving them back towards us. In a few minutes a tremendous crashing in the jungle, accompanied by the occasional shrill scream of a savage elephant, and the continued shouts of the mounted aggageers, assured us that they were bearing down exactly upon our direction; they were apparently followed even through the dense jungle by the wild and reckless Arabs. I called my men close together, and told them to stand fast, and hand me the guns quickly; and we eagerly awaited the onset that rushed towards us like a storm. On they came, tearing everything before them. For a moment the jungle quivered and crashed; a second later, and, headed by an immense elephant, the herd thundered down upon us. The great leader came direct at me, and was received with right and left in the forehead from a Reilly No. 10 as fast as I could pull the triggers. The shock made it reel backwards for an instant, and fortunately turned it, and the herd likewise. My second rifle was beautifully handed, and I made a quick right and left at the temples of two fine elephants, dropping them both stone-dead. At this moment the "Baby" was pushed into my hand by Hadji Ali just in time to take the shoulder of the last of the herd, who had already charged headlong after his comrades, and was disappearing in the jungle. Bang! went the "Baby;" round I spun like a weathercock, with the blood pouring from my nose, as the recoil had driven the sharp top of the hammer deep into the bridge. My "Baby" not only screamed, but kicked viciously. However, I knew that the elephant must be bagged, as the half-pound shell had been aimed directly behind the shoulder.

In a few minutes the aggageers arrived; they were bleeding from countless scratches, as, although naked, with the exception of short drawers, they had forced their way on horseback through the thorny path cleft by the herd in rushing through the jungle. Abou Do had blood upon his sword. They had found the elephants commencing a retreat to the interior of the country, and they had arrived just in time to turn them. Following them at full speed, Abou Do had succeeded in overtaking and slashing the sinew of an elephant just as it was entering the jungle. Thus the aggageers had secured one, in addition to Florian's elephant that had been slashed by Jali. We now hunted for the "Baby's" elephant, which was almost immediately discovered lying dead within a hundred and fifty yards of the place where it had received the shot. The shell had entered close to the shoulder, and it was extraordinary that an animal should have been able to travel so great a distance with a wound through the lungs by a shell that had exploded within the body.

We had done pretty well. I had been fortunate in bagging four from this herd, in addition to the single bull in the morning; total, five. Florian had killed one, and the aggageers one; total, seven elephants. One had escaped that I had wounded in the shoulder, and two that had been wounded by Florian.

The aggageers were delighted, and they determined to search for the wounded elephants on the following day, as the evening was advancing, and we were about five miles from camp. Having my measuring-tape in a game-bag that was always carried by Abdoolahi, I measured accurately one of the elephants that had fallen with the legs stretched out, so that the height to the shoulder could be exactly taken:—From foot to shoulder in a direct line, nine feet one inch; circumference of foot, four feet eight inches. The elephant lying by her side was still larger, but the legs being doubled up, I could not measure her; these were females.

The New Pilgrim's Progress

MARK TWAIN

From *Innocents Abroad; or, The New Pilgrim's Progress*, 1906

Mark Twain's *Innocents Abroad* was once the most widely read book in the United States that offered any real opinions on Muslims. Its true influence is impossible to ascertain; however, an author of his mass appeal inevitably informed popular views. *Innocents Abroad* sold 67,000 copies in its first year and has stayed in print ever since. Its astounding success earned Twain his next book contract and launched his career as a literary celebrity.

Twain (born Samuel Clemens) was hired by the *Alta California*, a San Francisco newspaper, to write humorous letters while traveling overseas in 1867. The trip lasted five months, and the letters ultimately became *Innocents Abroad*.

Primarily meant to be a European tour, Twain skipped through Morocco, Algeria, Egypt, Palestine, and Turkey. Not an adventure in the usual sense, the trip belongs in this collection because Twain was the first popular American author to be a tourist in countries where tourism was still in its infancy. Twain broke new ground by providing his readers with a look into a completely exotic and alien world. Although he was merely a tourist by the standards of his contemporary, Sir Richard Burton, Twain was doing what no one like him had ever done before.

His satirical and biting vignettes of the Islamic world have the wit and snarl of his commentary on Europeans and Americans. According to his introduction, his purpose was:

> . . . to suggest to the reader how he would be likely to see Europe
> and the East if he looked at them with his own eyes instead of the

eyes of those who traveled in those countries before him. I make small pretense of showing anyone how he ought to look at objects of interest beyond the sea. . . .

He looked at Muslims with the racist and caustic attitudes commonly found in the West at that time. Describing Istanbul: "Mosques are plenty, churches are plenty, graveyards are plenty, but morals and whiskey are scarce." Moroccan women: "I am full of veneration for the wisdom that leads them to cover up such atrocious ugliness. If I had a wife as ugly as some of those I have seen, I would go over her face with a nail-grab and see if I couldn't improve it." The review in the *Boston Telegraph* on December 15, 1869, sums up the book's reception in the United States: ". . . matter-of-fact record of travel in Europe and the East, delightfully flavored with humor and plentifully spiced with wit."

Twain was so blithely prejudiced because he lived in an age when racism of one kind or another was nearly ubiquitous. His views were typical of those offered in Victorian tourist guidebooks of his day; take, for example, this acidic generalization: "No one acquainted with Orientals expects the truth, unless it is in the interests of the teller, and to bear this in mind prevents disappointment."

Twain's skill as a satirist makes it difficult to determine his true opinion of Muslims, given that his purpose was to reflect perspectives he thought typical of Americans at the time. Accepting that his work influenced American opinion, even while it meant to entertain, is probably the safest conclusion. Calling him a racist and leaving it at that is too superficial. *Innocents Abroad* contains offensive jibes and epithets similar to those found in *The Adventures of Huckleberry Finn* and *The Adventures of Tom Sawyer*. No informed literary critic would claim that the issue of racism in those books was anything less than a complex one.

—J. H.

I never shall want another Turkish lunch. The cooking apparatus was in the little lunch-room near the bazaar, and it was all open to the street. The cook was slovenly, and so was the table, and it had no cloth on it. The fellow took a mass of sausage-meat and coated it round a wire and laid it on a charcoal fire to cook. When it was done, he laid it aside, and a dog walked sadly in and nipped it. He smelt it first, and probably recognised the remains of a friend. The cook took it away from him and laid it before us. Jack said, "I pass"—he plays euchre sometimes—and we all passed in turn. Then the cook baked a broad, flat, wheaten cake, greased it well with the sausage, and started towards us with it. It dropped in the dirt, and he picked it up and polished it on his breeches, and laid it before us. Jack said, "I pass." We all passed. He put some eggs in a frying-pan, and stood pensively prying slabs of meat from between his teeth with a fork. Then he used the fork to turn the eggs with—and brought them along. Jack said, "Pass again." All followed suit. We did not know what to do, and so we ordered a new ration of sausage. The cook got out his wire, apportioned a proper amount of sausage-meat, spat it on his hands and fell to work! This time, with one accord, we all passed out. We paid and left. That is all I learned about Turkish lunches. A Turkish lunch is good, no doubt, but it has its little drawbacks.

When I think how I have been swindled by books of Oriental travel, I want a tourist for breakfast. For years and years I have dreamed of the wonders of the Turkish bath; for years and years I have promised myself that I would yet enjoy one. Many and many a time in fancy, I have lain in the marble bath, and breathed the slumbrous fragrance of Eastern spices that filled the air; then passed through a weird and complicated system of pulling and hauling, and drenching and scrubbing by a gang of naked savages who loomed vast and vaguely through the steaming mists, like demons; then rested for a while on a divan fit for a king; then passed through another complex ordeal, and one more fearful than the first; and finally, swathed in soft fabrics, been conveyed to a princely saloon and laid on a bed of eider down, where eunuchs, gorgeous of costume, fanned me while I drowsed and dreamed, or contentedly gazed at the rich hangings of the apartment, the soft carpets, the sumptuous furniture, the pictures, and drank delicious coffee, smoked the soothing narghili, and dropped, at the last, into tranquil repose, lulled by sensuous odours from un-seen censers, by the gentle influence of the narghili's Persian tobacco, and by the music of fountains that counterfeited the pattering of summer rain.

That was the picture, just as I got it from incendiary books of travel. It was a poor, miserable imposture. The reality is no more like it than the Five Points are like the Garden of Eden. They received me in a great court, paved with marble slabs; around it were broad galleries, one above another, carpeted with seedy matting, railed with unpainted balustrades, and furnished with huge rickety chairs, cushioned with rusty old mattresses, indented with impressions left by the forms of nine successive generations of men who had reposed upon them. The place was vast, naked, dreary; its court a barn, its galleries stalls for human horses. The cadaverous, half-nude varlets that served in the establish-ment had nothing of poetry in their appearance, nothing of romance, nothing of Oriental splendour. They shed no entrancing odours—just the contrary. Their hungry eyes and their lank forms continually suggested one glaring un-sentimental fact—they wanted what they term in California "a square meal."

I went into one of the racks and undressed. An unclean starveling wrapped a gaudy tablecloth with his loins, and hung a white rag over my shoulders. If I had had a tub then, it would have come natural to me to take in washing. I was then conducted down-stairs into the wet, slippery court, and the first thing that attracted my attention were my heels. My fall excited no comment. They expected it, no doubt. It belonged in the list of softening, sensuous influences peculiar to this home of Eastern luxury. It was softening enough, certainly, but its application was not happy. They now gave me a pair of wooden clogs—benches in miniature, with leather straps over them to confine my feet (which they would have done, only I do not wear No. 13s). These things dangled uncomfortably by the straps when I lifted up my feet, and came down in awkward and unexpected places when I put them on the floor again, and sometimes turned sideways and wrenched my ankles out of joint. However, it was all Oriental luxury, and I did what I could to enjoy it.

They put me in another part of the barn and laid me on a stuffy sort of pal-let, which was not made of cloth of gold, or Persian shawls, but was merely the unpretending sort of thing I have seen in the negro quarters of Arkansas. There was nothing whatever in this dim marble prison but five more of these biers. It was a very solemn place. I expected that the spiced odours of Araby were going to steal my senses now, but they did not. A copper-coloured skeleton, with a rag around him, brought me a glass decanter of water, with a lighted tobacco pipe in the top of it, and a pliant stem a yard long with a brass mouth-piece to it.

It was the famous "narghili" of the East—the thing the Grand Turk smokes in the pictures. This began to look like luxury. I took one blast of it, and it was sufficient; the smoke went in a great volume down into my stomach, my lungs, even into the uttermost parts of my frame. I exploded one mighty cough, and it was as if Vesuvius had let go. For the next five minutes I smoked at every pore, like a frame house that is on fire on the inside. Not any more narghili for me. The smoke had a vile taste, and the taste of a thousand infidel tongues that remained on that brass mouth-piece was viler still. I was getting discouraged. Whenever hereafter I see the cross-legged Grand Turk smoking his narghili, in pretended bliss, on the outside of a paper of Connecticut tobacco, I shall know him for the shameless humbug he is.

This prison was filled with hot air. When I had got warmed up sufficiently to prepare me for a still warmer temperature, they took me where it was—into a marble room, wet, slippery, and steamy, and laid me out on a raised platform in the centre. It was very warm. Presently my man sat me down by a tank of hot water, drenched me well, gloved his hand with a coarse mitten, and began to polish me all over with it. I began to smell disagreeably. The more he polished the worse I smelt. It was alarming. I said to him—

"I perceive that I am pretty far gone. It is plain that I ought to be buried without any unnecessary delay. Perhaps you had better go after my friends at once, because the weather is warm, and I cannot 'keep' long."

He went on scrubbing, and paid no attention. I soon saw that he was reducing my size. He bore hard on his mitten, and from under it rolled little cylinders, like macaroni. It could not be dirt, for it was too white. He pared me down in this way for a long time. Finally I said—

"It is a tedious process. It will take hours to trim me to the size you want me; I will wait; go and borrow a jack-plane."

He paid no attention at all.

After a while he brought a basin, some soap, and something that seemed to be the tail of a horse. He made up a prodigious quantity of soapsuds, deluged me with them from head to foot, without warning me to shut my eyes, and then swabbed me viciously with the horsetail. Then he left me there, a snowy statue of lather, and went away. When I got tired of waiting I went and hunted him up. He was propped against a wall in another room, asleep. I woke him. He was not disconcerted. He took me back and flooded me with hot water, then turbaned my head, swathed me with dry tablecloths, and conducted me to a latticed chicken-coop in one of the galleries, and pointed to one of those Arkansas beds. I mounted it, and vaguely expected the odours of Araby again. They did not come.

The blank, unornamented coop had nothing about it of that Oriental voluptuousness one reads of so much. It was more suggestive of the country hospital than anything else. The skinny servitor brought a narghili, and I got him to take it out again without wasting any time about it. Then he brought the world-renowned Turkish coffee that poets have sung so rapturously for many generations, and I seized upon it as the last hope that was left of my old dream of Eastern luxury. It was another fraud. Of all the unchristian beverages that ever passed my lips, Turkish coffee is the worst. The cup is small, it is smeared with grounds; the coffee is black, thick, unsavoury of smell, and execrable in taste. The bottom of the cup has a muddy sediment in it half an inch deep. This goes down your throat, and portions of it lodge by the way, and produce a tickling aggravation that keeps you barking and coughing for an hour.

Here endeth my experience of the celebrated Turkish bath, and here also endeth my dreams of the bliss the mortal revels in who passes through it. It is a malignant swindle. The man who enjoys it is qualified to enjoy anything that is repulsive to sight or sense, and he that can invest it with a charm of poetry is able to do the same with anything else in the world that is tedious and wretched, and dismal, and nasty.

The Khan of Khiva

LIEUTENANT COLONEL
FREDERICK GUSTAVUS BURNABY

From A *Ride to Khiva*, 1878

James Tissot's elegant portrait of Lieutenant Colonel Frederick Burnaby, now in the British National Gallery, was painted in 1870. Burnaby's pose is stunningly natural. Decked out in the blue dress uniform of the Royal Horse Guards, sporting a military haircut and mustache, cigarette in hand, he leans back on a chesterfield. He exudes insouciance and worldly charm. Without knowing his story, the portrait hints at a plush, society life.

In reality, Burnaby personified the Victorian soldier-adventurer, seizing any opportunity to be in the field. He was a *Times* war correspondent in Spain in 1873, then in the Sudan in 1875. He was the first to complete a solo crossing of the English Channel in a hot-air balloon in 1882. But these were all easy achievements compared to his 1875 expedition to the Khanate of Khiva.

That year, he made his incredible journey from London, through Russia, to Khiva, now in Uzbekistan. This was one of the last so-called Turcoman khanates between Russia's southern frontier, Afghanistan, and China. Three Russian armies had conquered much of Khiva's territory in 1873, effectively closing it to travelers. Burnaby was among the last Westerners to visit the khanate before its fall to Russia, and he wrote about his dangerous journey in *A Ride to Khiva*. This account reproduced here was immensely popular, even published in a condensed magazine format.

A year later, Burnaby toured the Russian frontier and published *A Ride Through Asia* in 1878. Working for the British Red Cross, he witnessed the Russo-Turkish War in 1877. While his adventures made him a celebrity, he failed at politics and was defeated when he ran as a Conservative in the 1880 election. Though his junkets were officially billed as military leaves, no doubt Burnaby was also reporting to the British government. It was, after all, the age of the Great Game — Britain's and Russia's cold war over dominance of Asia and the Middle East.

Burnaby was killed by a spear in hand-to-hand fighting in the Sudan in 1885. It was a fitting end for one who had spent his life in pursuit of adventure.

—J. H.

The present Khan is the eleventh in succession of the same family. He commenced his reign ten years ago, at the death of the previous sovereign, the khanate descending from father to son, and not to the eldest male relative, as is the case among some other Mohammedan nations. The monarch receives the crown lands and gardens intact. With the rest of the nation, the property at a father's death is divided equally amongst his sons, thus doing away with the possibility of any one possessing a large extent of the soil.

The actual Khan, after paying his annual tribute to the Tzar, has 100,000 roubles, or about £14,000 a year, left for himself. He has no army to maintain, and some of the Turkoman tribes are recommencing to pay him taxes. This they do for fear lest otherwise it might be made a pretext for a Russian advance into their country.

The following day I rode out to visit the sovereign's gardens, which are about three versts from the town. He has five; each of them is from four to five acres in extent; they are surrounded by high walls, built of dried clay, with solid buttresses at the corners. Two large wooden gates at the entrance of the enclosure were opened by the gardener, a little swarthy man, clad in a dressing-gown of many colours, and with a long iron hoe on his shoulder. I was accompanied by the son of my host, and Nazar, when the former saying that I had the Khan's permission, the gardener stepped aside, and allowed us to enter.

The garden was remarkably well kept, and the horticultural arrangements much better than I expected to find so far from Europe. Here were to be seen long avenues of fruit-trees, carefully out and trimmed. There men were engaged in preparing the soil, which would be thickly studded with melons in the ensuing spring. Apple, pear, and cherry-trees abounded, whilst in the centre of the ground high scaffoldings, covered with trellis-work, showed where, in summer, the vines are trained. Under their grateful shade, cool walks are formed to protect the Khan and his ladies from the burning sun.

He has a small summer palace in this garden, to which he resorts, and where he holds his court in June and July. Trenches for the purpose of irrigation are cut in all directions about the grounds, whilst frequent mulberry-trees, terminating in thick clusters of the same, are interspersed throughout the garden.

The scene must be a striking one when the Khan, surrounded by his court and officers of the state, administers justice. For this takes place in the open, on a raised stone dais, which is ascended by a low flight of steps. There the delinquents are brought, and if they do not at once confess their guilt to their lord and master, he orders them to be taken to the moullah, a learned man, whose business it is to investigate into all such matters. The latter produces a copy of the Koran, and desires the suspected individual to swear his innocence; if this is done, and there are no eye-witnesses to prove the man's guilt, he is allowed to go free. Should he perjure himself, the Khivans believe that the vengeance of Allah will speedily overtake him, and that the retribution will then be much greater than any punishment which man's justice could inflict.

"But," I inquired, "are there never some wretches amongst you who will risk the wrath of Allah, and, perjuring themselves, be released to commit other crimes?"

"No," was the answer. "The fear of God's vengeance is happily too great to admit of such wickedness."

"But, supposing that there are witnesses who can prove that the person committed the crime, and he still denies it; what do you do then?"

"Why, we beat him with rods, put salt in his mouth, and expose him to the burning rays of the sun, until at last he confesses, and then is punished for his breach of the law."

After riding through the gardens which lie on the southern side of the city, and are on the road to Merve, we returned to Khiva, and visited the prison—a low building, on the left of the court which forms the entrance to the Khan's palace. Here I found two prisoners, their feet fastened in wooden stocks, whilst heavy iron chains encircled their necks and bodies. They were accused of having assaulted a woman, and two females were witnesses of the act; but as the prisoners would not confess, they were to be kept in confinement till they acknowledged their guilt.

On leaving the gaol, I rode to the principal school, and found it a series of little low rooms or open niches, which enclosed a courtyard. A large fountain, or basin for water, had been constructed in the centre of the open space, the corners of the court being surmounted by some high domes and minarets of coloured tiles similar to those in the Khan's palace. A moullah superintends each school, and under his supervision there is a staff of other teachers. The subjects taught are reading, writing, and the Koran, pages of which are committed to memory by the pupils. The teacher squats beside the hearth in the middle of the room, whilst the boys sit around him, and learn from his lips verses of their scripture. The parents pay for their children's tuition in corn, a certain number of measures being given to the instructor in return for his labours. A crowd followed us about, and some of the people were much surprised, seeing that I wrote from left to right, instead of from right to left, as I jotted down my notes in a pocket-book.

A succession of visitors awaited us on returning to our quarters, several moullahs, who had been to Egypt and Mecca, calling to pay their respects to the Englishman, who, like themselves, spoke Arabic.

In the meantime Nazar was making preparations for a start to Bokhara. Bread had been ordered, or rather a peculiar sort of little round cake, which substitutes the so-called staff of life at Khiva. The guide had promised to accompany us, and the camel-driver was thoroughly prepared to accompany me to the end of the world, so long as I gave him plenty to eat. I determined to remain one day longer, and then leave for Bokhara. This would be a twelve days' march from Khiva. From Bokhara I could go on to Merve and Meshed, where we should be in Persian territory.

I should much have liked to have remained some days longer at Khiva, but time was important. It was the 27th of January, and I was obliged to be back with my regiment on the 14th of April. However, *L'homme propose, mais Dieu dispose*; and the truth of this celebrated old French saying was prominently brought before me the next morning, for, on returning from an early ride through the market, where a great sale of camels and horses was taking place, I found two strangers in my apartment. One of them producing a letter, handed it to me, saying that he had been sent to Khiva by order of the Commandant at Petro-Alexandrovsk.

On opening the enclosure, I found a letter written in Russian on one side of the paper, and in French on the other.

Its contents were to the following effect: that the Commandant had received a telegram, *via* Tashkent, and that I must go the fort to receive the communication.

I was greatly surprised to find that any one took so much interest in me as to despatch a telegram so many thousand miles, and put himself to the expense of having the message forwarded from Tashkent, where the telegraph ends, to Khiva, a distance of nine hundred miles, by couriers with relays of horses. It must have cost a large sum of money sending that telegram, and I began to be a little alarmed, thinking that perhaps I should be asked to pay for it.

Again, what could have occurred of such great importance as to induce any one to telegraph? Could it be that General Milutin, the Russian Minister of War, had just remembered that I had called four times at his house, and that he had not been able to give me an interview, but that he was now prepared to grant one?

There was another solution which might also have been correct, and the thought suddenly occurred that perhaps Count Schouvaloff's brother, to whom the thoughtful ambassador in London had so kindly given me a letter of introduction, had by this time arrived at St. Petersburg, and wished to show me some hospitality.

Anyhow, there was the letter, and I must go to Petro-Alexandrovsk to receive the telegram. It was not a pleasant thought, after having gone so far, to have possibly to return to European Russia over the snow-covered steppes. It is a hard journey even for the Tartars, this fourteen days' march, with the cold at 20° and 30° below zero, and no shelter to be met with on the road. The Tartar and Khivan merchants occasionally, it is true, make the journey in mid-winter, but invariably wait till the spring for their return to Orenburg.

I had accomplished the really hard part of my journey, and every degree marched in the direction of Merve would have led me to a warmer clime. However, there was nothing to be done save to go to Petro-Alexandrovsk, and then, if the despatch were of such a nature as to oblige me to return, to retrace my steps.

The messenger who had brought the letter was eager for my immediate return to the fort. This, I said, was out of the question till the next day, as I wished to make some purchases in the town, and must also pay a farewell visit to the Khan previous to my departure.

A little later I rode to the bazaar, accompanied by Nazar and the guide, the latter not being at all pleased at our having to go to Petro-Alexandrovsk. He was very uneasy in his own mind about the consequences which might occur to him for having brought me to Khiva.

One of the men sent with the Commandant's letter was now continually in our wake, and I subsequently learned that a strict order had been sent to the Khan to have our party followed and taken to the fort, in the event of my having left the city.

On arriving at the bazaar we were instantly surrounded by merchants, all eager to dispose of their wares. On selecting the most respectable-looking man I could see, he led me into a large room at the back of his shop. Here, after he had offered us some dried fruit and tea, as indispensable to a Khivan tradesman when bargaining with a customer as coffee to a shopkeeper in Cairo, he proceeded to a large wooden box which stood in a corner of the apartment, and unlocked it with an enormous key which hung from his girdle. The key, as it turned in the lock, gave out a peculiar hissing sound, owing to some hidden mechanism in the interior.

"Do you want something for a young or for an old woman?" asked the merchant—Nazar having previously informed him that I wished to buy some female ornaments.

"If you want it for a young wife, look how beautiful this is—she would look lovely with it;" and he handed me a large gold ring, curiously set with small pearls and turquoises.

"This would be too large for her finger," I remarked.

"Yes," replied the man; "but not for her nose. This is for her nose."

"Lovely!" said the guide. "My brother-in-law's wife has one its very counterpart; buy it."

"Sir," said Nazar, "no girl could resist you, if you offered her such a present."

The whole party were much surprised when I informed them that in England we only put rings in the noses of the unclean animal.

The jewellery for sale was of a tawdry description; however, eventually I discovered a curiously-worked gold ornament, with long pendants of coral and other stones. After a great deal of haggling, Nazar succeeded in obtaining it for me at one-third of the price originally asked; the Khivan jewellers having very elastic consciences, in spite of the Prophet's injunction, that no true believer is to deceive the stranger within his gates.

On returning to my quarters I found the treasurer awaiting my arrival. He had heard the news of my enforced departure, and came to know at what time it would be convenient for me to pay my respects and say farewell to the Khan. Shortly afterwards I rode with him to the palace, when he first led the way to the treasury, and there presenting me with a dressing-gown, said that his Majesty had been pleased to beg my acceptance of this garment. It was a long robe, made of black cloth, reaching to the knees, and lined inside with silk and bright-coloured chintzes. Indeed, as I was afterwards informed, this is the highest honour that can be paid a stranger, and a halat or dressing-gown from the Khan is looked up at Khiva much as the Order of the Garter would be in England.

The sovereign expressed his annoyance that I had to leave his capital so suddenly. He then remarked—

"You will come back again, I trust; and pray tell all Englishmen whom you may meet that I have heard from the envoy I sent to India of the greatness of their nation, and only hope that before long I shall see some of them in my capital."

He was very kind in his manner, and shook hands warmly when I took my leave; the impression being left on my mind that the Khan of Khiva is the least bigoted of all the Mohammedans whose acquaintance I have made in the course of my travels, and that the stories of his cruelties to Russian prisoners, previous to the capture of his city, are pure inventions, which have been disseminated by the Russian press in order to try and justify the annexation of his territory.

Before leaving my quarters I endeavoured to persuade my host to accept a present in acknowledgment of the handsome treatment my party and myself had received at his hands. However, this was a fruitless task; the Khivan at once declined, saying that I was the Khan's guest; and that his Majesty would be very angry if he were to learn that I had tried to requite his hospitality by giving a present to his servant. Indeed, when I made it a personal matter my attempt was equally fruitless, and I left the city slightly pained at not being able to leave behind some token or other to show how much I appreciated his kindness during my stay at Khiva.

Ismail Deserts

LADY ANNE BLUNT

From *Bedouin Tribes of the Euphrates*, 1879

Lady Anne Blunt (1837–1917) was the granddaughter of Lord Byron, rake, adventurer, and poet, who died on a campaign against the Turks in Greece. Photographs of her suggest toughness, sensuality, and a sense of humor — qualities not unknown to Byron. She needed them. Blunt was the first Western woman to risk living and trekking as a Bedouin in the deserts of Mesopotamia (modern Iraq) and Syria. Because she immersed herself in Bedouin culture, her books revealed Bedouins to European readers in an unprecedented manner.

With her eccentric husband, Wilfred (a diplomat, poet, and diarist), she went on two expeditions into the deserts of Syria, Iraq, and Arabia between 1877 and 1880. The first expedition was launched in order to find pure Arabian horses to stock their stud farm in Crabbet, England. Her first book, *Bedouin Tribes of the Euphrates*, contained studies of the Shammar and Anazeh Bedouin cultures.

The Blunts broke with convention at every turn. Once in Baghdad they dismissed the advice of the British Consul, who thought they should spend time acclimatizing in the city. Instead, they entered the desert immediately, and in a short time they had become honorary members of the Anazeh and Shammar Bedouin tribes. "We thus acquired in a few weeks more real knowledge of the Desert and its inhabitants than has often been amassed in as many years spent in the frontier towns of Syria," Blunt wrote.

Her second amazing journey — amazing in part because she went on another so soon after her first — was a thousand-mile trek into central Arabia, recounted in *A Pilgrimage to Nejd* (1881).

Blunt is little known these days, far less so than T. E. Lawrence, whose experiences took place nearly forty years later. Unfortunately, the only figure remotely like her to reach the big screen is the sinister Lady Davenport, in the fictional Disney movie, *Hidalgo*. This is regrettable, because women experienced some of the greatest nineteenth- and early-twentieth-century journeys by Westerners in the Islamic world. Besides Blunt, examples include Alexine Tinne, who spent nine years exploring Egypt and the Sudan, and then died en route to Lake Chad in 1869. Ella Sykes rode through Persia in 1895 (her story appears in chapter 9 of this collection). These Victorians were followed by Gertrude Bell, Rosita Forbes (see chapter 22), Freya Stark, and others.

How might our view of the West's exploration and relationship with Islam be changed if the stories of these women were better known and celebrated in films and books, to balance the towering importance of T. E. Lawrence, the soldier-adventurer? A major shift in the perception of history could occur. Lawrence's wartime campaigns and experience among the Arabs add up to far less time and information gleaned about the Islamic world than the cumulative explorations of these women. Blunt lived in the Middle East much longer than Lawrence did. She died in Cairo in 1917 after having arrived in the Middle East in 1877. Her journeys, and those of the other women adventurers, mostly occurred in peacetime, with the cooperation and vital assistance of local Muslims.

Not a lesson to ignore.

—J. H.

To-day matters came to a crisis with Ismaïl, and he is gone. The two blacks also have left us. All last night and this morning Ismaïl was working the old tales of danger and ghazús, expatiating on the terrible nature of the desert north of us, contrasted with the delightfully inhabited regions of the south—want of water, want of grass, want of "Arabs," of all except plundering bands of Ánazeh, who, by his account, perpetually scour these inhospitable regions, robbing and slaying those who venture there. Ali and Hánna and the two Agheyl were much impressed by these sad stories, and even Daëssan occasionally chimed in, "He did not know the road; he did not know whom we might meet; he did not know where we should find Faris. Perhaps it would be better first to go to Ferhán, or at least to Naïf, who would send people with us. It was not all quite right between Ferhán and his brother; the Khábur was clean out of our road to Deyr," etc., etc. The weight of public opinion in the caravan was against us; and all we could say in support of our views was, that the camels were ours, and that those who liked might leave us. Of this, of course, there was no question among our own people, and Ismaïl was evidently loath to part with us—not, I fear, from affection, but from love of the backshísh he had so nearly earned.

We had no sooner started than it became evident that Daëssan had been "got at" during the night, for he no longer kept his course fairly, but suffered Ismaïl to lead him astray whenever our attention was directed elsewhere. Excuses were easy to give for this: "There was a súbkha in our way which would have to be turned by a circuit to the south-west; we had come too far to the north yesterday; he must go a little to the left to get his bearings." The contest between Wilfrid and Ismaïl soon almost became a physical one for the possession of the little man, one riding on one side and the other on the other, and each trying to edge him off to right or left, like the spirits of good and evil tempting a human soul. At last the crisis came. Ismaïl having stopped behind for a few minutes to say his prayers, Wilfrid profited by this to get a good point northward, so that when Ismaïl succeeded in overtaking them he was so much out of temper that he declared he would go no farther. The black man and the boy were already gone and out of sight, having made away nearly due south; so a halt was called, and we all sat down on the ground to discuss matters. The strong point of our case was, that physically we could do as we liked, and were free to turn the camels' heads to any point of the compass we chose; the weak one, that we could hardly go without introduction of any kind to Faris, and it was necessary that one or other of the Shammar should remain with us. Ismaïl's strong point was the desire we had expressed of paying Ferhán a visit, and the shame (*aïb*) it would be to pass so near his tent without stopping. The conversation, then, was something of this sort. *Ismaïl:* "You do not wish, then, to see the sheykh? Ferhán will not be pleased." *Wilfrid:* "We wish to see him, but where is he?" *Ismaïl:* "Out there with Naïf," pointing semicircularly round half the southern horizon. *Wilfrid:* "And Faris, where is he?" "Away on the Khábur, close to Deyr," pointing in almost the same direction. *Wilfrid:* "Nonsense, that is the road to Ána. I have an engagement to meet a friend at Deyr in five days, and I want to see Faris." *Ismaïl:* "Five days! it is quite close. The Pasha will send you there to-morrow." "But where is the Pasha?" "You see that hill on the horizon: come with me there, and I will show you his house." "Let us go; but mind, if I don't see it, good-bye."

There was not much danger in making this promise; and, although the hill (or rather the little indentation on the horizon) was some five miles out of our way, we thought it prudent to go so far with Ismaïl that we might not seem unwilling to see his master, whom we have no wish to offend (and passing close to a great man's camp without stopping is a serious matter); so we altered our course, and now held on nearly straight to the south. Ismaïl, seeing he had gained his point, had become good-humored; and we, wishing to part friends with him, explained the difficulties of our position as to Faris and his master, both of whom we had not time to visit. If the whole truth must be known, one of our principal objections to meeting the great man was that we had only one gold-embroidered cloak left, the one destined for Ferhán having been given to Smeyr, and we did not like to appear empty-handed at his tent. Daëssan followed in silence, for he is not much addicted to words, and Ali and the rest of our followers were of course in high delight. "In another moment we shall see the tents!" exclaimed the enthusiastic Hánna, "a lamb will be killed—perhaps a young camel; and we shall, at any rate, sleep among the Arabs to-night!" "Inshalláh!" they all chorused, and so we rode on.

The little hill, on nearer approach, turned out to be nothing but a mound transfigured by the mirage, and made to look great only from the surrounding level of the plain. Beyond it, however, the ground sloped away rapidly; and, in truth, it commanded a very considerable view. Here we halted, straining our eyes in every direction for the vision of black dots which should represent an Arab encampment, but nothing was visible for miles and miles. Ismaïl, however, was not so easily abashed. On the far horizon, perhaps fifteen miles away, rose a flat-topped hill, easily recognizable, and very likely really recognized by him. To this he pointed triumphantly. "There," he said, "is the house of Naïf, and there the Pasha abides." "A day's journey," we replied; "*you* will get there to-morrow, but *we* must go on our way." "At least," he pleaded, "go a little way toward it—as far as the tent you see down there." We knew there was no tent, but the object he pointed to was not far off, and we agreed to satisfy him; so, bidding the caravan wait, we galloped down the sloping plain. The object, on nearer inspection, proved to be a pile of bushes marking the spot where a tent had been, but long ago.

Just as we made this out, a string of camels hove in sight, a mile or two away. Ismaïl seemed alarmed, declaring there were horsemen with them; but we could see well enough this was not the case, and galloped on toward them, wishing to set the matter at rest as to the whereabouts of the Shammar, for the party seemed to be travelling from the south. We were determined, too, to get our information unadulterated by Ismaïl's coloring, and so let our mares out, and left him on his old kadísh well in the rear. As we rushed up to them at full gallop, with guns in our hands, it is not strange that the people with the camels should have been a little alarmed. They halted and formed square, as I may say, to receive our charge. They were ten men on dromedaries, armed with lances, but they had no fire-arms with them. We pulled up a few yards in front of them, and asked them whence they were, and whither going; to which they replied that they came from Ferhán, and were on their way to Tell Áfar, a town of the Sinjár, to buy corn. The camels were not laden. They informed us that Naïf's camp was, in truth, a little way beyond the flat-topped hill, the name of which was El Melífeh; but that Farhán had left it, and was, with his son Mijuel, a day's journey farther still. Ismaïl came up just as they told us this, and saw that the game was up; so, when the men had ridden away with their camels, he came to us and said, with a rather ghastly smile, that he must wish us good-bye here. He had to be at Naïf's tent before night; and if we would not come with him, why, he must leave us to our fate; he couldn't go with us farther north—he and Faris's people were not friends. We replied, "So be it," gave him a polite message to his master, and, to his great joy and surprise, a present for himself. We had gained our point, and could afford to be generous. So he wished us good-bye, and various blessings, between his teeth. Then, putting his kadísh into a feeble canter, he departed.

Circumstances had favored us, for Daëssan was behind, and the rest of our caravan out of sight, so that no discussion with any of our people had been possible, and when we returned we had only to announce Ismaïl's departure as a *fait accompli*. Daëssan, finding himself relieved from the burden of Ismaïl's presence, now made no objection to giving us the true direction, and the camels' heads were turned north-west, while our followers, after a few expressions of disappointment, lapsed into silence. We travelled on thus for two hours, regaining most of our lost ground. Wilfrid was then fortunate enough to discover a pool of rain-water, the first fresh water we had met with since leaving El Haddr, and there we filled our goat-skins. We should have liked to encamp beside the precious element; but Daëssan, saying that seriously there was danger in the country we were entering, begged us to go a little farther on. We are now encamped in a wady; far away from all living creatures, and nicely hidden from the surrounding plain. Ali, Hánna, and the rest are very serious and quiet this evening, and we hope to have an undisturbed night, having had troubles enough during the day.

We are now in the heart of Mesopotamia (just at the top of the second O in our map). The tents have not yet been pitched, for fear of distant eyes— for this is Tom Tiddler's ground, between Ferhán's people and Faris's, where nobody comes for any good.

The Aryans of Sarikol

ELLA SYKES

From *Through Deserts and Oases of Central Asia*, 1920

Ella Sykes, an upper-class Englishwoman, rode sidesaddle through Persia in 1895–96. This was the first of many incredible journeys she would undertake in her lifetime. The second was in 1915, when she rode from India, through the Pamir Mountains at altitudes higher than the Rockies, to China, then taking a train through Russia, and finally a ship to Britain. Yaks proved to be more useful than horses on parts of this trek. Sykes was the first Western woman to travel parts of Central Asia that few Europeans of her time had seen. Her most important accomplishment was not so much discovering new regions, but revealing those places and people to others through her books.

For both of these expeditions, Sykes joined her brother, Sir Percy Sykes. His career as a mapmaker, soldier, spy, and adventurer exemplifies the type of British officer who waged the cold war against Russian counterparts in the struggle known as the "Great Game." Sykes's journeys in Persia and Central Asia were far more dangerous because her brother, though officially a diplomat, was in fact an intelligence officer in a contest that often turned violent. He wrote his own books, but his sister's are the more engaging. Her three books are chatty and intriguing, and display observant intelligence, not to mention dogged toughness. First came *Through Persia on a Side-Saddle* (1897), then *Persia and Its People* (1910), and finally, *Through Deserts and Oases of Central Asia* (1920), which she wrote with her brother.

Lady Anne Blunt had set the standard for outrageous equestrian adventures in 1877 when she rode into the Iraqi desert to obtain studs for her horse farm. Blunt went into the desert disguised as a Bedouin, lived as a Bedouin, and, I suspect, never got the sand out of her soul even when she left the desert.

Unlike Blunt, Sykes was never inconspicuous, nor was she a particularly intrepid traveler. Her strength was in her inexhaustible endurance of harsh climates and rough living conditions. On no journey did she pretend to be other than what she was—an aristocratic Englishwoman—yet she didn't have a fleck of snobbery about her. Her tenacious capacity to explore exotic, foreign places—all the while hauling around extravagant baggage and maintaining her high standards of cleanliness and behavior—was stunning. She was always accompanied by a maid in Persia, and would only dismiss one if the maid was found incapable of withstanding the living conditions. Unlike Blunt, Sykes had no cultural or physical preparation for her entry into the Islamic world, but somehow she knew she was as tough as her brother.

Captain Percy Sykes originally belonged to a cavalry regiment in India. Then, after hunting expeditions in Kashmir, he was recruited for intelligence work. Like a character out of Kipling's *Kim*, he was sent as a spy into the Russian portion of Turkistan. His successful mission earned him a combined diplomatic and intelligence post in Kerman, where Russian agents were attempting to tip that region into their orbit. Unmarried at age twenty-seven, Sykes returned to England in 1894 and asked his sister to be his partner in setting up the Kerman mission. Percy and Ella Sykes returned there together in 1895.

Sykes's brief account of arriving in Persia details their journey by ship from Marseilles to Constantinople, from there to a port in eastern Turkey, and then on the Trans-Caucasus Railway through the Ottoman frontier provinces to Baku, in what is today the country of Azerbaijan. Then they crossed the wild Russian frontier region, and from Baku, the Sykes party traveled by boat across the Caspian Sea to a Persian port, Enzeli.

Her exhilaration upon arriving in Persia is delightful to read: "I realised that I was on the threshold of a new life, which I ardently trusted might have its quantum of adventures."

It certainly did. Her last adventure was in 1915 when she entered the Pamir Mountains.

—J. H.

On the return journey to Kashgar our first camp was at Issak Boulak, a secluded little valley high up in the hills. The name means Hot Springs, and we reached it by crossing a series of steep nullahs, up and down the crumbling banks of which our horses had to scramble, as our guide could find no track. At last we arrived at a fold of the mountains, within which was an orange-coloured stream fed by hot sulphur springs that gushed out of the hillside at a temperature of 150° Fahrenheit. My brother and I clambered up to the source of the water, and I dipped a finger cautiously into one of the two springs that were bursting out of the barren rock and pouring into a big pool below, which is visited by sufferers from rheumatism, who sit all day in the hot water. Sattur brought a can of almost boiling water for my bath, bursting into giggles as he poured it in, so mirth-inspiring did he find this labour-saving phenomenon.

Issak Boulak was an isolated spot at the back of beyond, and behind our camp a long twisting defile led into the very heart of the mountains, making me hope to come across some wild creature as we turned corner after corner; but the only sign of life was a hawk that swooped so low as to brush my hat. All the birds we saw during our tour were wonderfully tame. Hoopoes and choughs flew close as if to observe us, the pretty yellow wagtails merely hopped aside as we passed, the cheery desert-larks almost let us tread upon them, while pigeons and partridges had little fear of the gun.

At our halt at Subashi I had my first experience of riding a yak, or *kutass*. Though I had watched these creatures with their formidable horns moving with ungainly gait over their pastures and had laughed at the uncouth gambols of their calves at play, I had no wish for a more intimate acquaintance with them. But one morning, as we looked at the tremendous mass of Muztagh Ata, my brother proposed that we should try to reach one of the glaciers that hang on its mighty slopes, and accordingly we set off mounted on yaks. Instead of a bridle, the animal has a rope passed through the cartilage of the nose, and, though this is sufficient for the experienced, in the case of novices it is necessary to have the mount led. I sat astride on the peaked Chinese saddle, and found the movement of the *kutass* comfortable though slow, and we were soon working our way up the flank of the mountain without track of any kind. The ugly, good-tempered Kirghiz who led my yak wore a padded cotton coat striped with scarlet, blue, black and yellow; his long riding-boots were of red leather, and his velvet cap both lined and bordered with fur, while a cloth tied round his waist held his knife and various odds and ends, among which was a hunch of native bread. "I don't know Persian," he remarked to me in that tongue, and "I do not speak Turki" was my reply; but in spite of the language difficulty we understood one another quite well, and I did my part in urging my mount when it hung back and pulled at the nose-rope. It was a long stiff climb to reach the glacier, and all the yaks were panting, grunting and gnashing their teeth before we dismounted and stumbled over the mass of big boulders that were hurled in confusion one upon another just below the immensely thick curtain of ice. The altitude took my breath away, even the hardy Kirghiz complained of splitting headaches, and a big yellow dog, guardian doubtless of some flocks feeding on the scanty grazing below, made a sudden appearance and gave vent to the most lugubrious howls. The Kirghiz never venture into the fastnesses of Muztagh Ata, believing the "Father of the Snows" to be haunted by fairies, by camels of supernatural whiteness, and by the sound of drums, this last being possibly the thunder of avalanches. It was thrilling to be on the slopes of this great mountain, its crest as yet unscaled by any human being, in spite of the efforts of Sir Aurel Stein, and we were entranced with the magnificent mountain panorama from our point of vantage. As the descent was very steep we remounted our yaks, and my brother led off along the mountain side. But my guide was of an enterprising nature, and to my horror we started down what appeared to me to be a sheer precipice. Expostulations were of no avail; he turned a deaf ear to them; so I rammed my feet into the stirrups, leant back as far as I could, and clung to the pommel of my saddle, feeling that I might at any moment be flung over the head of my steed. I confess that my heart was in my mouth as my *kutass* accomplished the descent in a series of long slides, always recovering itself when I imagined that it was just about to fall headlong and bring us both to disaster. My opinion of it as a mount was unbounded, and it crowned its perfections by picking its way unerringly among the boulders that were piled up on either side of the glacier stream along which our route lay. Wild rhubarb was growing in profusion, and I made my boy gather it, as we had not tasted fresh fruit or vegetables for some weeks, and the Russian jam I had bought at Kashgar had fermented and gone off like bombs when the bottles were opened, though Daoud's apricot conserve had borne the long journey perfectly.

We had had a superb view from the flank of Muztagh Ata, but nothing to compare with that which we enjoyed from the shore of Little Lake Karakul that lies at the foot of this giant of the Pamirs. Here to the north stood up in all its grandeur the great mountain barrier separating us from Kashgar, which we had looked upon as some enchanting vision when seen at rare intervals from the roof of the Consulate. The "Father of the Snows" and its rival—the natives call it Kungur—rose sheer from the lake, in company with peak behind peak, all nobly serrated and wrapped in eternal snow. Guardians of the Roof of the World, their proud virginal crests, as yet untrodden by the foot of the explorer, offer an indescribable attraction to him who has felt the lure of the Inaccessible.

My Ride to Sheshouan

WALTER B. HARRIS

From *The Land of an African Sultan*, 1889

Walter B. Harris lived in, wrote about, and explored Morocco from 1886 to 1933. As a journalist and author of seven books, he garnered a wide readership in Britain and the United States. He first went to Morocco when the interior was largely closed to Europeans. When he died in Tangier in 1933, Morocco was divided between France and Spain, and Tangier was an international city controlled by Europeans in much the same way as Shanghai. Harris had decades of experience that gave his observations about Morocco a depth of understanding that few popular Western writers could claim for any Islamic country.

Harris's "My Ride to Sheshouan" is an adventure classic. Chefchouan, as it is now known, was forbidden to non-Muslims. Muslim refugees from the Christian *Reconquista* of Spain founded the city high in the Riff Mountains of northern Morocco. Built in the style of the lost Andalucian civilization of Islamic Spain, its pan-tile peaked roofs and walled medina are located beneath massive twin mountain peaks. It is one of the most beautiful towns in North Africa. Only three Europeans saw it before 1892: French explorer Charles de Foucauld, pretending to be a rabbi, saw it for an hour in 1883; Harris spent a skittish day there in 1889, costumed as a Muslim; and American missionary William Sumners was the next outsider, poisoned for his efforts in 1892.

Harris's stunt at Chefchouan took place early in his career and was just one of his many adventures. His most celebrated was in 1903, when he was kidnapped by the warlord Ahmed el Raisuni and freed in exchange for the release of Raisuni's men from the Tangier prison. That story was upstaged in 1904, when Harris covered Raisuni's kidnapping of American expatriate,

Ion Perdicaris. The Perdicaris incident became an international crisis when the United States sent forces to Morocco in an effort to free Perdicaris. This story appears later in this collection.

In the years before WWI, conflict and crisis in Morocco made headlines. Walter Harris was for English-speaking readers what Christiane Amanpour has been for CNN viewers watching the wars in Afghanistan and Iraq. He became a familiar guide to indecipherable events that portended worse to come.

—J. H.

◆ ◆ ◆

I do not know whether it was merely from love of adventure, or from curiosity to see a place that, as far as is known, has been only once before looked upon by Christian eyes, that I made up my mind to attempt to reach Sheshouan, a fanatical Berber city situated in the mountainous district of Northern Morocco, between the large tribe-lands of BeniHassan and the Riff. But whatever was my first impulse, this helped to bring me to a decision, the very fact that there existed within thirty hours' ride of Tangier a city into which it was considered an utter impossibility for a Christian to enter. That such a place can exist, seems almost incredible to those whose sole experience of Morocco is based on the luxurious Tangier hotels, and the more than semi-civilization of that town.

My mind once made up, it did not take long to prepare myself for my journey; and on a Friday of July in last year (1888) I might have been seen purchasing in the native Tangier shops the articles of clothing that were needed for my disguise, for any attempt to proceed thither in European dress must prove unsuccessful. The costume that I chose consisted of the white long shirt and baggy trousers of the Moors, a small crimson silk sleeveless jacket', the tarboosh or fez, and a jelaba or white-hooded cloak that envelops one from one's knees to one's head. Having successfully purchased these articles, my next business was to send for a boy, by name Selim, who lived in Tangier, but who was a native of Sheshouan and had previously been my servant. An hour later he came, looking very thin and down on his luck; I told him of my idea, and found him, much to my surprise, ready for a comparatively small sum of money to accompany me, and act as guide. I forthwith sent him into town, where he hired two mules with burdas, or Moorish pack-saddles, which were to be at my hotel at two o'clock the following morning. I then packed my luggage, a not very tedious proceeding, as it consisted merely of a small red leather native bag, which I wore slung over my shoulder, containing a toothbrush, a revolver, twenty-five rounds of cartridges, a few sheets of writing-paper, a pencil, and fifty cigarettes. Beyond this I only took a blanket, which was spread over the rough pack-saddle.

About three the next morning we left, and arrived at Tetuan, our first stage, distant from Tangier some forty-five miles, in about ten hours.

The journey from Tangier to Tetuan cannot be called one of extreme interest, though the latter part of the way, where the road leads one between the great mountains, swathed in forest and torn by torrents, is very fine. In fact all through Morocco, except the road I pursued the following day, and the valley of the Atlas mountains, there is not much that can surpass the Tetuan valley in grandeur of scenery. For the first half of the way the road is dull and uninteresting, passing over low, undulating hills, destitute of trees, nor is it until one reaches the slopes of the hill on the summit of which is situated the well-known Fondak, which forms the half-way resting-place for caravans, that things improve. The view from this spot is fine.

Here one always makes a halt for luncheon if one is making the through journey in one day, and for the night, if one is spreading it out over two. I have often pitched my tents at this romantic spot, and a fine camping-ground it made too, as there was abundance of wood for a camp fire, and the wild cries of the jackal at night added to the romance of the scene, making me, as I lay in my tent, almost think that I was back on the Ghauts of India again. The path after leaving the Fondak proceeds along the pass, and finally descends steeply to the level of the river below. This descent usually takes an hour more to accomplish, and rough work it is, as on all sides the path is blocked by great boulders of rock and stone.

Descended to the level of the river, the road improves, and, until one reaches Tetuan, is in good condition. In summer, and even in spring, nothing is more beautiful than the view here, the river with its banks crimson with gay oleanders, the cool shaded mountains, and the white town of Tetuan itself, half blocking one end of the valley, and beyond that the blue Mediterranean.

My first journey to Tetuan I shall never forget. We left Tangier about mid-day on the 1st of January, 1887. Our party consisted of Mr. and Mrs. T. Ingram, Jack Green and myself. We had sent our camp on ahead the day before, under orders to pitch at the Fondak, distant from Tangier only some five hours' ride.

It was a blazing hot day and accordingly we were all arrayed in the lightest of costumes.

We had not proceeded very far when T. discovered that his spaniel was missing, and rode back to fetch it, saying he would overtake us anon. Shortly before dark, between five and six, we began the ascent of the Fondak hill, all rather tired with the exertion of packing our camp off the day before, and the usual worry of a departure, besides which we had been shooting along the road, a tiring process under the hot sun. The idea of reaching the camp in a few minutes was most cheering, but when we arrived at the level ground no tents were to be seen. Meanwhile darkness set in.

We proceeded to the Fondak, and inquired of the Arabs if they had seen our camp. "Yes," they said, "it has gone on to Tetuan."

Here we were in pitch darkness in the wild mountain pass, half starved, and to add to our discomfiture, the thermometer fell suddenly and a frost set in. T. was nowhere to be seen, evidently he had lost his way. We took a few moments to consider matters, and came to the conclusion that at all costs we must push on.

Luckily there was a moon, but even with its aid the path down the boulder-strewn mountain side was anything but pleasant.

For hours we toiled on. The moon had set, we had no lights, and the cold was so intense that we were obliged to walk and lead our horses to keep any warmth in our bodies. About half-past ten, after ten and a half hours in broiling sun and frost, we came upon our camp, not in Tetuan certainly, but still no great distance from it. We found dinner ready, and our men in a state of terror, as it is not at all safe to travel over the Tetuan road by night.

Still T. did not turn up. We hoped that he had remained in Tangier, but though we spoke lightly of it, we were all very anxious.

About four in the morning he arrived, having been all the time on the road. He had lost his way, but finally found a guide, who led him across the country to the Fondak, in pitch darkness, and brought him safely into camp, with his horse dead lame. Our men caught it well for their disobedience in pitching our camp in the wrong place, and a few days later we parted with Larbi, the headman, who was to blame for this and many other misdemeanours, and gave the charge of the whole camp into Antonio's hands, a decided improvement. Nor had we any trouble for the rest of the journey, which lasted two months.

Tetuan itself is a picturesque town, though, like most Moorish cities, there is not much to be seen therein. Probably it inhabitants number some twenty-five to thirty thousand. In this city are found the finest houses in Morocco, as it was here that many of the Moors driven from Andalusia took up their residence, building themselves palaces according to their own hearts.

These houses are built round a square patio, and are generally two storeys in height, the upper storey possessing a balcony, on to which the rooms open. The patios are paved in marbles and tiles, and possess beautiful fountains, from which water is ever gushing. Palm and orange trees grow within, rendering the whole more a garden than a courtyard.

The city was taken by the Spaniards under Marshal O'Donnell in 1859, after a severe struggle with the brave natives, who, badly armed as they were, held it and the surrounding country against the invading foes for some months.

However, it fell at last, and Ceuta was added to Spain, while an indemnity of four millions of pounds was paid them. This indemnity has probably been one of the best strokes of luck the Sultan ever had, as the Spaniards, knowing that otherwise it would probably never be paid, seized the custom-houses, levying a ten per cent. ad valorem duty on exports and imports. This succeeded well, and a few years ago the four millions were re-alized. The Sultan, however, keeps on the duty, himself drawing the ten per cent now, and so enriching himself to the extent of some hundreds of thou-sands a year.

To return to "my ride to Sheshouan," on my arrival in Tetuan I put up at a small native fondak, or caravanserai, full of mules, camels and vermin, where I spent the night in my disguise.

The following morning we were up before dawn, and, fording the river near Tetuan, proceeded on our way. As soon as it was daylight, we began to pass Moors coming into town with vegetables and wood, laden on donkeys; and I was pleased to find that my disguise was sufficiently satisfactory as to lead them to assume that I was an Arab, and to salute me with the salutation, never offered to a Christian—"Salaam 'alikûm." After about two hours on the road, we passed through the village of Zenat, perched high on the mountain side, a pretty, picturesque little place, half hidden in its groves of olives and oleanders, with tiny streams and miniature waterfalls in every direction, and rocks clustered with maidenhair fern. When we had left the village behind, the road led us along the mountain-side at a great distance above the valley beneath, till, an hour later, we descended by a winding path, forded the river, and proceeded up the valley on the left-hand bank. Up to this point the coun-try had been fertile and well cultivated, and the fields full of men and women gathering in the harvest; but now we had entered the country of the wild Beni-Hassan tribe, and the aspect entirely changed; instead of fields, nothing but steep mountains, covered with arbutus and other stunted growth, being visible, except ahead of us, where the great bare rocky peaks of the Sheshouan mountains stood out boldly against the morning sky.

The next object that we passed was a ruined fondak, or caravanserai, not unlike that which exists halfway between Tangier and Tetuan, but entirely de-serted and out of repair. It was near this fondak that my first adventure befell me. We had been overtaken by two Beni-Hassan tribesmen, who, I had no-ticed, had scanned me very closely—far more closely than I appreciated; and I was not particularly pleased to suddenly discover these two, and a third, who was holding a chesnut horse, stationary about two hundred yards in front of me, engaged in conversation, and now and again turning in my direction. There was no other course than to proceed, which I did. On nearing them, the owner of the horse placed it across the road, completely blocking my way, while his two companions took up their position on either side. On my reaching them, one, seizing my bridle, told me I must go no further, while a second pulled me from my mule by my jelaba or cloak. I knew that if I uttered a sound my chance of reaching Sheshouan was at an end, so, grasping my revolver firmly under my cloak, for the double reason of having it ready in case of necessity and keeping it from the sight of my assailants, I remained dumb. My Arab boy proved himself on this occasion—as he did on several afterwards—to be quite worthy of the confidence I had placed in him, for, lying in a calm and collected manner, he asserted that I was a Moor from Fez.

"Why does he not speak?" asked one of the men.

"Is it likely a Moorish gentleman would speak to robbers who attack him on the road, and insult him by pulling him off his mule?" responded Selim; "but he will be revenged, for when the Sultan comes" (referring to the approaching visit of the Sultan to Tetuan), "he will come here and lay your country waste."

Thereupon the men, with a still incredulous look, relinquished their hold of me, and mounting once more, I proceeded on my way. An elevation having rendered us invisible to the tribesmen, we thought it as well to place a more satisfactory distance between ourselves and them, so whipped the mules into a gallop, and were soon some way ahead.

Turning a corner, we suddenly came upon a band of some twenty or thirty Beni-Hassani working by the roadside. These we passed without any difficulty, though the minute or two that we took to pass through them was scarcely a pleasant time, as I expected every moment to hear out first assailants shouting to them to arrest my progress. Then we again proceeded at a gallop over terribly open country; I say "terribly open"—for I felt sure that before many minutes were over I should need some place of concealment. We were crossing the high table-land that exists between the Zenat and Sheshouan valleys—an elevation that is entirely ignored on most of the maps of the country—and the only spot that would offer any cover was a stream, the banks of which were overgrown with oleanders. For this we at once made, and, entering the bed of the stream, I dismounted and hid myself amongst the shrubs, while Selim led the mules to a spot some little way further up the river.

By this time the three men who had first stopped me had reached the band we had seen at work, and informed them of their belief in the presence of a Christian; and as I had expected, a few minutes later some dozen Arabs appeared in sight, running along the path we had just travelled over. In five minutes they had found our mules, and were questioning Selim as to my whereabouts. From my hiding-place I could overhear sufficient of the conversation that passed between them.

"Where is the Christian?" they asked.

"What Christian?" said Selim.

"The Christian who was with you."

"There was no Christian with me."

"Who was with you?"

"A Moor; the son of Abdul Malek from Fez, who is going to Sheshouan to see some of his mother's people."

"Bring him here."

"I don't know where he is."

Then for a minute or two the talking was carried on in whispers, and I saw my boy and an elderly mountaineer leave the group and wander off engaged in conversation.

A few minutes later I was discovered and marched forth from the river-bed to a large tree growing near by on the plain, where I found myself alone with a dozen or so wild-looking fellows. I knew that to deny I was a Christian was useless now, so I informed them at once that I was one, and that I was on my way to Sheshouan, handing them meanwhile (much to my grief) some of my cigarettes. They seemed very much surprised at the calm way in which I took matters, and not a little amused; and five minutes later, conversation was being carried on in an animated but amicable manner. Suddenly my boy

appeared on the scene, and never in my life have I seen a face of greater surprise than he wore then, on finding me seated in the group of mountaineers,
who a minute or two before had been telling him to bring me out from my
hiding-place, presumably to kill me—and not only seated there, but apparently on the best of terms.

On my rising a few minutes later to proceed on my journey, they begged
me to go no further, assuring me that if I were discovered I would for certain
lose my life, and that even their own people would kill me if they detected
that I was a Christian. I told them that I had made up my mind to reach
Sheshouan at any risk, and bade them adieu, shaking hands with all of them,
but closing my ears to their ill-omened warnings.

We had soon left the watershed, and once more the path led us along the
steep mountain-side, the new valley running almost due south, while that we
had left ran in the opposite direction. From where we were now we obtained
a glorious view, rivalling any scenery I have seen in Morocco, with the exception of some of the valleys of the Atlas mountains, which it much resem-
bled. Thousands of feet into the now sunset sky the great mountain of
Sheshouan reared its rocky crags; while far below, purple in the evening
shadow, lay the wooded and cultivated valley, with its rapid turning and twisting here, there, and everywhere like a thread of silver.

We were now at no great distance from Sheshouan, so, concealing ourselves in the bushes, we awaited the setting of the sun. As soon as he was
down we resumed our journey, and an hour later, in bright moonlight, crossing the sharp ridge of a hill, came suddenly upon Sheshouan, and found ourselves in the soko, or market-place, situated outside the walls of the town.
Crossing the soko at a brisk trot, we entered the town by the Bab-el-Sok, and,
proceeding through several streets, passed under a dark archway. Here dismounting, we knocked at a door, which, being opened, we entered the house
of my guide's parents. In the dark they did not recognize me as a Christian,
in fact it was not till some minutes later, when we had secured the mules in
the patio of the house, and ourselves in a large bare room, that my boy con-
fided in them. They were not at all pleased to see me, but they knew as well

as I did—and therein lay my safety—that my detection meant death to their son for bringing me, as well as to myself. Half an hour later, having partaken of some food, and rested a little, for we had been sixteen hours *en route* from Tetuan, I left the house, and with Selim's father walked through the town.

Sheshouan, which is a large town covering more acreage than Tangier, and possessing seven mosques and five gates, is magnificently situated on the slope of the mountain, which rises from the town almost perpendicularly to a great height. The houses are different from those of any other city in the country, as they do not possess the general flat roof, but are gabled and tiled with red tiles, which gives the place more the appearance of a Spanish than a Moorish town. But what to the natives is the great attraction of Sheshouan is the abundance of water; for issuing from caves far above in the mountain-side are three waterfalls, whose water is so cold that the natives use the expression that "it knocks one's teeth out to drink it." I tasted it, and found it too cold to be pleasant drinking. From the pool at the bottom of these three falls aqueducts carry the water to the numerous mills which are clustered there, after turning the wheels of which it continues its course to the many fruit-gardens for which Sheshouan is famous.

After about two hours' walk in the town, we returned once more to the house, where I was only too glad to roll myself in my blanket and surrender my weary body to sleep. All next day I lay in hiding. During the afternoon we decided that my safest means of leaving would be after dark in the disguise of a woman, as that would render me almost entirely hidden from sight under the enormous haik that completely envelops womankind in Morocco.

About sunset my boy returned from purchasing some fowls and eggs for supper, looking very much upset and in tears. I was sorry to see this, for up till now he had behaved splendidly, though his mother had been in one long fit of hysterical crying ever since I had arrived—a circumstance which was not warranted to improve anyone's spirits. Even when I saw Selim in this state, I never suspected anything was wrong except that his spirits had given way under the strain, and it was quite casually that I asked him what was the cause of his trouble.

"Oh, sir," he cried, "it is all up. Those Beni-Hassan men have told that they have seen a Christian on his way to Sheshouan, and all the town is on the alert to catch you."

I went at once to the tiny window and looked into the street. It was full of men hurrying to and fro. Twice I heard the question asked, "Have you seen the Christian?" My prospects certainly did not look golden; but nothing could be done for an hour or so, till it was dark; and on an empty stomach one can do very little, so I set to work and cooked and ate my supper. I had not much appetite, but I made a point of eating half a roast fowl and drinking a large jugful of milk, meanwhile carefully considering my plans in my mind. First, I determined to abandon the woman's disguise, as being of a suspicious nature, and instead borrowed a torn and ragged mountaineer's brown cloak.

Supper was over, and in half an hour more it would be sufficiently dark for me to leave. What a wretched half-hour that was! Selim was in tears, his mother in hysterics, his father sulky; in fact, the only persons who kept up any show of spirits were myself—and I confess that it was nothing more than a mere "show" of spirits—and a man whose help had been sought, a native of a mountain village some hours distant, and who all through never lost his cheerfulness, though the risk of losing his own life, a risk that he was voluntarily running, was very great.

At last the half-hour was over, and all our plans completed. Mahommed, my new-found friend (and verily a friend in need), was to accompany me out of the town by the principal gate, thus hoping to excite less suspicion than if we attempted to escape by one of the less important and more obscure exits, while Selim was to proceed by another way and meet us outside the soko. The mules we left for the present, arranging for Selim's father to bring them early in the morning to our next hiding-place, the cottage of Mahommed, situated in a village some four hours distant.

My disguise was light and airy, far too light and airy for such a cold night, consisting as it did merely of a brown jelaba and a pair of slippers. Creeping quietly through the door, we left the house, and walked through the now crowded streets to the gate. Every now and again I felt an uncomfortable, creepy sensation, as I heard the hurrying natives saying to one another—and saying it once or twice even to my companion and myself, "Where is the Christian?" "Have you seen the dog of a Christian?" At the gate was a guard placed to stop me; but in my disguise I passed them successfully and entered the soko, where men were passing to and fro on the look-out for me. Here, to avoid suspicion, we seated ourselves cross-legged on the ground, and remained sitting for several minutes, it seemed like an hour. While in this position a native came and seated himself next to me, and carried on a short conversation with my companion. Every moment I expected detection—it seemed an impossibility that I could escape. Then we rose and were once more *en route*.

Soon we had reached the spot where Selim was to have met us, but there were no signs of him. We sat down on some rocks and waited, but he did not come. Then Mohammed left me to search for him, and I was alone, but completely hidden among the ferns and stones. While he was away, a man passed me so closely that his jelaba touched my knees; but he went on without perceiving me. A few minutes later Mahommed and Selim appeared, the latter having mistaken the trysting-place.

We at once set off at a brisk walk across country to Mahommed's cottage. For four hours and a half we walked in the cold night, over the most terrible ground. We had not been on our way half an hour, when I slipped in crossing a stream, and got my shoes soaked with water, which rendered them impossible to walk in. From that moment, till we arrived at the cottage, I walked barelegged and bare-footed, pushing my ankles, already raw from sunburning, through the sharp thorny bushes, till the blood was trickling down over my feet. At last we reached the village, and creeping from tree to tree, Mahommed reconnoitring ahead, we entered the cottage, I was at once taken to my hiding-place, a kind of cellar, but very clean, where, half an hour later, when I had bound up my legs in some strips of sacking, we ate a supper of native bread and goat's milk, and very good it was too. My kind friends then left me, and were soon slumbering in another part of the cottage—their snore reaching me even—in my cellar. I felt better; though far from safe, yet I was out of Sheshouan. I opened my red-leather bag, and drew out some cigarettes; then rolling myself in my blanket, I lay and watched the blue smoke curl up and up till it was lost in the darkness. Never did I enjoy a cigarette so much as then, and were I a poet, I would have written an ode to that benefactor of mankind, Nestor Gianaclis. It was not long, however, before I fell asleep, worn out with the excitement of the day, and the long night walk; nor did I wake till late the next morning. My breakfast — bread and eggs and milk — was brought me at once, and I received the welcome news of the arrival of my mules.

Luck, however, was against me, for one of the very Beni-Hassan men who had accosted me on the road turned up in the village by some evil chance and recognized my beasts. However, Mahommed denied that they belonged to Christians; but the suspicion of the villagers was aroused, and again I was in great danger.

It had been our intention to proceed on our way when the sun set, but towards evening we discovered that the villagers were on the look-out for me, and that it would be unsafe to leave before the moon went down, about midnight.

That day and evening seemed very long, but Mahommed never lost his cheerful mien, and kept me interested by telling me stories of himself — how he was the head of a robber-band, and only a few months before had shot two rich Moors, whom he had robbed, and whose mules he had stolen. Never for a moment did I mistrust him, as I knew that, whatever he might be, his ideas of hospitality — the greatest virtue the Arabs possess — would render impossible any treachery. The only reason I can think of why he should have rendered me such services was his love of adventure, for he positively seemed to enjoy the risk he was himself running in saving me. There was no monetary reason in his acts; for on my parting from him the next day, he absolutely refused to take what I offered him, and it was with great difficulty that I persuaded him even to accept payment for the food, &c., I had partaken of in his house.

At last the moon went down, and accompanied by Mahommed I set out, again creeping from tree to tree and hedge and hedge, once even taking refuge in an empty stable, till the village and the guard around it were safely passed. Then Mahommed hid me in a clump of trees while he returned to the village, and, with Selim, brought out my mules. The cold was intense, in spite of its being July, and I felt cramped and sore indeed as I crouched down, not daring to move a muscle. So an hour passed, then my eyes were gladdened with the welcome sight of the men and mules. Selim and I at once mounted the beasts, while Mahommed walked ahead to show us the path. When dawn appeared we were well on our way, and an hour or two after sunrise had left almost all danger behind us. At the ruined fondak, which we reached after about eight hours' ride, Mahommed left us and turned back. Never did I grasp a hand to say good-bye with more kindly feelings than I did that of this stalwart, handsome mountaineer, who had risked his own life and had saved mine. I tried to thank him in fitting words, but he stopped me, and said, "It is nothing. It is nothing." Four hours later the white walls of Tetuan were in sight; and thirteen hours after leaving the village, tired and hungry, with bloodstained legs and torn clothes, I passed through the gates with a sigh of relief such as I have seldom sighed, and felt myself —at last!—safe from all dangers.

The following evening I arrived at Tangier, to receive the hearty congratulations of my friends, and a severe blowing up for risking my life in such an unwarrantable way.

To Marrakesh on a Bicycle

BUDGETT MEAKIN

From *The Land of the Moors*, 1901

"Nothing is more deceptive and annoying than the Moorish idea of distance."

Today, it is called Essaouira, but it was once known as Mogador, Magazan, and Mogdoura; these are all names for one of the most beautiful towns on the Atlantic coast of Morocco. In 1900, pockmarked, crenellated umber walls held salt-white buildings against the rocky shore; roads were unknown, and a simple lifestyle prevailed. It was here that Budgett Meakin, a British resident of Tangier, decided to begin a unique journey by bicycle.

Meakin belonged to a prominent British family in Morocco. His father had founded the *Tangier Times*, where Meakin worked as an editor-reporter. By 1906, his impressive list of books and articles made him the most authoritative British expert on Morocco—and his interest and affection were genuine. "I like the Moors," he wrote, "with all their faults, and am not ashamed to confess it."

Meakin had traveled through much of Morocco, often passing himself off as a Muslim or a native Jew. His decision to ride a bicycle from Mogador to Marrakesh was not quite the same sort of adventure. While he seems to have done it mostly because it amused him, the effect this journey had on his written impressions of Moroccans is profound.

At the time of Meakin's journey, Marrakesh was the limit of precise European knowledge in this region. Roads, in the European sense, did not exist. The wheel—and certainly not the bicycle—hadn't been part of the Moroccan

landscape for centuries. Riding a bicycle in this part of the world clearly iden-
tified Meakin as an Englishman. His writing records the Moroccans' response
to his *Nasrani* (Christian) contraption: the bicycle essentially made him inex-
plicable and dangerous. The Pasha of Marrakesh banned him from riding inside the city because the bicycle did not "belong [t]here."

Although Meakin was an intrepid and sensitive traveler who scolded
other writers for inaccuracies and disrespect, he could not escape the fact that
he was strikingly European in a country that was afraid of the outside world.

Twelve years after Meakin's journey, the French were building a road
from Casablanca to Marrakesh. It was probably best, given the way he felt
about the country, that he did not live to see its completion.

—J. H.

Whether cycling without roads is pleasant or not, depends, like
so many another question, on the way in which you look at it.
For my part, I enjoyed it in Morocco immensely, but the
other man—for there were two of us—found it less funny. To begin with, I
was a novice at "wheeling," having had but one week's practice, and had not
learned what a good road means to the cyclist; whereas my friend had just
been cycling through France. Then, too, knowing the country and speaking
the language, I derived full benefit from the remarks overheard, which often
lost much in translation. But the inexhaustible good-humour and wit of my
comrade, Dr. Rudduck, kept us bright, and one realized fully the force of
the Moorish proverb: "Choose your companion before your road." The novelty was something, too, both for us and the natives, although when at times
we had perforce to walk, it was rather trying to be pitied by passers-by, who
wondered why we had not hired mules to transport such awkward "luggage"
as our machines.

Not only has Morocco no roads, it has also no inns or hotels after leaving the coast, and the prospect of unprepared native quarters was not exactly
relished, especially as we knew from experience what they were like. So we

schemed to carry what we could on our machines, which were rigged up with frames and carriers on which we were able to pack some sixty pounds apiece. Thus, indeed, we started, but soon relinquished our loads to a horseman whom we had engaged for the journey.

Nevertheless, from time to time I had occasion to reload my machine—a "Rover," which, with carriers, etc., weighed 40 lbs.—till it and I and the baggage together scaled 300 lbs., in which condition I rode it easily over pavements and stony roads, or up slight hills. On my return, in crossing Paris like this, the greatest interest was aroused, and I was more than once asked if I were not moving house! A well-filled 18in. "Gladstone" on the frame behind; a good-sized hold-all above the handles; a luncheon basket below, containing spirit-lamp, kettle, and tea things; a packed valise inside the frame, with a sun umbrella strapped alongside; a water-can between the cranks, and a tin of oil below the seat, formed the full equipment: I found it enough.

Such tracks as there are in Morocco are those formed by beasts of burden, eight or nine inches wide, frequently worn so deep that our pedals struck on one bank or the other in descending, sometimes with such sudden force that the machine was lifted off the ground. Often so many stones or so much sand filled the track that we had to run outside on the grass or ploughed land, over which I soon got accustomed to bowl with ease, if not pleasure. Such careful guiding too, was required on account of these stones, that I expected to be duly qualified for tight-rope riding upon my return. Often the tracks led down into gullies, into which one would wildly plunge—since they were almost always dry—rising up the other side with a bound that was most delicious.

Other variations in a ride which might have grown monotonous were constantly afforded by the wonder and astonishment of all whom we encountered. The time was that of harvest—in May—and right and left the reapers started up with shouts to one another and raced after us. Some, no doubt, thought we were "flying devils," but they could not make out our machines.

"But what sort of beast are you riding? We thought it must be a 'drinker of wind,'"—whereby is denoted a certain fleet camel used on the desert, seldom now seen in Morocco.

"Why, dear no; it's only a mule, a Nazarene mule, you know,"—for everything outside Morocco is either called Roman or Nazarene.

"You don't mean to say so! How do you breed them?"

"Well, you can see for yourself from its speed that its mother must have been a gazelle, and from these round parts and iron that its father must have been a reaping-hook."

A moment's stare while trying to realize whether this could be the truth or not, and out they burst in a hearty laugh, for the Moors do enjoy a joke, and this was one which specially appealed to them, so to every new-comer it was repeated as fact in most solemn tones. Others, taking up the idea, would ask particulars as to its feed, and whether it kicked, or had any evil habits.

"Stand away from his heels there!"

"Hold his head, Mohammed, and see that his girths are tight!"

"Whew, what a stirrup! Why, they're not the same length! Pull them tight? Now then, the Nazarene's mounting—clear away!"

Then all would set off to race us, girding up their loins and promising great things.

"Wait a bit, though! It's not a fair start!"

But we were clear of a crowd to which we had no desire to return, and, as far as the ground would allow, forged ahead. Sometimes we offered fabulous prizes to any who might outstrip us, riding sedately alongside of some old farmer, whom we tempted to spur on his mare till both panted, while we coolly spurted ahead with "good morning!"

Whenever we overtook such riders, we had to yell our warnings, for our bells were not understood, and on several occasions, in spite of precautions, caused such alarm to fellow-travellers that they and their mounts parted company, one dashing over the plain, the other picking himself up to see what had happened.

Once I met an old man whose donkey so suddenly shied at the apparition that in a moment he found himself seated where there was no fear of falling. I really felt sorry, but was hesitating whether I should stop to be abused or not, when, looking backward, my machine ran into a tuft of grass and seated me likewise, to the unbounded delight of a party of natives, while the old man and I looked at each other solemnly.

Another time, while riding across the market at Tangier, a Moor who tried to get out of my way, as women do even in England, by running right across my track, tripped over his cloak at the critical moment, whereupon I landed head foremost into the soft heap he provided, but before he could collect his brains or his limbs I was mounted, and the crowd enjoyed his discomfiture richly, for neither of us was damaged.

On no occasion did we suffer rudeness or interference at the hands of the Moors, notwithstanding the prognostications of our friends, though their inquisitiveness often proved amusing. Sometimes, if they could get near, they would turn the nut of the tyre valve, or threaten to try our "Dunlops" with their daggers, assured that if not pork sausage, they must be made of pig-skin, since they were the work of pig-eating unbelievers. But they liked the idea of air for fodder, especially as a famine was threatened, and they were urgent in their requests for a ride, which no assurance of danger could stay.

"Let me try, Consul; there's not a horse in the province that I can't ride; I'll break her in."

At one halting-place our only way out of difficulty was to declare that none should on any account be permitted to try but the sedate and portly governor whose guests we were, who would sooner have stood on his head. Our only real trouble was when we had to wheel our machines—which occurred so often that my companion thought we ought to call it a walking tour with bicycle variations,—when the crowd was apt to grow unpleasantly large and close. While standing we could keep their curious fingers at bay, but walking we could not. One day, at lunch beneath a hedge of cactus, all the wonder and amazement of the circle around us was dispelled by a travelled Moor, who exclaimed scornfully: "Bah! *These* are nothing: what do you look at *them* for? Why, these things have only *two* wheels, and in Algeria I have seen things with *four!*"

Their wonder is to be explained, since in Morocco there are practically no wheeled vehicles; of one thing, however, all had heard, that the "Romans" have a wonderful contrivance by which they get about with incredible speed, known in Morocco as the "land steamer," which they naturally took our innocent "cykes" to be.

"Alas! Alas! Woe is me! The Christians have taken our country at last; why, here's a railway train! Woe to me! Woe to me!"

Those who felt less desponding, although no less certain, yelled at us lustily: "Give them fire! Give them fire!" and from the remarks overheard I found that my red-cloth-covered water-can was usually taken for the furnace. None could conceive how moving the pedals could make them go.

As for accommodation at night, the less said the better. The first night we made for a governor's residence, whither we had been preceded by a mounted messenger from the governor of Mazagan, whence we started, an old friend who had not only given us a dinner, but had come out to see us off. On arrival we were shown into the bare and comfortless guest room. Already a Jewish trader was installed there with his baggage, and after a while came tea and sugar and candles for all. Then, after a visit from the governor, supper, a big dish of stew with abundant bread. After this we lay down and slept, when the fleas would permit us, even the case-hardened Jew complaining next day that they had kept him awake, so it may be guessed how we suffered. Next day the old governor, fat, grey, and nearly blind, wrapped in his blanket and white-hooded cloak, came round to be doctored while we doctored a punctured tyre—our first and last, since the stones on these tracks being worn and unbroken, the tyres do not suffer in this way anything like so much as in England.

But from the heat and jolting they suffered more than ever tyres were meant to stand. On both our machines the rear tubes gave way at the joints, but when replaced by tropical "Dunlops," caused us no more trouble, although in one case a 30 in. tube had to do for a 28 in. wheel. Towards noon the heat of the ground and the sun was so great that the air in the tubes extended and puffed them until we could let off a good rush, and yet leave them tight. Most days, however, we rode in the early morning and late afternoon, enjoying a much needed mid-day rest where we could. Jæger-clad, *cap à pie*, I was as independent as could be of changing temperature, though at night it grew piercing cold in contrast to the heat of the day. And once, having failed to overtake our man with his load, when taking refuge in an Arab tent, alongside of a calf and chicken, we were fain, in the dark, to roll ourselves on the ground in a native blanket, so filthy that when day broke we could not look at it.

When we got our tent up, and could cook our own supper, everything went well, but when we had to rely on what we could get, we needed all the appetite the day had given us. The most sumptuous fare in the country was a musty flavoured preparation of barley, interspersed with chunks of mutton or chicken and eggs *ad lib*. Milk could only be obtained when we arrived at the moment of milking, before the new was mixed with the old, though the resulting sour beverage was almost always to be had, and the Doctor liked it. Bread we had with us, and water we carried also. Once or twice we obtained oranges, and on several occasions we fell in with governors or other officials who invited us to join them at well-cooked and well-served repasts, with abundance of sweet green tea.

At last, after several days, between walking and riding, we reached Marrakesh, and one morning bowled up to the door of the Southern Morocco Mission, where we were most hospitably entertained. The already familiar bazaars of the city offered a never failing supply of artistic scenes and interesting studies, with their robed and shrouded figures, men in colours and women in white, an unending succession of picturesque types: its narrow, winding streets, lined with cupboard-like shops, and its extensive covered markets, were in turn invaded by the bicycle and camera, as witness these pages.

Such consternation was caused, that rumours of it even reached the ears of the late Wazeer Regent, who sent a message to us requesting us not to ride within the walls, and giving notice that such things did not belong to Morocco. But we had had our ride, and still continued to enjoy ourselves, although the doctor had determined never again to cycle in Barbary.

Morocco, the Land of the Extreme West

ION PERDICARIS

from *The National Geographic Magazine*, March 1906

In his fury Raisuli determined to capture me and hold me for ransom."

On the night of May 28, 1904, shouts from the kitchen disrupted an elegant dinner in the palatial villa home of American expatriate Ion Perdicaris, three miles from Tangier, Morocco. According to Perdicaris, a small, balding, aristocratic man in his sixties, shouting drew him to the kitchen. Fully expecting to mediate yet another row between his German housekeeper and French chef, he headed downstairs, followed by family members.

Instead of a domestic argument, he found rifle-armed Berber tribesmen led by Ahmed el Raisuni, a notorious warlord. The intruders beat Perdicaris's stepson unconscious. When Mrs. Perdicaris resisted, she was knocked down a flight of stairs. The warlord helpfully announced who he was: "I am Raisuni—*the* Raisuni!" He told his Berbers to saddle the finest horses in the Perdicaris stable and ride into the indigo night with two captives: Perdicaris and Varley, his stepson. Varley was almost immediately released, but there was a ransom demand of 70,000 Spanish silver dollars from the U.S. government for the safe return of Perdicaris.

U.S. President Theodore Roosevelt was in the midst of a reelection campaign and chose to employ his "big stick" philosophy. He immediately ordered a naval squadron and a unit of Marines to Morocco. Secretary of State John Hay declared, "Perdicaris alive or Raisuni dead"—although many preferred to believe that Roosevelt himself made this statement.

Nine weeks of standoff ensued: U.S. troops and ships in Tangier Bay versus Raisuni in the mountains. Perdicaris returned to Tangier when the U.S. paid the ransom. The whole episode was farcical, since Perdicaris was not even an American citizen—he had renounced American citizenship during the Civil War to keep property in the Confederacy—a fact that the U.S. government kept secret until 1933. Roosevelt's use of military force during an election campaign would have been embarrassing if Perdicaris's real citizenship had been revealed.

Early-twentieth-century Morocco was a hornet's nest, as France, Spain, and Germany vied for influence and outright control. Sultans were deposed, and pretenders to the throne raised armies and carved off regions for themselves. Morocco was not in decline; it had bottomed out.

Perdicaris belonged to a rarified species of European and American expats who were busy reviving Tangier as a Biarritz in North Africa. Diplomats, avoiding the inconvenience of the three inland capitals, built charming legation mansions and enjoyed a rich social season. Along with these villa dwellers were the usual scoundrels, mercenaries, traders, and exiles drawn to a land of chaos and opportunity.

Perdicaris became a community leader, sitting on committees and dealing with the Moroccan pasha on behalf of the expats. He built two palatial residences: a country villa on the Cape Spartel road called Idonia (where he was kidnapped) and a town house called the El Minzah, so sumptuous that it is a luxury hotel today. His autobiography, *The Hand of Fate* (1921), suggests he was an aimless egomaniac who had found a self-important niche for himself in Tangier.

Raisuni's capture of Perdicaris in 1904 was motivated by vengeance against his kinsman, the Pasha of Tangier. Raisuni was a *sherif*, descendant of the Prophet Mohammed, and had an army of Berber followers. From a mountain base, he had taxed, extorted, and robbed throughout northwest Morocco. Then in 1896, an invitation to dinner by his kinsman turned out to be an ambush. He was captured and sent to the horrible prison at Mogador. His kinsman was rewarded by being made the Pasha of Tangier. The Pasha of Mogador had

Raisuni hung in manacles in the kasbah, exposed to the deadly sun, in an effort to kill him. But he did not die. Raisuni was chained to iron bars and put in a dungeon, even chained to a corpse in hopes that he would catch a lethal disease, or starve to death. He survived, and escaped—but only briefly.

Raisuni's followers had smuggled a metal file to him in a loaf of bread. The plan was for him to meet a boat on the shore and be rowed safely up the coast. Filing through the cell bars took weeks; when Raisuni finally reached the appointed spot outside the city walls, there was no boat. Returning to town, he killed a guard with his chains. After a shootout and street fight with soldiers, he was recaptured. Inexplicably, in 1900 he was released, even though the authorities still regarded him as a rebellious homicidal maniac.

Raisuni was intelligent, ruthless, and violent, making him a dangerous man in the years of anarchy after the great sultan's death in 1894. Prophecy foretold he would be sultan. A tribal army of thousands believed he was a sherif. Raisuni's savvy understanding of foreigners became evident during the events of 1904, when he chose Perdicaris as the ideal high-profile victim. These stunts raised Raisuni's status in Morocco, made headlines in London and New York, and ultimately, made him wealthy. The ransom went to build his palace at Asilah, known as the House of Tears.

In turn, Perdicaris capitalized on his own adventure, going on speaking tours and writing about his experience, including an article for *National Geographic* in 1906 from which this excerpt is taken, and his autobiography in 1921, *The Hand of Fate*. Note that he uses "Raisuli," the alternative spelling of Raisuni's name.

—J. H.

T he memory of that evening is indeed associated with an ineffaceable sense of horror. We had gathered in the drawing-room directly after dinner, when we were startled by loud screams from the servants' quarters. Followed by my stepson, Mr. Cromwell Varley, whose wife and two daughters, just home from school at Geneva, completed, with Mrs.

Perdicaris, our family circle, I rushed down a passage leading to the servants' hall, where I came upon a crowd of armed natives.

Even then we did not realize our danger, but thought these intruders might be a party from a neighboring village. Our night guards were supplied from this hamlet, and we supposed that they, like ourselves, had rushed in to learn the cause of the uproar, which we, at the moment, attributed to some renewal of a quarrel that had broken out on a previous occasion between a young German housekeeper and our French chef de cuisine, when the latter, irritated by some insulting allusion to the French defeats at Metz and Sedan, had attacked the housekeeper, when, as now, we had been startled by her screams.

As I turned to inquire of these natives who crowded about me as to what had occurred, I saw some of our European servants already bound and helpless and, at the same moment, we ourselves were assailed by these intruders, who struck us with their rifles. At the same instant our hands were roughly twisted and bound behind our backs with stout palmetto cords that cut like knives.

Varley, who made a fierce resistance, was handled with more violence. Indeed I thought the rifle blows would split his head, while his hand was cut to make him let go his hold upon one of the gang, whom he had liked to have strangled.

At this moment the housekeeper, hearing our voices, rushed across the hall from her dining-room, where she had locked herself in, and, just as we were driven out of doors, we saw a blow aimed at her head and she fell to the floor. This was the last we saw, then, of any one in the house where I have never since set foot.

Once outside, our assailants endeavored to drive us down to the stables, but we managed to make our way toward a guard-house, where a couple of government soldiers were stationed rather as gatekeepers to attend visitors than for any purpose of defense.

By a lamp in front of this building we saw our guards, our gardeners, and other native servants under cover of the rifles of another party of mountaineers, while a little apart stood their leader, a man of fine presence, attired in the handsome dress worn by the native gentry. One of my men was reproaching this personage bitterly for this unprovoked aggression.

The leader of the mountaineers raised his hand and, in low but emphatic tones, declared that if no rescue were attempted nor any disturbance made, no harm would befall us and in a few weeks we should be safely back among our people, adding, "I am Raisuli! the Raisuli!"—this, as I afterward discovered, being his clan appellation, since this chereef, or native nobleman, is known among his own followers as Mulai Ahmed ben Mohammed, the Raisuli.

On hearing him declare his name I felt at once that the affair was possibly more serious than I had hitherto anticipated, since the presence of this insurgent chieftain meant more than a mere summons to surrender any money or valuables in the house, and that some political object had probably dictated this attack—one which had been so unexpected and suddenly executed that neither our guards nor our grooms and gardeners, nor the Spanish workmen employed upon the estate, nor we ourselves had been able to make any defense, all of us having been simultaneously attacked and overpowered before we were aware of any impending danger.

Raisuli had indeed been reported to be on the warpath for some time past, but as his operations had been confined to outlying native villages or to the smaller towns, no one imagined he would attack any one in the immediate neighborhood of Tangier—where I myself, as president of an international commission that administered the affairs of the town, was in a position to requisition by telephone the entire available military force.

Approaching him, bound as I was and in evening dress, I said to him in Arabic, "I know you by name, Raisuli, and I accept your safe conduct, but we cannot go with you thus. We must have our overcoats, hats, and boots."

"Which of your servants shall I have released to return to the house for what you require?" replied Raisuli.

I selected Bourzin, the younger of the guards, on duty that evening. On indicating Bourzin, his bonds were cut and he was released; but as he did not immediately reappear, Raisuli became impatient: still he allowed another of my servants, a Spaniard, to also be released, and the latter quickly executed his commission. We had not time, however, to put on our boots before we were hurriedly made to mount.

Several of our horses had been brought up from the stables, but either because it was feared that Varley might escape or because he had been wounded, he was put upon a mule which the mountaineers had brought with them, while I was allowed to select which of my animals I would ride. As I apprehended a long journey, I chose the youngest and most spirited of my horses.

Before we mounted our hands were freed, upon giving our parole that we would not endeavor to escape. This was an immense relief, for those palmetto bonds cut into the wrist, while the constrained position of our arms amounted to torture.

We were not, however, allowed to hold the bridle ourselves, but were led off by the mountaineers, whose rough handling threw my horse into such a frenzy that it was with difficulty that I could keep my seat.

Just as we were starting, Bourzin reappeared and volunteered to accompany me, to which Raisuli assented, and this attendant was also allowed a mount.

Two of the mountaineers clambered upon Varley's horse, a big chestnut, which was not saddled, while the saddle which had been hastily placed upon my horse was one that had been cast aside and the girths were rotten.

As I learned afterward, this selection was due to a mistaken attempt of one of my grooms to save our saddles. He did not realize that they were required for our own use, and when he had been ordered to produce the saddles, had thrown this one to the mountaineers, declaring that the good saddles were all under lock and key at the house—a mistaken zeal, which cost me, later on, a serious accident.

Thus we were led off along the dark avenue beneath the overhanging branches of the trees.

"At least," I thought to myself, "At least the ladies know nothing of this horrible misadventure!" since I pictured them as still awaiting in the drawing-room our return from the servants' hall, to explain the uproar and the screams of the women.

Very different, however, had been the alarming experience of the other members of the family during the few minutes which had elapsed between our leaving the drawing-room and our departure with the mountaineers. As we learned six weeks afterward, the ladies had presently followed us from the drawing-room, but when they reached the servants' hall we had already been driven out of doors.

As Mrs. Perdicaris endeavored to join us, one of the mountaineers, seizing her, threw her violently backward, down a half flight of stone steps onto the pavement, while Mrs. Varley was pitched on top of her.

The women servants, who alone had not been bound, assisted the ladies to rise, and one of the women rushed past the mountaineers to the telephone, and before these savages realized her intention she called up the central office at Tangier, telling them of the attack and of our capture. Before she could say more she was torn from the instrument by the angry natives.

At the same moment the screams of a pretty native servant struggling with the men, who were dragging her off, aroused my wife, who, despite the fact that she was seriously hurt from her fall, rushed to the woman's assistance and Ayesha's cowardly assailants, fearing Raisuli's displeasure, hastily retired, balked of their proposed prey.

Mrs. Perdicaris was then herself assisted to the front hall opening upon the portico or pergola, where she came upon Bourzin. Instead of bringing us our things, Bourzin stopped to reassure my wife, inventing a statement to the effect that I knew the leader of the band and had in the past rendered Raisuli a great service, and that we were now amicably coming to some arrangement, but should any disturbance be made, that all of us, both the family and the servants, might be killed.

As my wife listened she heard my voice from without as I addressed Raisuli and, noticing that I did not speak in tones either of excitement or alarm, she concluded that Bourzin was telling the truth; consequently she waited near the door for my return, and in the meantime Bourzin slipped away, unnoticed, to rejoin me.

Needless to say, the ladies waited in vain for our return, and when at last they ventured out onto the pergola all was silent. We had disappeared.

As for ourselves we were led rapidly along the avenue leading away from the direction of the town, our horses being forced over the dry stone wall which encircles the property and driven along by many a blow from the rifles of our escort, as the men dragged the unwilling animals over rocks, through the underwood and brambles, and across the numerous water-courses, down toward the plain of Bubana to the west of the town.

How different the familiar locality, the scene of many an exciting steeple-chase or game of polo, looked as we now negotiated its water jumps and barriers in the darkness. Here and there we came unexpectedly to the steep cuttings of water-courses or to deep pools, which our captors made no attempt to turn or to choose the easy places; but as the fellow who held my bridle would hesitate upon the verge of such descents, my horse, pressing forward to escape the blows from the rear, would either step upon the heels of the man in front or push him unexpectedly over the edge, when all three of us would come rattling down into the water, into which we splashed, stumbling over the big boulders, each such incident terminating in a sharp blow upon my horse's nose, administered by the angry native so soon as the latter recovered his footing.

Ultimately I was, however, grateful even for these unpleasant interludes, since I was thus kept from reflecting upon the ulterior anxieties implied by our capture, owing to the effort to keep my seat in the saddle.

After circling around the town at a distance of several miles, our party struck across the fields toward the east, making in the direction of the track leading to Tetuan. Here the going was easier and we had more time to consider our situation. Varley and I, however, were intentionally kept apart from each other.

Later on we found ourselves for a few moments within speaking distance, and my companion asked how I thought this business likely to end.

"From what I have heard of Raisuli's character," I replied, "I hope we may not be ill-treated, for should it be deemed necessary to starve or torture us into signing for a heavy ransom, I believe we shall be left to these ruffians. So long as Raisuli himself is in view, I do not think we need apprehend any violence."

"I do not see him anywhere at present, do you?" inquired Varley.

The men who led our animals now warned us to be silent. It was therefore with a distinct sense of relief and satisfaction that, just as dawn broke and when a halt had been called on a hillside, we saw Raisuli himself emerging from the gloom.

As he rod up I recognized the horse on which he was mounted as one I had lately purchased for my wife. This horse had been admirably broken to the saddle, but so soon as he was left to his own devices he became a terror to the grooms.

What, then, was my surprise to see the horse kneel in order that Raisuli might dismount, and, after the latter had thrown the bridle carelessly over the horse's neck, the animal stood, never offering to move as Raisuli advanced toward me.

Hastily dismounting, I approached the chieftain, insisting that I should be allowed to communicate with my friends, explaining to Raisuli that I was an invalid and that unless I could procure the remedies I required he might at any moment have a dead prisoner instead of a live one on his hands.

Raisuli made no answer; he merely drew forth from beneath his mantle a carnet or book, from which he extracted a sheet of European note paper, an envelope, and a pencil, which he handed me, none of these being articles used by natives.

I at once wrote to my wife, and then asked if my letter could be sent to El Minzah, our town residence, whither I presumed that my wife would have gone after what had occurred at Aidonia on the preceding evening.

Raisuli asked me whether I could guarantee that his messenger would not be arrested at Tangier.

I answered, "Certainly! My people will realize that any such detention would injure me!"

Hereupon he called one of his followers and taking the man aside gave him his instructions.

From where I stood I could see that the messenger did not at all relish these orders. However, after further insistence, the man looked up to Raisuli with an expression of devotion, and, stooping, kissed his leader's mantle in token of submission.

I then bethought me also of writing to the young Wazani chereefs to come up and negotiate my release. To this second request Raisuli did not so easily accede. However, ultimately he produced further paper and envelopes, and the messenger, taking both my missives, mounted one of my mules and rode back to Tangier.

We were now furnished with turbans and Moorish haiks or mantles, as the party did not wish to have it seem that any strangers or Europeans were with them. As the sun rose above the hills these mantles and the turbans added to our discomfort, as the heat became more and more oppressive.

About one o'clock we were halted for stream, and the two natives who preceded me, mounted on Varley's horse, allowed the animal to drink.

In vain I endeavored to prevent the man who was leading my gray from approaching the chestnut, as both horses were great fighters; but the thick-headed mountaineer, paying no attention to my admonitions, led my horse into the stream.

In a moment the two animals were upon each other, while the natives were falling about in the water, which was full of great boulders, in the midst of which, the two horses reared and bit and fought each other, while I kept my seat as best I could under these trying circumstances.

Luckily I did not fall and ultimately both horses and their leaders were dragged out onto the further bank by the united forces of the entire party and we proceeded on our way.

About one o'clock we were halted for luncheon in a valley between the hills, where there was neither shade nor cool water to drink, and the only food produced consisted of a few very gritty dried figs, a little hard and pungent cheese made from the milk of goats, and a glutinous and limp, yet exceedingly tough, galette or cake, which is the only form of bread used by the poorest natives. The few mouthfuls I tried to swallow sickened me, so we were only too thankful to mount as soon as we could.

In vain I tried to learn where we were going. Raisuli had remained in the rear and the surly mountaineers would not answer our queries.

The ascent, whither our course now led, became steeper as we penetrated further among the hills, and about four o'clock I met with the accident I had so long apprehended.

As we came to the bank of a rapid torrent, that was confined between steep and slippery rocks, my gray took the water jump; but not so did the sullen native who held the bridle; consequently there was a crash and, my horse rearing to recover himself, the rotten girths parted, and away went both the saddle and rider, backward down the steep declivity. It seemed to me yards before I brought up on a ledge of rock with, as I for the moment apprehended, a broken back and dislocated thigh. Here I lay quivering with pain until Varley came up, and, a little later, Raisuli. I told him of how the man's stupidity had nearly cost me a broken limb.

Raisuli reproved the man in question, and this fellow was replaced by another guide or jailer. I was hoisted with difficulty upon the saddle, now fastened on by palmetto cords, and we proceeded upon our melancholy journey. I felt I could not long endure the pain due to my fall, since my leg was already swollen from the thigh to the instep, while I was also numb with the weariness of this protracted ride, which had already lasted throughout the entire night and the better part of the day.

Every hour the country grew wilder and the road more abrupt. We only passed within sight of one miserable village, clinging to the steep hillside, and here the women and children came out to hoot and jeer at us, evidently realizing the situation and rejoicing over our sorry plight. Nor could I learn how much longer this weary march might continue to tax my failing strength; yet all this was trifling compared with what was yet to come.

A little later we reached the crest of a hill, from which we looked down upon a wooded vale, beyond which rose a rock-crowned eminence. Pointing to these bristling crags, my attendants told me that beyond these heights lay the village which was the object of our journey.

It seemed to me, wearied as I was, that it was impossible that I could endure so many more hours of fatigue and pain; but there was no help for it, since short of this undiscoverable village there was, it seemed, neither food nor shelter to be obtained.

Descending into the wooded valley, we crossed a stream, and the party halted beneath the giant oaks which stretched their wide-reaching arms above our heads. Here we halted for an hour's rest before we began the steep ascent—a path which took us up through a narrow cleft or gorge at the back of a great mass of the cliff that apparently had slid forward during some cataclysm of nature, leaving this open breach. Passing behind the fallen mass of rock, we climbed the narrow gorge, so narrow that we had great difficulty to protect our knees as our horses struggled up the steep. And this was the gateway, the portals, giving access to Raisuli's lair.

We had yet several hours before we could reach the village of Tsarradan, situated on the southern shoulder of this mountain called Nazul. As the evening light faded, the track, which led often along the outermost edge of these lofty heights, overhung such precipitous descents that a single false step of my horse, which was now trembling with fear, might have cost me my life.

It was not until near midnight that we reached the hamlet, and I was deposited in a miserable hut composed of two rooms. The thatch had in part been blown away, and when, a little later, it came on to rain we were in a deplorable plight, since the floor of beaten clay soon became a soft ooze.

Thus we passed the night, without beds or any convenience. Of sleep I knew nothing, since, between the pain from my fall and the annoyance caused by innumerable creeping pests, I did not close my eyes. Indeed, this expedition cost me sixty hours without sleep and almost without food.

Raisuli, becoming alarmed at the report of his men as to our condition, appeared at the door of our hut on the second day after our arrival and asked whether he might enter. I was only too glad to see him and, holding out my hand, I bade him welcome. He seemed greatly relieved at my tone and manner, expressed his regret at finding me in such a condition, and added that had he known that I was in such feeble health he would have endeavored to capture some one else!

This was but indifferent consolation, after all I had suffered. Still, when Raisuli went on to say that we were to consider ourselves not as prisoners, but rather as hostages, I confess that I felt relieved.

"Your horses and the arms I have taken from your dependents," he continued, "will all be returned to you. I ask nothing from you!"

I did not, however, feel so pleased when he explained that prior to our release he would exact from those who had inflicted so many wrongs upon himself and his people the following conditions:

First.   The withdrawal of the body of troops now operating against him at the foot of the hills.

Second. The removal of the pasha, or military governor, of Tangier from his post.

Third.   The release of all the men of the three Kabyles, or hill tribes, under the leadership of Raisuli who were at the moment confined in the prisons of Tangier or elsewhere.

Fourth. The payment of an indemnity of seventy thousand dollars, to be recovered against the Oolad Abd-el-Saduk.

Fifth.   That Raisuli should be made over-lord of the villages of Zeenats and Breeje!

As Raisuli concluded, I felt like saying, "Why not ask to be proclaimed, out and out, Sultan of Morocco?" In fact it seemed to me that it was quite as likely that the Sultan, Abd El Aziz, would agree to renounce the throne in favor of Raisuli as to accede to such conditions as the latter proposed to demand before consenting to our release. I literally felt my heart sink as I was thus informed of the nature of these conditions. I did not then know, however, of the orders which, even at that very moment, had been issued here in

Washington; thanks to which energetic action on the part of our government my release was subsequently secured.

But, to return to my talk with Raisuli. "The indemnity you ask from the Abd-el-Saduk family," I said, "will ruin them."

"Precisely," he replied. "They have inflicted worse than death upon me. It is precisely in order to be revenged upon them that I have carried you off."

He then proceeded to recall the circumstances of his own capture by the then Pasha of Tangier, Abd-er-Rahman Abd-el-Saduk, an incident that all at Tangier knew of at the time, some nine years prior to my present misadventure.

Raisuli, then as now, had been up in arms against the government, owing to an attempt on the part of the Pasha of Tangier to force upon the tribes of Beni Emsauer, Ben Idder, and Beni Arose a creature favored by the Abd-el-Saduks, as kaid of their district, an appointment in contravention of the arrangement sanctioned by time and custom, whereby these Berber tribes were entitled to the nomination of candidates to these posts, from which candidates the Sultan's government selected the governors, or kaids, of the district.

Abd-er-Rahman having failed in his attempt to establish his creature as kaid over these three tribes, united under the leadership of Raisuli, sent to the latter proposing an amicable settlement of the points at issue.

The latter, trusting to Abd-er-Rahman's safe conduct, accepted the pasha's invitation, and while seated at the latter's table was seized, in violation of the governor's solemn assurance, bound, and sent to Mogador, where Raisuli was chained in a sitting posture to the wall and where he thus remained four long years, during which he was never able to stand during the day nor to lie down at night.

The object of this cruel punishment was to cause Raisuli's death, the cowardly pasha not daring to openly do away with his prisoner, whose release from this horrible suffering was due to a member of one of the foreign legations at Tangier. While on a special mission to the capital this official had informed the Sultan of the circumstances of the case.

Abd El Aziz immediately issued an order to release Raisuli from his chains, excepting the fetters or anklets which confined his feet. Subsequently, after five years' confinement, Raisuli was unconditionally restored to liberty.

His property, mostly in flocks and herds, had, however, been appropriated by his agents or partners.

Failing to obtain justice, Raisuli had called together some of his more faithful adherents and had raided the zereebas or farms of his faithless associates, two of whom had subsequently been killed in an attempt to surprise Raisuli, himself.

This incident had again placed Raisuli under the ban. Forces were sent down from the capital with orders to bring in Raisuli, dead or alive.

It was these circumstances that had led the latter to effect my own abduction in order to bring the pressure of a threatened intervention by one of the powers to bear upon the Sultan and thus enable Raisuli to demand a free pardon for himself as a condition of my own release and also the payment of a heavy indemnity in order to be thus revenged upon the treacherous pasha, the cause of all his troubles.

That the Moorish authorities were fully alive to the necessity for immediate action was shown by the arrival the very next morning of an emissary from Hadj Mohammed Torres, the Sultan's delegate minister of foreign affairs at Tangier.

Torres had entrusted these negotiations to a cousin of Raisuli himself, a certain Sid Hassan. In accordance with Raisuli's suggestion, I gave this agent a note to Minister Gummere, the American representative at Tangier, together with other letters to my family.

This opportunity, which Raisuli allowed me without any restriction, proved an inestimable blessing, and the knowledge that I could thus communicate at pleasure with family and friends relieved the situation of its worst feature. I had always had a peculiar horror of being carried off and held to ransom, a misfortune which is almost more maddening to the family and friends of the victim of such outrages than to himself. Therefore I felt grateful to Providence that since such a misfortune had overtaken me, I had at least fallen into the power of the most kindly and gentle of brigands imaginable. Indeed, I had never conceived of such a situation as that in which I found myself.

In so many respects the man interested and attracted me in spite of all my natural motives for dislike. Raisuli was at once so gracious and dignified, not to us only, but to his own wild adherents, who evidently idolized their chieftain, whose position among them seemed that of the head of a Highland clan in the olden times.

He could not bear to hear a child cry, while on several occasions I noticed his care even to avoid allowing the bees collected on his cup to drown, as I saw him lift them out with his spoon or finally empty the cup itself onto the grass. Then, too, he was so quick to see the humorous aspect of a situation, while his repartee was as immediate and to the point as though he had been born in County Galway itself. In fact I discovered to my consternation that I was beginning to like the man in spite of my natural resentment. I found myself unconsciously accepting his contention that he was not a mere brigand or cattle-lifter, but a patriot struggling to rescue his Berber followers from the tyranny of the corrupt chereefian officials. His charm of voice, the natural poise and dignity of his manner, his self-control under provocation, all betrayed a superior character. He is in fact a born leader and with a certain statesmanlike quality. He deplored the condition of his country, the feuds which separate the tribes, the many deeds of violence, and the blood so uselessly shed.

In fact, this strange experience while in camp with Raisuli at Tsarradan began to assume an aspect of unexpected and idyllic charm. The life of the natives; the little touches of more gentle human character; the tiny child who offered me fruit, which I at first declined, until I noticed the expression of disappointment and mortification upon the boy's face, and then the radiant and almost ridiculous satisfaction of the little fellow when I pretended to enjoy his half-ripe offering; the many attempts of the wild people about me to propitiate me; their curiosity as to our own manners and customs, as when one venerable inhabitant of the village led me gently aside to inquire why we walked so energetically up and down the village green. "For health's sake," was my reply. "Indeed?" said the old Mohammedan, "and may I ask how many such daily turns, up and down, it may require to keep a Christian in good health!"—all afforded matter of interest and reflection. And then when the first answer from our home reached us, and we learned that already cablegrams had been received from Washington announcing that the squadrons under Rear Admirals F. E. Chadwick and Jewell, then coaling at the Canaries, had been ordered to Tangier to secure our release—and, above all, when I read the telegrams from the United States showing the wide interest so generously taken in our misadventure—when we realized all this, words cannot describe the emotion called forth by these evidences of interest and good will.

The next great excitement was the arrival, about a week later, of the relief expedition headed by the two young chereefs, Mulai Ali and Mulai Ahmed, sons of the late grand chereef of Wazan and of his English wife. Their approach was heralded by discharges of musketry, fired, as Raisuli informed me, by the inhabitants of the various villages on the route, a different route to the one by which we had been conducted. These discharges were to give Raisuli notice that strangers were entering the district, for "not only are you the only foreigners," said the chieftain, "who have set foot among these Beni Arose people, but we do not even allow natives from other localities access, unless in some especial case like the arrival of these friends of yours, and," he added with a grim smile, "who are also distant relatives of my own!"

When at last the long line of men, mounted and on foot, with its train of baggage animals, appeared we were not a little gladdened by the sight.

Mulai Ali, the elder brother, pitched his camp near at hand, and after a long conference with Raisuli, the younger of the Wazani chereefs returned to Tangier to communicate to our own officials the state of affairs.

Not only had our friends sent us a handsome tent, with furniture and supplies of every description, but also a cook and servants to wait upon us, so that we suffered henceforth no undue hardships of any sort, while the presence of Mulai Ali, who speaks both English and French, was a most welcome addition, although our intercourse with "The Boss," as Varley and Mulai Ali dubbed Raisuli, diminished materially.

Another event also tended to augment my anxiety, which was the arrival of two very evil-looking emissaries from Bou Hamara, the pretender to the throne, and who wrote urgently, insisting that Raisuli should entrust us to his, Bou Hamara's, care. I had so suffered from my tiresome ride to Tsarradan that I felt I would far rather be shot where I was than be dragged off to die upon the road to Taza, situated in the very heart of these cruel mountains.

Raisuli explained that the Pretender wished to secure our persons to use as a shield in case he himself should be too hard pushed by the Sultan's troops.

While standing near Raisuli one day on the village green, of which we were now allowed the freedom, one of his followers came up from Tangier, almost breathless from his haste, to report the arrival of the two American squadrons. The man described how the eight frigates had entered the bay, one after another. He told of the anxious deliberations of the Moorish authorities and of the alarm of the native inhabitants, who feared the town might be bombarded. The man declared that the place was *mkloub*, or upside down.

I watched Raisuli with anxiety, lest apprehending the landing of marines, with a view to our relief and his own capture, he might endeavor to drag us to some more distant and inaccessible retreat. What was then my surprise when looking up with a bright smile, he said, "Well, I think I can now congratulate you!"

"I do not understand you," I replied.

"I mean," answered Raisuli, "that the presence of these vessels will lead the authorities at Tangier to make such representations to the Sultan as may result in his acceding to my demands, and then you will be able to return to your friends."

This calculation of the insurgent leader was soon proved to have been justified, since a runner carrying a dispatch, one of four copies of the same document, each carried by a separate courier, was held up by some of Raisuli's partisans, and thus we learned the, to us, grateful information, which was confirmed by the arrival of Sid Hassan a few days later to say that His Chereefian Majesty had been most graciously pleased to accede to the demands which Hadj Mohammed had forwarded to Fez.

Raisuli was now confronted by the problem as to what disposition he was to make of the seventy thousand silver Spanish dollars which he demanded for our release. Here at Tsarradan there were no iron safes, nor so much as a house with a cellar, while the thatch of skaff, or dried reeds, the only roofing of the houses, offered but poor security should he leave so much coin stored in a village where he himself was but a transient sojourner.

To the great amusement of Mulai Ali, and to my own considerable astonishment, the solution of this troublesome question which Raisuli proposed was that "La Senora," as the natives called my wife, should receive the seventy thousand dollars from Torres and deposit the money to her own credit in Tangier at the bank where we were accustomed to cash our checks, and that he, Raisuli, might then draw upon Mrs. Perdicaris as occasion should require.

I, however, entirely declined to request my wife to accede to this singular proposal, and when I explained to Raisuli the suspicions to which such an arrangement might expose us, he at once said that he would be the last to wish to place us in such a position.

It was finally arranged that the younger of our Wazani friends should bring to a certain village half way between Tangier and Tsarradan twenty thousand dollars in silver and the remaining fifty thousand in certified checks on the Comptoir d'Escompte, the French bank at Tangier, together with the prisoners whose release Raisuli had demanded, and that our captor should accompany us to this village, of which the Sheik, El Zellal, was one of his adherents. These negotiations occupied some time and led to many journeys of Sid Hassan back and forth from Tangier to Tsarradan.

After six weeks, and on the evening preceding our departure, we strolled from the village green with Mulai Ali; nor were we now, as had always hitherto been the case, accompanied by any of Raisuli's men. During our walk we fell into conversation with a native from another village, and who made some allusion to two unfortunate Spanish children, for the boy at least was but a child, though his sister was fifteen. This brother and sister, the children of a poor charcoal-burner, had been stolen about two years prior to our own adventure, nor had they been recovered, despite the pressure exerted by the Spanish authorities at Tangier.

We now learned to our horror that these unfortunate children had been carried off by the very man in whose hut we had spent so many sad hours, and that they had not only occupied the very room where I slept, but that after a long detention they had been ultimately killed in the garden and were buried not far from where our horses were tethered. This discovery showed the lawless character of these Berber followers of Raisuli, and also that we ourselves had been in more danger than we realized, had any mishap to Raisuli occurred while we were among these savages, for such these Berbers really are, possessing neither a written language nor any of those elements of culture or refinement which almost every other white race boasts.

I confess that during this our last night in that wretched hut, the scene of the sufferings and humiliations of those unfortunate Spanish captives, I scarcely closed my eyes.

The next morning it was still dark when our men began loading the pack-mules, and we reached the crest of the mountain, which lay between us and Tangier, just as the sun rose. Never have I anywhere witnessed a scene of more wild and fantastic charm. A slight mist hung about the base of the rocks, whose peaks and turrets were now flecked with crimson or lilac, now shaded with purple, by some passing cloud.

On our left rode Mulai Ali, arrayed in a silk bournous of spotless white, followed by all his men, while on my right Raisuli bestrode his gray charger. The dark, thick cords of twisted camel's hair crossed about his white turban, and the cartridge belt over his broad chest made him look every inch a man of daring deeds.

Upon this occasion Varley and I rode our own horses, or, rather, I rode the black horse which Raisuli had ridden on our way from Tangier, and as we climbed again, but in how different a mood, those rocky steeps I told the latter of my surprise at the horse's behavior. A smile played upon the chieftain's lips as he answered, "Oh! that is easily explained! Did you not know that before you purchased that horse it belonged to me?"

"I did not, nor," I added, "do I seem to have known as much of your affairs as you evidently knew of mine! Still," I continued, "this does not entirely explain the very different behavior of the horse. I can understand that you could, by the use of spur and bridle, compel the horse to kneel in order that you might dismount, but I am still at a loss to account for his standing obedient and motionless when you had left him to his own devices!"

"This is also easily explained," said Raisuli. "The fact is," he continued, "you Roumi are of too easy a disposition. You spoil your wives, your children, your servants, and even your very horses. These animals," he said, "are quite intelligent enough to know that they must obey *our* wishes, even when we are not in the saddle!"

"If these are your views of how we should deal with men, women, and even with animals, I will mention the fact to the Sultan when I next see him," I replied jocosely.

"Yes," continued Raisuli, in the same strain, "and if His Chereefian Majesty indulged in fewer European fads, and had a little more grip, and would use the spur more freely, *he* would have a better seat in *his* saddle," referring to the expression that the throne of the Sultan should be his saddle.

We continued during the entire morning in a northerly direction. Our path after taking us over the lofty crest of Mount Nazul and through the forest of almost primeval oaks beyond, again led us along the crest of a line of hills—a path at times so narrow that we were compelled to proceed in single file. At such moments our escort trailed out over half a mile or more, passing between steep slopes or even abrupt precipices on either side of us. From these heights we could see the distant sea and the Spanish coast beyond, and at last Raisuli pointed out to me a white fleck upon the distant sands of the nearer African coast which he said was Tangier.

About noon we found ourselves looking down upon a village many hundred feet immediately beneath us. Here a halt was called. This was the eyrie of El Zellal, a semi-fortified place, hanging on to the steep hillside, half village, half Zereeba.

Raisuli sent forward some of his followers on foot to be sure that no government troops were hiding within the village, the approach to which was through a tall gateway of masonry, and when his men reappeared, signaling that no foes were concealed within, the chieftan turning to me said, "Do as you see me do!" As he spoke he spurred his steed violently; whereupon the animal, squatting upon his haunches after the manner of a dog rather than that of a horse, slid down the steep descent.

Congratulating myself that my own horse, having been trained by Raisuli, probably possessed the same accomplishment, I followed suit, as did the other mounted members of the party, and presently we all found ourselves gaily tobogganing down the steep hillside and through the gate right into the village, where we had some difficulty in pulling up at the entrance of the residence of El Zellal himself, so abrupt was the incline or downward grade.

Here we were detained, owing to the absence of Mulai Ahmed, the younger Wazani chereef, who did not arrive at the appointed hour with the ransom and Raisuli's men who had been released from prison—a delay due in part to the difficulty of bringing with him, in addition to other impediments, a huge mule litter to carry me, should I not be able to endure so many hours in the saddle.

In the meantime we waited amid a solemn silence, except when some much-required food was served, and as we sat there it might have seemed more as though we were in some house of mourning rather than in one so shortly to become the scene of our eagerly desired liberation.

At last the mules bearing the silver dollars, carefully packed in boxes, arrived; but now luncheon was again served in honor of Mulai Ahmed, and must be partaken of, after which the bullion was counted in another room.

Here I was presently summoned, and invited to seat myself between

Raisuli and Mulai Ahmed, while a group of the more important natives, including El Zellal, as well as men from other localities, were ranged around the room.

"The silver," said Raisuli, addressing me, "has been counted—twenty thousand dollars, as stipulated, in Spanish dollars; but these letters," showing me as he spoke a check book containing certified checks on the Comptoir d'Escompte, the French bank at Tangier, "of the value of these, which are supposed to represent fifty thousand dollars, I know nothing. However, I will accept them on your personal guarantee, but on that condition only."

When I had examined the checks certified by Torres and by El Gannam, the Sultan's delegate minister of finance, I gave the required assurance verbally, and Raisuli, leading me to the door, where I found my horse waiting for me, bade me adieu, saying that he had learned to look upon me as a friend, and that he hoped I cherished no ill feeling on account of my detention. He furthermore assured me that should any danger menace me in the future, that no only he himself, but any of the men of the three tribes under his orders, would hasten to my relief.

Thus I left him, and pushing on as rapidly as we could we were soon in the midst of the large armed escort which had come from Tangier to see us safely home. It seems there had been some rumor of an intention on the part of other tribes to secure our persons after we should have left Raisuli and to hold us for further ransom.

Fortunately our further journey suffered no delay other than that caused by the transport of the litter, of which I was most thankful to avail myself, since I had twice suffered while at Tsarradan from severe nervous prostration.

This reminds me to mention with a grateful heart that my wife having applied to Admiral Chadwick, when she learned of my second attack, to inquire whether a surgeon could be detached from one of the vessels under his command, every medical officer in the fleet at once volunteered to go and attend me, even though warned that they might be themselves detained by Raisuli.

We did not reach Tangier until long after dark. As we were pushing forward in the gloom of evening a company of native cavalry, which had been sent out to report our arrival, galloped up, and so soon as they discovered we were of the party, turned and hastened back to announce our coming, as to which there was even yet grave anxiety. An hour later and we could see the town lights, and also those on the mastheads of the vessels in the bay, and we could even make out that these were answering signals from the United States consulate in the town. Yes, our friends now at last knew that we were near at hand.

I struggled out of my litter and onto my horse and presently galloped through the gateway of my home, amid the acclamations of friends and neighbors. As I descended from my horse Admiral Chadwick himself, who had with Minister Gummere awaited my arrival even until this late hour, for it was now nearly midnight, grasped me by the arm, and thus was I literally restored to my family by the gallant officer in command of the fleet which the United States government had so generously sent to my rescue. But for this strenuous and successful intervention I might still be detained among those mountains. Upon this point I insist the more, since it has been suggested that we owed our rescue to other agencies.

To the joint exertions of my friends, Minister Gummere, and to the British Minister, Sir Arthur Nicolson, I am deeply indebted — indeed, I can find no words adequate to describe what I owe to them, as well as to Admiral Chadwick, not merely for their untiring efforts on behalf of Varley and myself, but for the sympathy and solicitude of which my wife was the recipient throughout these long six weeks, so much more trying to her even than to ourselves, since she indeed was the greater sufferer.

With this expression of my gratitude to the government and to the people of the United States, I conclude this account and beg to thank you also for the indulgent patience with which you have listened to so long a narrative.

Loading a Camel

CAPTAIN A. H. W. HAYWOOD

from *Through Timbuctu and Across the Great Saraha*, 1912

Captain A. Haywood's 1909 journey from Sierra Leone to Algeria was part of a new trend in Western exploration of northwest Africa. Nearly all of Islamic North Africa was now under European control. Traveling in regions that by this point had been ostensibly "pacified" by French colonialists somewhat reduced the perils of crossing the Sahara. In 1909 Morocco was still independent, and Libya remained a province of the Ottoman Empire. But by 1912, France and Spain had partitioned Morocco, and Italy had invaded Libya.

Fifty-four years had passed since Barth entered Timbuktu in 1855, disguised as a Muslim. Haywood's Timbuktu was a flyblown, gritty outpost in French-controlled Mali. He traveled much of the way on the Niger River aboard *Rene Chaille*, a charming steamship named for a French Saharan explorer. In 1806, a journey on the Niger had cost Mungo Park—the first European to visit the Niger—his life when he was ambushed and killed. A century later, the Niger had become a commercial highway.

Haywood was a British officer on five months' furlough from his posting in British West Africa when he began his journey. His trek through Mali, Niger, and Algeria (all French territories at the time, at least on maps) is recorded in *Through Timbuctu and Across the Great Sahara*. Haywood carried an arsenal, because Tuareg tribesmen on his route remained hostile. But Haywood's journey is a benchmark: Western explorers now had more detailed geographical knowledge of the Sahara and a marginally better chance of not being killed by locals. By 1909 tenuous French conquests curbed the Tuaregs' ability to prevent Westerners from traveling the desert.

Nonetheless, Haywood was forced to alter his route through the Sahara because according to French officials, raiders from Morocco—still independent—made crossing from Timbuktu unsafe. He was forced to head north from the Niger at Gao, 270 miles farther west along the river. He was probably the first Englishman to cross the bleak, harsh Sahara from Gao, in Mali, to In Salah in Algeria.

During WWI, aircraft and motor vehicles would change Saharan exploration, bringing speed and the capacity to fly over the terrain to map and photograph it, not to mention, to subdue its people. The development of railways and roads also made travel faster and opened regions to Europeans that in Haywood's day were inaccessible.

In 1909, however, Haywood traveled by train in Sierra Leone; in Niger and Mali, by river steamer and canoe. Camels carried him across the Sahara—something he greatly enjoyed. He was a keen observer of this animal's idiosyncrasies and wrote about them appreciatively. During Haywood's trek, there was not an automobile or aircraft to be found. He was a traveler and writer in the twilight of an era, among the last adventurers to explore the Sahara without benefit of these modern machines.

—J. H.

T he preparations to be made for a journey across the Sahara are many, as I soon found out at Gao. It was not merely a question of arranging for the hire of camels and the services of a guide, but various other points wanted careful attention.

To start with, the baggage had to be made up in loads suitable for camel transport, and, naturally, on a pack animal a far more accurate adjustment of weights is necessary than is the case with carriers. Besides, I found that cases of provisions, my tin travelling bath, and even my camp table (Uganda pattern), were the reverse of being comfortable loads on the desert camel, although they had been very compact for transport on porters' heads. All these things had to be either left behind or put into leathern bags, called "mesoued." A bag is quite the easiest form of baggage for a camel to carry. Two of these can be slung over the pack-saddle, and the weights easily adjusted by taking something out of the heavier and adding it to the lighter one. No ropes are necessary to tie a "mesoued" on to the saddle, while boxes and such-like loads have to be strapped round with cords, and tied on to hooks on the pack-saddle. These ropes, however strong, break sooner or later, with the result that your cases fall with a crash to the ground and the contents are probably scattered in all directions.

As this was my first experience of the desert I had to learn all these little points, but, fortunately for me, my French friends helped me with much practical advice, making my task much easier. I had to retain some of my cases, however, as sufficient bags were not forthcoming, and I rather unwisely decided to retain my bath. Although water would be scarce on the way, I could not help thinking that the luxury of a bath when I did arrive at a well would be too great to forego!

I replenished my stock of rice so as to have sufficient to ration my servant and guide, and at the same time I carefully overhauled my tinned provisions. My supply of the latter was decidedly low, but there were no means of increasing it now; besides, I had made up my mind to live on the simplest fare, such as farinaceous food, in order not to augment unduly the number of camels in my caravan by having too many loads. I had, however, to arrange for sufficient rations to last till my arrival at Insalah, in about seven weeks' time. I was informed that at the oasis of Insalah I should be able to reprovision myself for the remainder of the desert journey.

Another most important item for consideration was the means for carrying water. Big glass demijohns are impracticable in the desert. They make the water hot, and are extremely likely to break, should a camel drop its load, or even if the beast should knock up against one of his fellows, in his usual clumsy manner. The French use two kinds of water-carriers. The one mostly used, and invariably used by the nomads of the desert, is a leather water-skin, called "guerba," which is generally porous, and therefore leaks to a certain extent, but keeps the water cool, and is easily slung on a camel's back.

The other kind is an iron or aluminum cylindrical vessel, which can be locked if necessary, and cannot break. The water therein contained gets very hot, but is never wasted as in a "guerba." I was obliged to take "guerbas," as no metal carriers were available. And I provided myself with eight of these.

In connection with the subject of water, which is, indeed, *the* vital item in desert marches, I had to arrange to have some means of drawing water from a well. This is a more serious problem than may be thought, for wells in the Sahara are often seventy yards or more deep. In one case I recollect there was a well over 330 feet deep! To draw water from such a depth a long rope of hide is required, at the end of which is attached a leather bucket, called "délou." Spare material of all kinds must be carried, as a caravan must be absolutely self-contained from start to finish, and any omissions in calculating requisite stores are likely to be heavily paid for in the desert.

All gear has to be thoroughly tested as to its strength and durability before embarking on a journey, and this is a matter to be attended to personally, for a native cannot be trusted.

Of course, two most important items are the camels and the guide. My animals belonged to the Kountah Arabs, who wander in that part of the Sahara north of Gao, while the guide was also a Kountah Arab, named Sidi Mahomed. I had a second guide for the journey as far as Kidal, a Tuareg, from the Ifora country, through which I should pass.

The camels were rather a sorry-looking lot of animals, whose aspect was not reassuring to a person about to start on a long desert march, but the Kountah chief, from whom I hired them, vouched for their ability to take me and my belongings safely to Kidal. I had no intention of keeping these camels or the guides beyond Kidal, but would hire a fresh caravan there. The Commandant kindly helped in this matter by sending a camel-runner in advance to the officer commanding the post at Kidal, to prepare camels and a guide for me. These camel-couriers travel much faster than a caravan. We calculated to take twelve days over the journey, whereas he would accomplish it in five or six. The courier's mount is a fast-trotting camel, which at a pinch can cover about fifty miles a day.

On the 23rd of April all was ready, and I decided to start that afternoon, so as to avoid marching in the day when it was hot. As I gazed for the last time at the broad, calm bosom of the Niger, flowing gently by the walls of Gao on its way to the sea, I could not help feeling rather serious, and wondering when I should again see running water, if, indeed, ever. Before me was the unknown mystery of the great Sahara Desert, and in it I was to pass many long and weary days before I should arrive in a country watered by running streams. How often should I not long for a glimpse of the cool, rippling river I was now look-ing on for the last time! For days I must be content with the sight of a well, if I was to see any water at all; and, at the time, I hardly realized how welcome the sight of that well would be. About 4 p.m., as the sun was losing its power, having bidden adieu to my good hosts at Gao, I prepared to start.

All the Europeans at the station were assembled to see me off. I fully be-lieve most of them thought I should never reach my destination. I promised the Commandant to write to him as soon as I reached Insalah to announce my safe arrival so far. There were many cameras raised to get a snapshot of my party before their departure, and then we were off.

The camels after this march began to show signs of fatigue; several, too, had got terribly sore backs. These sore backs had not altogether developed on the march, for I had noticed them suffering from barely healed wounds be-fore we left Gao. I had been assured, however, that it was very rare to get a hired camel without a tender place on his back, so there seemed to be noth-ing to do but accept the situation. I used to dress their wounds daily with iod-oform and cotton-wool, but it was almost as painful to me to see them loaded as it must have been to themselves. I lightened the loads as much as possible, but most of my kit had to be carried if I hoped ever to reach the other side of the Sahara, so I had to harden my heart and ignore the pain they must have sometimes endured. The Bambara soldiers, when charging a camel, are quite callous. But they do not, and I suppose never will, understand the beast. Being negroes, they are totally unconscious of the pain animals can suffer. Of course, it must be said that they are not natives of a camel country, and so are handicapped by a lack of knowledge of the beast, when they are enlisted in camel corps. I think they never quite appreciate the necessity for giving the camel a regular number of hours daily in a pasturage whenever it is possible, and they certainly are not as careful about watering him as are the nomads of the desert, who are brought up from their childhood to look after camels.

The camel is a curious-tempered animal. He seems to have the same characteristic as most desert nomads. He dislikes mankind cordially, and takes no pains to disguise the fact.

To mount a camel he must be made first to squat on the ground. This is accomplished at the expense of some time and temper, by pulling his head towards the ground by means of the string in his nostril and ejaculating frequently a soothing noise similar to what is used by a nurse when she tries to induce a baby to go to sleep. The camel at last obeys, with many grunts and "protests." The next operation is to mount. The first point is to seize the rein in your right hand and place this hand on the front of the saddle. At the same time you must seize the camel's nostril in your left hand, turning his head inwards until the nose nearly reaches the front of the saddle. Every movement on your part will call forth numerous deep growls of protest, but one soon gets accustomed to this, and takes no notice of it. When, however, you seize the nostril and pull his head round he will roar as if he were being tortured to death. It is advisable to place the left foot on the slack part of the rein on the ground, or he may take you by surprise and suddenly jump up.

Having successfully accomplished all these manœuvres, you should rapidly throw the right leg over the saddle, lifting the left foot from the rein and placing it on his neck. The camel will then generally—but not always—rise with a most disconcerting jerk, growling loudly all the while. This is perhaps the most awkward, and even dangerous, moment for the unwary novice. On rising the camel first throws his head and body forward and then backward with lightning-like rapidity, when the rider must conform by equally rapidly jerking his own body in the inverse directions, otherwise he will inevitably lose his balance and be hurled on the ground. The Saharan camel is not a well-trained animal, so it behoves one to be careful when first attempting to mount an unknown beast.

After having mounted the rider will not persuade him to cease his angry grumbles for some little time. If he refuses to rise, as he sometimes does, the only plan is to tap more or less violently with the feet on his neck; but in every case the golden rule is to have patience, for of all the brutes in creation which have been tamed to do man's will, the camel is surely the most trying. I have sometimes spent ten minutes in endeavouring to make a camel rise, when I was in a particular hurry to be off. Beating is quite ineffectual, and only serves to humble one's pride. A camel's hide is pretty tough, and he cares little for the blow from a thick stick or whip.

The camel never seems really happy unless he is absolutely left to himself. Far away from mankind, and unobserved, he eats and eats till he is gorged, and then lies down to sleep. If man is at hand he will never eat as well as when by himself; the presence of a human being seems to have a strange effect on him. This has been often proved by noticing the difference between camels left at their pasturage in perfect liberty and those which are guarded by men while feeding. The former regain condition comparatively quickly, while the latter, besides taking longer, will probably never return to such good form as their more fortunately placed brothers who are grazing quite at liberty. When near a man he constantly seems to sulk and not to make the best of himself. I have known camels in the Sahara, who had not had anything to eat for several days, refuse their food after being ill-treated, seemingly preferring to die than to accept any favour from the person who has beaten them.

Although camels can go several days without water, yet, when they do drink, they are gluttons for it. They drink an abnormally large quantity at a time, and will return to drink two or three times in the day until satisfied. Camels suffer a good deal from indigestion, and this is probably due to the huge quantities of food and water they consume.

It was the custom to hobble our animals at night, and I recollect how on one occasion on this march to Kidal, my plans for the next day's journey were upset by a freak on their part. We halted one night, rather tired after a long march, about eleven o'clock. The road was rough, as we had entered into a mountainous, rocky country, and it was impossible to move any further until the sun rose, the moon having just set. It so happened that there was an excellent pasturage in an "oued" close by, and into this the camels were turned after being hobbled for the night.

I awoke next morning at daybreak to find all except four of the brutes had disappeared. They had wandered off, moving, as they do when hobbled, by a series of little jumps, in the direction from which we had come the previous evening. I sent a party to track them. They had gone back a distance of fifteen miles to our last halting-place, and were found quietly grazing there, quite unconcerned at the trouble they had given us! The incident made me lose a valuable day. It was not the slightest use to get angry, so I resigned myself to such incidents quite meekly at last. Camels will wander extraordinary distances in search of water when very thirsty. I heard of a case where two camels had gone back a six days' march to the previous well, when, had they only known it, the next well was only one day's march ahead! Usually they have a keen instinct for the presence of water, and when they have been to a well, along a certain route, they will recollect the road in a wonderful manner.

Cases of guides having lost their way, and having then trusted themselves to the memory of the camel, by allowing him to go in the direction he selects, are frequently repeated. The camel in such cases generally, although, of course, not invariably, brings the caravan safely to the well. It must be understood that this will not occur unless the animal has followed that route on previous occasions, and further, that he must in such cases usually be within a few miles, at most, of the well.

One rather unpleasant feature about these Sahara camels is the number of ticks they collect. These loathsome insects find a habitation on all camels, and are difficult to destroy.

The question of the different herbs of the desert leads one to consider the subject of how and when camels should be allowed to graze. I found I had a lot to learn about this, and it is a most important item in the education of the desert traveller. Since one's mobility, and frequently one's life, must depend on the state of the camels in the caravan, the subject is obviously worth studying. Of course, in some cases forced marches are absolutely necessary, as when crossing a waterless tract of desert with little water on the camels. But in most cases the welfare of the camel must be studied as carefully as possible. Now, it has been noticed that the camel will eat better at certain times of the day than he will at others. Between the hours of 11 A.M. and 3 P.M. camels do not graze. They generally lie down and rest at this time. Further, they do not graze between about 2 a.m. and sunrise. They will, practically, graze all the rest of the twenty-four hours. Experience has also shown that they graze better on moonlight nights than when it is dark. With these data as a guide, one can regulate the time of marching so as to allow the camels to graze at suitable hours. The authorities say that the animals should be allowed four hours' pasturage at the very least during the twenty-four.

Another point to be remembered is that camels ruminate, or chew their food, for some time after grazing. Time should be allowed for this. When not grazing, and particularly at night, camels can often be observed chewing. They will go on scrunching their massive jaws for hours together, while squatting on their hunkers round the camp after dark.

Camels are strange beasts, passing the comprehension of man in many ways. I often used to watch them in their pasturage, and think what antediluvian creatures they appeared to be. The camel seems to belong to a prehistoric age, and should be classed with the giraffe, elephant, and hippopotamus, to my mind. He is a sad sort of animal, seeming never to take any enjoyment in life. Even when in perfect liberty, grazing, he does not look happy. He only then seems to be a little less discontented than usual. But with all his peculiarities and vices a camel is a necessity in desert travel, and I suppose we should be grateful to him for enabling us to cross these inhospitable tracts. Without the camel the Sahara would be even less known than at present.

While at In Ouzel I had to make a careful overhaul of my equipment. The portion of desert now close in front of me was the much-dreaded Tanezrouft, and a journey across it at any time of the year was not a thing to be lightly undertaken, but more especially was this the case during the hottest season.

The Tanezrouft extends between the 23rd and 26th parallels in the Central Sahara, forming a tract of desert in which there is no water, to all intents and purposes no grazing and, what is still more inconvenient in many ways, not even any firewood. The consequence is that all these necessaries must be carried for a distance of about 200 miles. The width of this waterless region varies in different parts, but at the point where I was going to cross it I must expect to take about seven days to accomplish the journey. This is a tract which must be crossed as rapidly as possible in order to reach the wells on the north side, for a camel in hot weather cannot exist more than about eight days without water; moreover, the water-skins are calculated to leak to the extent of one-tenth per diem, from which it is evident that a full water-skin would have lost the whole of its contents by the tenth day, even if none of the water in it had been drunk. It follows that any delay over and above seven days, in the passage of this dreary bit of desert, would be extremely perilous for the safety of the caravan.

From the above considerations it is obvious that it was imperative to be most careful that all details connected with the equipment and organization of the little caravan should be put into first-rate working order. It was unfortunate that I had been ill at this rather critical time, but I had in person seen to as much as possible, and had left everything else in the competent hands of Mahomed.

Broken saddles required to be repaired and thoroughly overhauled, girths had to be mended and renewed, water-skins must be carefully tested to see they did not leak more than the normal amount, while camels' wounds had to be dressed. Besides, the whole of my kit really needed overhauling, but owing to the sandstorms constantly blowing, it was impossible to do this. Our greatest difficulty was with the saddles, for many of these had the wooden framework broken, and this required to be firmly lashed in order to make the saddle serviceable.

There are two or three different patterns of pack-saddle used in this part of the Sahara. The French-made one is much solider than the native article, but in some respects is less adapted for use with camels, and likely to give them a sore back if not carefully attended to. The French saddle, called the Gao pattern, consists of a wooden triangular frame, made of two horizontal bars on each side, which are connected by two transverse pieces at the sides, the apex of the triangle being formed by a further horizontal bar. This saddle fits on to the camel's back on the top of two well-stuffed panels which are filled with cotton-wool. On the framework are fixed two iron hooks on each side, so that baggage can be slung on each side of the frame. In most cases the two panels are sewn together, a hole being cut in the middle to allow of the camel's hump protruding. I found that the chief drawback to these saddles was that the panels were often not long enough; consequently, if a load was used which projected lower than the panel on the animal's side, he was certain to get chafed by the constant friction of the article against his skin. I saw some nasty wounds which had been thus inflicted, and these were always difficult to heal.

The native type of saddle, called the "arrej" in Arabic, is a far simpler affair, made on the same principle but with two light pieces of bamboo fitting over each side of the camel, and connected by two diagonal bamboos. This saddle also is kept from pressing on the animal's back by means of a cushion of date-palm fibre, while no girth whatever is used.

Owing to there being no girth, a very nice adjustment of loads is required to preserve the balance. I have seen some curious sights with this saddle, too, when a camel has been coming down hill. If he trots disaster is almost inevitable, for he jogs his saddle out of place, and equilibrium between the loads is lost, so that they fall to the ground, saddle and all.

Riding-saddles, called "rahla" in Arabic, are of two kinds—the Arabic and the Tuareg saddle. These simply consist of a round piece of wood for the seat, covered with leather, and a peak in front as well as one behind. In the case of the Tuareg "rahla," which is by far the most comfortable, the peaks are higher and the seat wider in circumference. The shape of the peak in the Tuareg saddle is rather strange; it is in the form of a cross. The best of riding-saddles are hard and uncomfortable if the length of march is above the average. I used to fold a blanket over mine to soften somewhat the discomfort caused by the hard wood. I never saw a saddle of European manufacture, but have no doubt that something far more comfortable could easily be made.

Approaching a Perilous Pass

P. T. ETHERTON

From *Across the Roof of the World*, 1911

The Karakoram Mountains, northern British India, 1910. P. T. Etherton was having tea with the *mir* (Persian for *emir*, the local ruler) and his son. Their discussion topic: ". . . flying was becoming an established fact, and that ships were being made to sail in the air." The mir had decided he wanted an aircraft "to explore the skies."

In 1931, Etherton would be on the first aircraft to fly over and photograph Mount Everest—but in 1910, he did it the hard way. He climbed through the "Roof of the World"—the highest altitudes inhabited by humans, many of whom were Muslims—to kill wapiti, bear, ibex, and roe deer. "It had long been an ambition of mine," Etherton wrote, "a big-game shooting expedition into Central Asia, a scheme as bold as it was comprehensive, since it included the Pamirs, the Thian Shan, and the Great Altai Mountains, thence through Siberia to the Trans-Siberian Railway."

Etherton described his thin-air expedition and shooting spree in *Across the Roof of the World* in 1911. His narrative starts dreamily in the hill stations, where he lodged in cozy bungalows and islets of comfort such as the Chambers Hotel. He traveled by a two-wheeled cart called a *tongas*, his gear in a smaller version called an *ekka*. His vocabulary was British Raj speak. Lunch, for example, was *tiffin*. This was the frontier of empire, the rampart of the land of memsahibs and sahibs.

Beginning in British India, he led his group up into the Karakoram Mountains and the Yarkand Pass. In 1910, the region was a frontier zone between the British Raj and the Russian and Chinese empires. Etherton's column of servants and yaks entered his version of heaven on earth: the Tien

Shan (Thian Shan to him), known to the Chinese as "Heaven's Mountains." Almost 500 miles wide and 1,740 miles long, the Tien Shan Mountains form the spine of Central Asia. Coming out of the mountains, Etherton visited gritty desert cities in Chinese and Russian Turkistan. Once in Russia, he took the Trans-Siberian Railway to Europe.

Across the Roof of the World is reprinted here for several reasons. Etherton was one of the world's greatest adventurer-authors. In addition to his military career in India, he was also British Consul General in Chinese Turkistan. A selection of his book titles reflects his incredible résumé: *In the Heart of Asia* (1925), *Adventures on Five Continents* (1928), *First Over Everest* (1933), *Across the Great Deserts* (1948). Few adventurers can claim more experience and insight than Etherton.

He is also included because his treks took him through another region of the Islamic world that remains hazy to Westerners: Hunza, where he entered the Karakoram Mountains, was a tiny kingdom ruled by mirs, belonging to the Ismaili sect of Islam. On his journey to Siberia, he encountered Muslim nomads—Kazaks, Kirghiz, and Turcoman—and included them in his narrative.

Recently, Westerners were introduced to the complex ethnic groups in Muslim South and Central Asia through news reports about the Allied assault on Taliban-governed Afghanistan. Etherton's expedition traveled through this very region, now broken into five Muslim majority countries— Afghanistan, Pakistan, Tajikistan, Kazakhstan, Kyrgyzstan—and Muslim regions of China and Russia. Today, there are officially 18 million Muslims in China, which is a gross underestimation; it's more likely that there are at least 40 million, more than the population of Iraq.

Across the Roof of the World is an insightful look at Muslim China before decades of oppression and persecution pulverized a culture that is only now experiencing a revival.

—J. H.

One great advantage in fording the Yarkand is the fact that the bed is smooth and firm wherever one can touch it, so there is no distressing blundering and struggling amongst huge boulders and rocks, every one seemingly put in its particular position as a pitfall for the unfortunate traveller.

Now, to attempt the crossing of a big and rushing river a good acquaintance with the fords conducting from one side to the other is essential, though even this knowledge is sometimes stultified by the seething current which catches the forder in its folds, throwing him about like a cork, and lucky he be if not washed away and drowned. The guide professing to be well up in river lore of this nature was deputed to take the lead, and pilot us through the billows, a post not appealing to him, but one which force of circumstances compelled him to fill. The yak tackles most fords with comparative ease, on this occasion further justifying his reputation as a wader of rivers of a high order. More than once mine was carried off his feet, but with an admirable coolness he breasted the current, battling against it until bottom was touched.

On the far side I rested the yaks before despatching one back with the guide who brought over the baggage animals, an operation pleasanter to look back upon than watch, since the chances of all one's worldly goods being swept irretrievably away are very strong.

In the jungle amongst the reeds and willow trees I halted awhile, before commencing the ascent of the Tupa Dawan, the path leading high up above the right bank of the river. I partook of a frugal lunch inside an old ruined log hut there, a rough structure, doubtless built many years ago judging from its dilapidated condition.

It was a long and stiff pull to the summit of the Tupa Pass, over a bare and otherwise desolate stretch of ground sloping down at an extremely steep angle to the river bed far below. The summit is likewise bare and in addition covered with fragments of rock.

A descent of about 1,500 feet takes one into the nullah, the head of which leads over into the Kulan Urga Valley by a high and exceedingly difficult pass.

The path winds down in a succession of zigzags to the nullah in question, these running directly under one another, a fact we were summarily apprised of by miniature avalanches of stones caused by the yaks above us, for Nadir and I had, as usual, gone on ahead.

I camped that night some four miles up the nullah leading to the Qoqoi Qotchkor, with the intention of pushing on at dawn and getting over the pass, the guide saying it was high and very difficult. This man, like all natives high and low, assured me the pass was "not far," and that we should reach a Kirghiz encampment in the valley on the other side by evening. His ideas on the subject of distance were limited, as I was destined to discover by practical experience. Just how much "not far" represented in his computation was at the moment a problem I could not solve but I certainly was sanguine enough to hope the close of the day might see us in the valley on the far side.

It was a quiet, restful spot where I camped, a grassy patch by the brook, whose rippling waters flowed almost noiselessly down the narrow valley, a pleasing contrast to the rush and roar of the Ili Su. I spent the evening in re-packing and arranging the loads in readiness for the ordeal of the morrow, since I was sure it would be a formidable one. Whilst thus occupied some fresh yaks arrived in accordance with arrangements made the previous day, when I had despatched one of the Kirghiz drivers with orders to that effect. This worthy had disappeared into the hills with the object of rounding up fresh transport, though from where I knew not, but he had assured me scattered groups of Tajiks and Kirghiz lived in even these inaccessible parts, and that from them he would be able to secure other yaks capable of tackling the ground ahead leading down to Yarkand. He omitted to mention the main reason of his anxiety to secure fresh animals was that it would permit him to return to the Pamirs with his own yaks, and thus avoid the probable loss of his life on the perilous Qotchkor Pass.

The yaks with me were suffering from exhaustion and the hardships of the march down the Ili Su, and were consequently quite unfit to tackle the still more difficult portion of the route ahead. The arrival of the fresh animals gladdened the hearts of the yak men from the Pamirs, and mighty pleased they were to turn back and avoid treacherous and unknown routes with their manifold dangers. When I paid them off the next morning in solid coin of the realm their faces beamed with delight, and we parted the best of friends, they to return to the snows and wind-swept uplands of the Pamirs, I to cross into the Kulan Urga and Asgar Sai Valleys on my way to Yarkand.

I started that morning soon after half past five, the road lying through a narrow valley some seventy yards broad, with grass patches and wood jungle here and there. The ground on both sides ran up in a series of grassy slopes, intersected by many side ravines and gullies, whilst beyond the grass it was rocky, approximating more to the nature of cliffs.

Shortly after leaving camp we sighted burhel on the grass slopes of the right bank. They did not seem to be in the least surprised at our sudden appearance, merely contenting themselves with moving slowly off up-hill, halting every now and then to gaze back, probably wondering what strange creatures we could be, for I doubt if they had ever seen much of man before. Higher up we sighted another herd coming down the hill from the right slopes of the valley and which, crossing some distance in front of us, went off up-hill on the opposite side. Both here and in the Ili Su I saw a number of burhel, but high water in the rivers and the possibility of being shut in for the summer did not permit of my tarrying; indeed as it was we had to trek fast in order to avoid being held prisoners by the rapidly rising water.

As regards the Ili Su it might repay sportsmen trying this spot for burhel, since it is only a day's march from the Taghdumbash Valley, and as no one ever shoots there some good trophies would doubtless be obtained.

The Ili Su is also reputed to hold ibex, but whether they would repay pursuit is another question. Certain it is I saw no large heads either there or on the Taghdumbash Pamir, though as to whether any frequent those uplands or not I can express no definite opinion.

At 8 o'clock I halted for a light breakfast, the while giving the yaks time to forge ahead, for the ground we were then entering upon was more stony and arduous, and a yak, though very sure, is at the best of times a slow moving creature. At 10 o'clock I left the last patch of grass and wood jungle behind and entered a narrow, stony ravine, whose sides reminded me of the Ili Su. The way was littered with huge boulders over which we had to scramble, there being no visible track and a prolonged climb it was over this rocky débris at an ever-increasing gradient. The ravine from now onwards became wilder and more rugged, its dark sloping sides covered with moraine and the detritus of avalanche-swept shale, whilst beyond the ground stretched away up into the region of eternal snow. Amidst such a scene of rugged grandeur and sombre immensity we toiled upward, at noon reaching a point where the nullah bifurcated, one branch leading to the north, the other being the road I was to follow, and the one the guide had informed me was "not far." There was grass on the only open patch at this parting of the ways, so we rested there, gathering energy for the wilderness of rocks and boulders ahead. It was a long, unbroken ascent over masses of slate and shale, where to gain a footing at all was a work of art, the labour intensified by its sliding propensities, causing much blundering and struggling on the treacherous surface.

Such a road, leading as it did, at a steep angle, over heaps of detritus and ground that is one vast moraine, is most distressing for the baggage animals, and their struggles over the terribly rough going were pitiable to behold. As mentioned before the rarity of the atmosphere at these high altitudes puts a great strain on men and animals alike, and the hard work entailed by such precipitous ascents causes the heart to beat like a sledge hammer, and one gasps for breath in the attenuated air. It had always been my practice never to hustle the animals over such ground, but allow them to go their own pace, a slow, but withal a sure policy, working out better than any attempt to rush them through. At the same time it obviates a heavy mortality consequent on continued exertion combined with great height and its attendant evils.

The secret of success in crossing high passes lies in ascending them slowly, with due regard to the respiratory organs, which at high altitudes, and the resulting lack of sufficient oxygen, can only perform their functions under difficulties still further accentuated by any attempt to force the pace.

At two o'clock we were a long way below the summit, apparently further off than ever, but the guide still stuck manfully to his guns and declared we were now quite close. The ascent, now over a long and exceedingly steep moraine, momentarily became more laborious and exhausting. A pony I had brought from the Ili Su had to be left behind at the last patch far below, as, though marching unladen, he was quite unfit to proceed even over the ground further down, which in comparison to that we were now on was a mere bagatelle. The inconceivably rough going was too much for him, but the yaks on the other hand bore the ordeal well, accustomed as they are to live at considerable heights, although it was only at the cost of much puffing and grunting, and frequent halts to gather breath for renewed attempts.

At half past three we crossed patches of frozen snow, just beginning to melt under the warming influences of the sun, and reached a basin shut in by the surrounding heights. Some 400 feet above we could discern the razorback crest denoting the summit of this appalling pass. It was a last supreme effort up a slope approaching so nearly to the perpendicular that it seemed a hopeless task trying to gain the top. But patience and perseverance have their reward, and at a quarter past four I stood on the summit, calculating the height with my instruments to by 17,400 feet, and the highest pass I had yet crossed. Having reached that altitude one is quite content to go no higher, unless there be something tangible at the end of it in the shape of a good trophy of ibex, burhel, or other horned denizen of the mountains.

From the top a grand view unfolded itself, a panorama of peaks and glacier stretching away north and south over the mighty Mustagh and Kuen Lun Ranges. It was a fine display of snow-capped heights, with great spurs running out parallel to the main ranges, the valleys and ravines in between being lined along their lowest levels with a thin silvery thread denoting a rushing torrent flowing from its glacier bed above. There in the distance stood out bold and exceptionally well defined the Ili Su Pass I had crossed some days previously, and the peaks on either side of it, whilst farther south one could distinguish the giant summits of that grand chain of mountains, the Mustagh Range, rising above the Raskum Valley, the highest peaks attaining an altitude of more than 26,000 feet.

Turning to the east and looking over that portion embracing the Kulan Urgu Valley, down which I was now to travel, almost the same scene of savage grandeur met the eye, with the exception that the peaks were not so high, nor the line of snowy summits to complete as that spreading itself out to the gaze in the Karakoram and the Mustagh from the western aspect of the Qotchkor Pass.

Soon after reaching the summit one of those remarkable changes of weather common at high regions came on, and in the place of a cloudless sky and brilliant sunshine, a dark and driving mist supervened, boding ill for the descent and causing us to hasten preparations for the downward journey. The summit of the pass was a narrow razor-backed ridge, with a huge snow-cornice overhanging the eastern side. The descent looked exceedingly steep and dangerous, and the snow-cornice, frozen solid, offered no means of getting down to the slope beneath. The yak men went along the top endeavouring to find a way for the animals, whilst I assisted Piro and Giyani at tightening ropes and generally readjusting the loads in order to facilitate the downward passage of the laden yaks.

Presently the drivers returned and reported the only practicable path through the snow-cornice was a difficult one, and asked me to inspect it before allowing the yaks to proceed. This I did and it certainly seemed very hazardous as there was merely a 12-inch ledge leading down at a most acute angle for twenty feet, thence a long, stony slope supervened for a distance of quite 2,000 feet to the bed of the ravine, the surface being covered with shale and frozen as hard as steel. I gave orders that the path through the snow-cornice should be enlarged as much as possible, and that the yaks should be assisted down by all the men, of whom I had eight. This was done with the aid of the tools we possessed, and the path widened slightly to the commencement of the slope, which was frozen so firm that it seemed impossible for any animal to maintain a footing. The wind, now rising ominously, drove the mist across the summit, confining the view to a matter of some fifty yards at the most, and filling my party with the direst forebodings. The path having been prepared I marshalled all hands, and with the object of testing it sent an unladen yak ahead to prepare the way for the others, and make as secure a hold in the treacherous surface as could reasonably be expected.

The laden animals were then passed down in succession, assisted by everyone, some holding on to their tails, whilst others at the lower side steadied their progress and prevented any sudden precipitation down the slope. By the time this dangerous part was successfully negotiated, it was 5 o'clock, and a dark misty afternoon. Already the feeble light was rapidly waning, night coming on apace as it ever does in the East, and I began to realise nothing could get us to the foot of this incline without disaster. We were now on the eastern slope, where it became necessary to proceed with the utmost caution, to save yaks and men from an untimely descent to eternity.

At times the mist would lift somewhat, revealing only that sweeping slope going down it seemed to us to the bottom of the earth. The surface was as slippery as glass, and I did not like the outlook at all, as the ground was certainly the worst we had been on, while the gathering gloom, foretelling the approach of darkness, rendered the task of getting the laden animals down a well-nigh superhuman one.

On reaching the summit I had scanned the whole valley to the east but saw no sign of habitation, nor indeed any traces of the Kirghiz encampment the guide had assured me existed just below. It was then too late to visit any of the trouble on he who had committed us to this desperate country, doubtless out of ignorance, so I merely contented myself with bringing down my invective on the author of our impending misfortunes. All that remained to be done was to find a way out of the difficulty and endeavour to reach the foot of the pass in safety if possible.

To add to our embarrassments the cold wind increased, turning everything into a state of frozen rigidity, so that the fleeting moments became of vital importance. It was impossible for the laden yaks to maintain a hold, some slipping thirty feet or more on the glassy surface, only recovering themselves when a friendly rock intervened to break the force of their descent and afford them a chance to regain a footing. Yaks are fine mountaineers but it seemed as though one were asking too much of them in the descent of the Qotchkor.

We had brought the animals down about fifty feet when one of them slipped again, and although desperate efforts were made to save him, it was useless on a slope continuing for full 2,000 feet. I was a little distance below endeavouring to hack a path in the icy surface so as to alleviate in some measure the difficulties of getting the transport down. As the yak slid backwards I hoped against hope he would be able to pull himself up, since he carried my most important kit, negatives, uniform, and presents destined for Chinese officials in Turkistan. One of the yak men was holding on to the halter rope and it looked as though he too would be dragged to certain death, but having gone about seventy feet at a tremendous speed, he let go and saved himself by cannoning into a rock, somewhat bruised but otherwise safe. The yak, however, continued his headlong flight, and by the time he had slid the first 150 feet was gathering a terrific impetus that nothing could check. I realised there was no chance of his saving himself on that glacial surface, so resigned myself to the inevitable. It was indeed a bitter moment to stand there and listen to the crash of my boxes being literally smashed to matchwood, coupled with feelings of regret at the untimely death of the poor beast. The Kirghiz above were in an agitated state of mind, weeping and wailing, calling on Allah to save them, and generally behaving as though their last hour had come. I at once gave orders for the remaining yaks to be off-loaded, and the kit stacked on the spot, intending to come up the next day and man-haul everything down. I left Piro in charge, directing him to bring the unladen yaks on a rapidly as possible to the Kirghiz encampment, still a long way down the valley, in search of which I now set out with Nadir and Giyani. On the way we endeavoured to get an idea of the direction the fallen yak had taken, but the gathering gloom and mist overhanging the slopes beneath the summit prevented our seeing anything of him. We went down several hundred feet following parallel to the course of his descent, but beyond the same terrific slope, of seemingly illimitable depth, could see nothing, so concluded he must have fallen a tremendous distance, in which conjecture we were right as was proved by our investigations the next day.

Some 2,000 feet below the summit we passed a solid wall of frozen snow and ice, now rapidly developing into a glacier that would probably in future years come down the valley and block up entirely the path through the ravine, though at the time there was no immediate indication of this. From here we passed through the bed of the ravine, a mass of rocks and shale, and then over a gravel and mud-strewn moraine rendered heavy and sodden by the fast-melting snow. A further descent brought us to open grassy slopes with a narrow ravine on either side through which flowed streams fed from the snows above, finally uniting at a point further down the valley.

I searched the entire ground here hoping to sight the Kirghiz encampment I had heard so much about from the guide, but nothing could be seen except the rocky bed of the streams and the walls of dark moraine above them. Continuing for some distance we reached the confluence of the streams, thence went along the valley on the right bank, where the grassy slopes were covered with numerous well-defined tracks hollowed out by the Kirghiz flocks.

Further down, and a good nine miles from the summit, we heard the barking of dogs, denoting the camp we were in search of. Descending into the valley and rounding the corner of a spur jutting out from the main ridge, we came on it, a solitary yurt with a small stone hut, the only sign of human habitation in this dark and gloomy wilderness. It was 9 o'clock when we reached the yurt tired and weary, but the Kirghiz, with characteristic hospitality, placed it at my disposal, the occupants disappearing through a low door into the stone hut close by, like rabbits into a warren.

We were glad to rest awhile after sixteen hours hard work over what may be termed one of the most difficult passes in the world. I, together with Nadir and Giyani, enjoyed a meal of barley boiled in milk, which a pretty Kirghiz girl prepared for our delectation. I then sent off for reinforcements from a Kirghiz camp, some miles away, in an adjacent nullah, and later in the night despatched a second man to hasten their arrival, since I wished to return to the dreaded pass the next day and go over the ground where the yak had fallen, in the hope of recovering some of my property, particularly the negatives and photographic plates, articles I could ill afford to lose. After supper

Nadir proceeded to appropriate sundry numdahs and felt rugs to provide me a couch for the night, while he also brought in firewood from a stack near the yurt, and which had been cut from the willow jungles found in the valley down stream.

We gathered round the blazing fire and, warmed by its cheery glow, discussed the day's events and the outlook for the morrow. The dancing light lit up the interior of the yurt, the primitive though warm and comfortable dwelling of the Kirghiz nomad. The walls were decorated with the usual embroidered cloths, whilst from the staves of the wickerwork constituting the frame on which the yurt is built depended a native guitar, not indeed of the type met with in Europe, but yet one that could give forth melodious music when manipulated by a master hand. Along the sides of the yurt were bowls hollowed out of wood, forming the eating and drinking utensils of the owners, while part was curtained off, serving the double purpose of a place of repose for the lady of the yurt, and pantry, which contained bowls of milk and cream covered with dirt and dust, always a strong feature in the nomad's dwelling. I enquired as to the country I had now to traverse, and the information gathered indicated it as being of a formidable nature, but I was not perturbed, having already covered much ground beset with many difficulties.

The Kirghiz here were greatly interested in my adventures down the Ili Su and on the Qotchkor Pass, parts of the universe they had never visited, and I doubt if they ever will, especially after my description. The loss of the yak seemed to be a serious calamity in their eyes, for the docile creature represents much worldly wealth to them, the mere fact of my having lost an important kit not appearing to be anything like so disastrous as the loss of its hairy carrier.

At dawn the next morning the Kirghiz reinforcements had not arrived, but at 6 o'clock Piro and the yakmen came in. They had spent the night at the foot of the pass amongst the rocks and boulders, having found it impossible to make any headway in the darkness, while in addition men and animals were tired out from the hardest day's work they had ever experienced. Soon after their arrival, as the Kirghiz had still not put in an appearance, I collected all available hands and, leaving only Piro and his party in camp, set out for the pass. It took us five hours to get there over a road which would have made the patient Job weep tears of grief and sorrow. Arrived at the foot of the glacier we had encountered on our way down the previous night, I marshalled the party into line with the object of working up hill and thoroughly searching the slope. Fortunately it was a fine day with another of those cloudless skies, prominent in the East when clear weather is the order of the day, so there was still a chance something might be recovered.

Judging from the mist and clouds enveloping the pass and the ravine below it the evening before, I had looked upon a fall of snow as highly probable. This would have rendered the search doubly severe, since most of the articles might have been buried, and all traces of the yak's descent obliterated. But luckily for me nothing untoward happened, and with fine weather to carry out operations I confidently expected to see again some of my missing goods and chattels.

The first thing we found after commencing the upward march in line was a copy of Napoleon's Memoirs with the cover torn off, and after this articles came to hand fairly fast, including, amongst others, a History of the Russo-Japanese War, with the maps out and scattered about over the icy slope. Shortly after our own arrival we sighted the Kirghiz reinforcements coming rapidly up the narrow ravine. They had reached the yurt soon after my departure, pushing on at once to my assistance, mounted on fresh yaks, who tackled the rocks and boulders in a way that did one good to see. These men were in charge of a most excellent Beg, or head man, and getting them into line we worked gradually up the slope. There were fourteen all told, the new arrivals, armed with ropes and ice axes, wearing a business-like air. It was impossible to do anything on the frozen slope without the aid of ropes and ice axes.

We found the yak fully 2,500 feet below the summit, wedged in between blocks of ice, with his head jammed in a tiny crevasse through which raced an icy cataract. He was naturally in a mutilated condition, pieces of skin having been torn off from contact with jagged rocks, and several teeth missing, some of which the Kirghiz actually found during the subsequent search. The tremendous distance he fell must have broken every bone in his body. Not a vestige of the two boxes attached to him remained, only the loading ropes still trailing by his side.

A Bloodthirsty Band of Brigands

ERNEST H. GRIFFIN

From *Adventures in Tripoli: A Doctor in the Desert*, 1924

September 1912: A stormy night, somewhere off the coast of Tunisia.

"As I worked the pump," wrote Ernest Griffin, ". . . lightning showed me the staring faces of the Arabs as they squatted, huddled in their blankets, round the stern of the boat, and I thought in their glance I detected an element of contempt—contempt that fear of death should so drive a man that he should continue to struggle against the plain decree of God."

Griffin was certain the *Boudelbous*, the ratty schooner taking him to Tunisia, would sink. Stripped, "ready for the final plunge," with his revolver, coat, and water bottle tied to a plank that would float when the ship went down, he desperately worked the pump. Ultimately, the *Boudelbous* did not sink, and Griffin landed safely in Sfax, French Tunisia. Before long, he had brought medical equipment and supplies to Ben Gardane, on the Tunisia-Tripoli border. Tripoli (now Libya) was then a province of the Ottoman Empire under invasion by Italy.

Griffin had traveled to Libya in 1912 to lead the British Mission, a medical relief group, behind Turkish lines. Sent by the British Red Crescent Society, founded in British India, his purpose was to offer medical services to Muslims who might be unreceptive to the Red Cross, with its Christian and European associations. At the time, Griffin knew little about the country and less than a smattering of Arabic and Turkish.

Griffin was forced to smuggle himself into Libya during the night, as sea routes were patrolled by the Italians. (The Turks had to supply their troops by smuggling via French Tunisia.) His guide navigated the desert at the border, "steering entirely by the flash of Italian searchlights that were being operated vigorously from one of their forts." His first impression of the war was the westernmost Turkish outpost at El Assa. Hospitable officers "gave proof of their broadmindedness by getting out a bottle of absinthe, strictly, of course, for the benefit of their Christian guest."

Eventually, Griffin and Dr. Martin Turnbull of the British Mission arrived at El Yefren, in the mountains. They set up a hospital where they spent most of the following year. Griffin soon found he could not be neutral; Turks and Arabs became his friends, and he was sympathetic to their cause. Living in mountain towns and desert oases, he came to admire a people whose lives lacked nothing that a little assistance from the outside world could not remedy. He was bitterly disappointed when he had to lead the pullout of the British Mission back to Tunisia, to the sound of Italian artillery pulverizing Libyan resistance.

Griffin survived the Libyan war, and then the Great War. In 1924 he published his compelling Libyan experiences in *Adventures in Tripoli: A Doctor in the Desert*.

—J. H.

I was now feeling very tired, and Mohammed, taking the hint from my loud and unchecked gaping, volunteered to do the first watch of three hours. But my luxurious repose on the soft sand was not destined to be of long duration; for no sooner had I fallen into a dreamless slumber than I was awakened by the loud report of a camel-gun, followed by the whine of rifle bullets speeding over the bivouac. In a flash we were all awake, and grasping our arms lay down behind the boxes and loads, which formed an excellent zareba.

Although the moon had not yet risen the surface of the desert showed up clearly under the soft light of the stars. At first I could see nothing; then suddenly the running figure of a man came into view. As the fusillade in front of us was growing in intensity and the bullets were coming unpleasantly close, I felt it was time for definite action, so lifting my revolver against the charging man I was just about to fire a round when Saad yelled out that the Arab was his cousin. Leaping the boxes he collapsed on the ground, and I could see at a glance that he was badly wounded; blood was running down his face from a large cut on the scalp, and his left arm hung useless at his side. Having gulped down some water he explained to Saad that he had heard we were in the vicinity, and on his way to join us had been set upon by a band of robbers who were watching the movements of our caravan.

The firing had now ceased, so far without a shot being fired by my men; but suddenly big Sambo shouted out that the enemy were approaching and discharged his blunderbuss. This acted like a lighted match in powder, and at once the camel-men poured a ragged volley into the unseen enemy. Despite the fact that I felt rather annoyed at the loss of sleep, I could not help feeling strangely exhilarated, for it is not every day that one can take part in a scene of this sort.

A cloud of thick, black, acrid smoke overhung the caravan, half concealing the figures of the Arabs as they thrust home the charge with their ramrods. Out of this cloud burst tongues of flame, as the old muzzle-loaders were fired, to the alarm of the camels, who swung their heads in panic. At my feet knelt the chief camel-owner, who chose this moment to beg me to make good his loss if one of his camels should be hit. In competition with him was the shouting of the wounded man, who complained that he was bleeding to death, while a third Arab, well sheltered behind my tin uniform case, seized the opportunity to inform me that he did not wish to continue in the service of the Mission and would be glad to receive his wages and depart!

As "star-shells" were not included in my medical stores I was forced to wait patiently for the rising of the moon before I could tell what there was in front of us. At length Saad volunteered to go out on patrol to see if he could find out anything. He returned after about half an hour, bringing with him an old camel-gun with bloodstains on the stock and a couple of loaves of Arab bread that he had found lying in the desert. It certainly did not look as if we had inflicted heavy loss on our assailants; and pleasant as it was to think that we had really been attacked by a bloodthirsty band of brigands and had beaten them off, when I reviewed the whole matter in cold blood I came to the conclusion that we had interfered in a vulgar little robbery just in time to save a man's life, and had then got a few rounds from the discomfited thieves, who perhaps hoped to drop a camel or two. Still, some of my followers held other views, and a few weeks later I heard a servant of the Mission describing to an Arab notable in Sfax how we had beaten off an attack made by a hundred well-armed Tuaregs! He forgot to add, however, that the enemy were dressed — in buckram!

At daybreak I extracted the charge of filth from the wounded man's arm, set his fracture and made him as comfortable as possible. In return he gave me rather grave news. It seemed that the Arabs guarding the coast had heard of Bahrouni's flight, and seeing no further chance of receiving provisions had determined to go home; so, hungry and desperate, they were streaming across the desert, robbing all who were not strong enough to resist them. This was serious for us, since their line of retreat to the hills crossed our road at right angles. As he informed me that Sheikh Sauf was still at Bechoul, I determined to march directly on that place, and not to Juesh as I had first intended. I comforted myself with the thought that Sheikh Sauf would know I was somewhere on the desert between Bechoul and El Yefren and would send some reliable men to meet me.

As the wounded Arab had no further use for his Gras rifle, I purchased it from him, together with a bandolier of cartridges; with these I armed Saad, after giving him some elementary instruction in the action of the piece. Since I now had fifteen well-armed men and a good supply of ammunition, I had little reason to fear the result of an encounter with any small groups of Arabs, always providing the camel-men stood firm; but I knew from bitter experience that these latter were a shifty lot of ruffians and very little reliance could be placed on them.

No sooner had we got the horses saddled and the loads adjusted than a violent altercation arose among the Arabs. Together with Mohammed, I rode up to them to find out the cause of the trouble, and soon learned that the Arabs from the plains were sure that the hillmen were concocting some nefarious scheme, as they were always together in a group and speaking Dje-belli among themselves, a language the others did not understand. I settled the matter by prohibiting the use of Djebelli and threatened to dismiss with-out backsheesh anyone heard speaking it.

At midday the camels were so tired that I was forced to agree to a halt, eager as I was to push on. We unloaded near a large patch of young corn, and the general undoing of the bonds of discipline was clearly to be seen when the Arabs allowed both horses and camels to crop freely the green shoots of what they now contemptuously called "Italian corn".

The sun was now very hot, so I had my personal luggage piled as high as possible in order to make a shelter from the fierce midday rays. I was just squatting down on a piece of carpet when Saad came up to me and pointed to an approaching patch on the desert. Getting out the field-glasses, I focused the group, and was soon able to make out the figures of perhaps sixty Arabs, some on foot, others on horseback or on camels. I shouted to the head driver to bring in the camels, who were feeding in the corn, and together with Sambo, Mohammed and Selim, commenced making a rough breastwork with the boxes.

We were in a splendid position. A good well lay within twenty yards of us, and some large boulders together with our stores gave fair protection from rifle fire. We could hold off a large force if only the camel-men remained loyal. Suddenly I heard a sort of groan burst from the head camel-man. He was looking in a dazed fashion at the newcomers; his jaw had dropped and his face was ashen-gray. Terror and amazement were depicted on his face.

I focused the approaching Arabs again and was just about to utter the ill-omened word, when Saad forestalled me: "Tuaregs!" The word probably conveys little to the ordinary traveller, but on the Sahara it stands for the very personification of lying, thieving, cheating and murdering. Sex-Bolshevism has dominated the tribe for many years, and the men appear to do exactly what the women tell them. When the stock of luxuries and food gets low in their camp the warriors are urged by their wives to go forth and loot a cara-van. Although I had seen a few of this tribe near Zavia, I thought that they had all returned to the interior, but now there was no mistaking their masked faces and the little high saddles on their fast camels.

For a while I looked at them fascinated, and then turned round to see how my Arabs enjoyed the prospect. A rough ring had been made by boxes, stones and sacks, inside which the camels were knelt. To my gratified amazement the head camel-man came up to me with Mohammed, made the usual grasp at my hand to kiss it, and informed me that everyone was prepared to fight to the end, as we could expect no mercy from these people. In return I thanked him for his loyalty and assured him that we could easily beat the enemy off, if it came to a fight. I gave instructions that no one was to fire without orders, and in any case the muzzle-loaders were to be reserved until the enemy was right on top of us.

In accordance with the custom of the country the band stopped about two hundred yards off and sent two of their number up to parley. These halted about thirty paces away and commenced a shouting match with Mohammed. Seated as I was on a piece of carpet outside the zareba, I could hear quite clearly what was being said. It appeared that the envoys wished to speak with the foreign doctor. I told Mohammed quietly to let them come up but to watch them carefully. I had my revolver in the bosom of my shirt and a rifle at my side. When the two came up I saw at once that they were ordinary Arabs, but a more villainous-looking pair of men I never before cast eyes on. They had left their rifles behind, but carried large flint-lock pistols and knives in their belts.

For a while I took no notice of them but continued reading that illuminating advertisement which is given away with every bottle of Eno's Fruit Salt, as I had no wish to appear in an undignified hurry. At length I looked up and asked them what their business was, and in answer one of them started a long harangue, of which I understood nothing and Mohammed very little, owing to the peculiarity of dialect. The other envoy now spoke and he was able to make himself understood. The upshot of his speech was that they were travelling from the coast to the interior and were all dying of hunger—was I prepared to give them something to eat? In reply I said I should be very pleased to do what I could for them, as we had been sent by pious Moslems to help them, but unfortunately it would not be very much as my stock was low.

During this discussion the other Arab had been edging nearer and nearer the ring of boxes in order to see how many rifles we had. When Mohammed under my instructions ordered him away he laughed in an insolent fashion and made some rapid remarks to his comrade. The latter now changed his conciliatory tone and in a hectoring manner told me that they wanted not only food but clothes and money. Waving his hand to the main body in a scarcely veiled threat, he said that they were many and meant to have their wishes. I had just absolutely refused to give them any money, while willing to concede food and half a dozen blankets in order to avoid bloodshed, when matters came to a crisis. The second Arab had now moved to the well, and seeing big Sambo about to draw water he went up to him and asked for a drink. Not thinking what he was doing, Sambo laid down his blunderbuss on the coping-stone and held the skin for the man to drink out of. In a trice the Arab snatched up the gun and started walking away with it, the object of the manœuvre being of course to see if we would show fight. I was unable to do anything myself, as I was completely covered by the little group standing round, but Selim jumped up, covered the man with his rifle and ordered him to halt. The Arab at once threw down the gun, laughed heartily and tried to pass the matter off as a joke. The man in front of me now burst into abuse, and the pair walked away, waving their arms to their friends. This I took to be a signal, and I was just preparing to retreat into the barricade when, quite unnoticed in the general hubbub, two new figures rode up. One was an elderly man with a long grey beard, who sat his horse with dignity and had a look of authority in his eyes. He asked me what the trouble was, and, after Mohammed had translated my reply, got off his horse and sat on the mat beside me. Before going any further I told the cook to make some tea as fast as possible, as I was anxious to secure the support of the old man by the ties of bread and salt.

The old Arab now introduced himself as the sheikh of that district, and said he was very sorry to see us in any trouble, as he had very good cause to be grateful to the Mission for the care we had given his son when the latter had been wounded. But the times were very troublesome and there were a lot of bad people about; moreover, all his men were with Sheikh Sauf and he could not offer us protection. He thought it would be better for us to give presents to the bandits rather than stand the risk of fighting, and he pointed out that it would be easy for the enemy to sit down and wear us out by sniping. In reply I told him it was only a matter of hours before Sheikh Sauf's gendarmes came to escort us, and that I utterly refused to give anything away except food, which it was my duty to distribute by the laws of the Holy Prophet. The sheikh thereupon said that the tribesmen in front of us were very cunning and unmerciful, and if we were beaten would leave no one alive. At this cheerful news I scarcely knew what to say, as the day was so warm, the atmosphere so clear, the sky so blue, that it seemed a distinct pity to leave it all. It ended in my saying to the sheikh that God was Merciful and Compassionate and what was written would come to pass. The sheikh quite agreed with this pious statement, although he was just commencing to qualify it with a phrase beginning with "but" when Saad brought up tea. At first the old man was reluctant to drink, but, encouraged by the loud *"Bismillah!"* with which I prefaced my own cup, his scruples vanished, and he not only drank the full number of glasses allowed by etiquette, but thoroughly enjoyed a box of fancy biscuits that I had saved for any important occasion. Having accepted a tin of cigarettes and the remainder of the biscuits, he called for his horse, saying he would go across and speak to the bandits. He mounted and rode off to where his fellow-countrymen were gathered.

During his absence I improved as much as possible the defences of the camp. Large stones were rolled up against the boxes as a protection against rifle fire; skins and water-pots were filled and provisions laid out. I promised the camel-owner full indemnity for any camels killed or injured and told the men that if they should be wounded in the service of the Mission they would be properly looked after until they were restored to health, and amply compensated for any injury.

Although I felt quite sure of the position, at the same time I could not help feeling rather excited, and when Mohammed brought me my dinner I found it was all I could do to masticate it; still, I made up by drinking large draughts of tea. As well as the young Arab's money-belt that I was still wearing, I had a fairly large sum in Turkish gold in my pockets, and I was now anxious to make quite sure that none of this should fall into the hands of the enemy in case our caravan should be overwhelmed. With this end in view I picked up the large bell-mouthed blunderbuss that big Sambo usually carried and retired with it to the shadow of some rocks, where one by one I loaded the coins into its huge barrel, ramming on top large paper wads. One shot and the money would have been scattered to the four winds of heaven!

The next hour passed very slowly, and I was indeed thankful when at last I saw the sheikh returning. He told me that he had spoken earnestly with the men and that they had agreed to leave us unmolested if we would supply them with a little food and attend to their wounded. The old man was inclined to be rather apologetic as to the attitude of his co-religionists, and he was greatly relieved when I told him I did not expect a very high standard of morality from soldiers who were perishing of hunger. Anyone who has seen even the best European troops retreating after a serious reverse will, I think, agree that these poor Arabs should not be too severely judged.

Taking with me a large parcel of cigarettes as a peace-offering, despite Mohammed's protests, I walked across with the sheikh to cast an eye over the wounded, little Sambo marching in the rear with a towel and a large galvanized bowl. There is always a certain amount of moral satisfaction to be gained by thrusting one's head into the lion's jaws, and I can quite understand how easy it is for a travelling showman to get a volunteer in any village to be shaved—or even married—in a cage of forest-bred tigers.

At all events, I was soon surrounded by some of the roughest and wildest looking men it is possible to imagine. But except for patting my gloves and scrutinizing my dress generally very closely they treated me with the greatest deference. Protected only by my sacred calling I walked freely amongst these men who a few minutes before had been ready to cut my throat.

Having treated the three wounded men, I made them each a present of cigarettes and then called to Sambo for a bowl of water to wash in. As I had taken the precaution to place crystals of permanganate of potash under my finger nails, the water rapidly became blood-red in colour to the gratified amazement of the onlookers. Then, as the whole band looked so miserable and hungry, I determined to do what I could for them. I bought a sheep from the sheikh to provide them with a good dinner, and added as well flour, tea and sugar. Finally, selecting three who looked the most depraved of the lot, I presented them with a copy of the Koran apiece. Having thus ministered to their spiritual and bodily needs, I was able to leave them with a clear conscience.

The sheikh now invited me into his tent to take food, and although I was most anxious to push on I felt it would be ungracious to refuse after all he had done for us. Inside his quarters there were two men clad in gendarmes' uniform who complained bitterly to me that Bahrouni had paid them no wages for over three months. The sheikh told me that, so far as he knew, they were both good men, and strongly advised me to take them with me as far as the frontier, as he felt sure we should need protection on the way. I therefore agreed to give them thirty francs each and their food to take us as far as Sheikh Sauf's camp, or, in default of this, to the French frontier. I must confess that Mohammed did not like the look of them and urged me not to take them. He proved to be right, for they turned out to be a pair of unmitigated scoundrels and a source of danger instead of a protection.

Toward the City of Emperors

JOHN REED

From *The War in Eastern Europe*, 1916

American journalist John Reed was greeted by the porter at his Istanbul hotel in August 1915. America had not yet entered WWI. As a correspondent for New York's *Metropolitan Magazine*, Reed and Canadian illustrator, Boardman Robinson, had traveled the war-wracked Balkans before arriving at the Ottoman capital.

"Excellency," the porter said in French to Reed, "the secret police have been here to enquire about your Excellency. Would your Excellency like me to tell them anything in particular?" The porter, of course, expected a bribe. Reed was in a city churning with spies and intrigue.

Istanbul, situated on the Bosporus—the narrow waterway between Europe and Asia—was the most strategically located capital city in the world, as well as the capital of the largest Islamic state in history. Nevertheless, Reed had come to a city and civilization on the brink of apocalypse. By 1918 British victories over the Ottomans forced them to surrender. Within a few years, nearly five centuries of the Ottoman Empire ended; the Islamic Sultanate was overthrown, replaced by the Republic of Turkey, a secular state with a new capital at Ankara. Britain and France stripped the empire of its Middle Eastern provinces. Constantinople became like Vienna, the former capital of the Austro-Hungarian Empire also defeated in WWI: a picturesque mausoleum of its extinguished importance.

Reed is best known for his book about the Bolshevik Revolution, *Ten Days that Shook the World*, published in 1922. This work has eclipsed his earlier books, which is a shame. *The War in Eastern Europe*, which contains his Istanbul jaunt, is at least as pertinent to today's geopolitical situation. Reed's book reminds us that the physical "frontier" between the West and the Islamic world is found in Europe and Asia. His portrait of Istanbul shows that Rudyard Kipling's maxim—"East is east and West is west"—does not always hold true.

—J. H.

The handsome great sleeping-cars bore brass inscriptions in *svelte* Turkish letters and in French, "Orient Express"—that most famous train in the world, which used to run from Paris direct to the Golden Horn in the prehistoric days before the war. A sign in Bulgarian said "Tsarigrad"—literally "City of Emperors"—also the Russian name for the eastern capital that all Slavs consider theirs by right. And a German placard proclaimed pompously, "Berlin-Constantinopel"—an arrogant prophecy in those days, when the Constantinople train went no farther west than Sofia, and the drive on Serbia had not begun.

We were an international company: Three English officers in mufti bound for Dedeagatch; a French engineer on business to Philippopolis; a Bulgar military commission going to discuss the terms of the treaty with Turkey; a Russian school-teacher returning to his home in Burgas; an American tobacco man on a buying tour around the Turkish Black Sea ports; a black eunuch in fez, his frock coat flaring over wide hips and knock knees; a Viennese music-hall dancer and her man headed for the café concerts of Pera; two Hungarian Red Crescent delegates, and assorted Germans to the number of about a hundred. There was a special car full of bullet-headed Krupp workmen for the Turkish munition factories, and two compartments reserved for an *Unterseeboot* crew going down to relieve the men of U-54—boys seventeen or eighteen years old. And in the next compartment to mine a party of seven upper-class Prussians played incessant "bridge": government officials, business men, and intellectuals on their way to Constantinople to take posts in the embassy, the Regie, the Ottoman Debt, and the Turkish universities. Each was a highly efficient cog, trained to fit exactly his place in the marvellous German machine that ground already for the Teutonic Empire of the East.

The biting irony of life in neutral countries went with us. It was curious to watch the ancient habit of cosmopolitan existence take possession of that train-load. Some ticket agent with a sense of humor had paired two English-men with a couple of German embassy attachés in the same compartment— they were scrupulously polite to each other. The Frenchman and the other Britisher gravitated naturally to the side of the fair Austrian, where they all laughed and chattered about youthful student days in Vienna. Late at night I caught one of the German diplomats out in the corridor gossiping about Moscow with the Russian teacher. All these men were active on the firing-line, so to speak, except the Russian—and he, of course, was a Slav, and without prejudices. . . .

But in the morning the English, the Frenchman, and the Russian were gone—the breathing-place between borders of hate was past—and we fled through the grim marches of the Turkish Empire.

The shallow, sluggish, yellow Maritza River, bordered by gigantic willows, twisted through an arid valley. Dry, brown hills rolled up, on whose slopes no green thing grew; flat plains baked under scanty scorched grass; straggly corn-fields lay drooping, with roofed platforms on stilts starting up here and there, where black-veiled women squatted with guns across their knees to scare away the crows. Rarely a village—miserable huts of daubed mud, thatched with dirty straw, clustering around the flat dome of a little mosque and its shabby minaret. Westward, a mile away, the ruins of a red-tiled town climbed the hillside, silent and deserted since the Bulgarians bombarded it in 1912, and shot off the tips of the two minarets. The crumbling stumps of minarets stood alone on the deso-late flats, marking the spot of some once-living village or town whose very traces had disappeared—so quickly do the ephemeral buildings of the Turks return to the dust; but the minarets stand, for it is forbidden to demolish a mosque that has once been consecrated.

Sometimes we stopped at a little station; a group of huts, a minaret, adobe barracks, and rows of mud-bricks baking in the sun. A dozen gayly painted little *arabas* slung high on their springs waited for passengers; six or seven veiled women would crowd into one, pull the curtains to shield them from the public gaze, and rattle giggling away in a cloud of golden dust. Bare-legged peasant *hanums*, robed all in dull green, shuffled single file along the road, carrying naked babies, with a coquettish lifting of veils for the windows of the train. By the platform were piled shimmering heaps of melons brought from the interior—the luscious green sugar-melon, and the yellow *kavoon*, which smells like flowers and tastes like nothing else in the world. An ancient tree beside the station spread an emerald shade over a tiny café, where the turbaned, slippered old Turks of the country sat gravely at their coffee and *narghilehs*.

Along the railway, aged bent peasants, unfit for the firing-line, stood guard—bare-footed, ragged, armed with rusty hammer-lock muskets and belted with soft-nosed bullets of an earlier vintage still. They made a pathetic effort to straighten up in military attitudes as we passed. . . . But it was at Adrianople that we saw the first regular Turkish soldiers, in their unfitting khaki uniforms, puttees, and those German-designed soft helmets that look like Arab turbans, and come down flat on the forehead, so that a Mohammedan can salaam in prayers without uncovering. A mild-faced, serious, slow-moving people they seemed.

The brisk young Prussian who got on at Adrianople was strikingly different. He wore the uniform of a Bey in the Turkish army, with the tall cap of brown astrakhan ornamented with the gold crescent, and on his breast were the ribbons of the Iron Cross, and the Turkish Order of the Hamidieh. His scarred face was set in a violent scowl, and he strode up and down the corridor, muttering *"Gottverdammte Dummheit!"* from time to time. At the first stop he descended, looked sharply around, and barked something in Turkish to the two tattered old railway guards who were scuffling along the platform.

"*Tchabouk!* Hurry!" he snapped. "Sons of pigs, hurry when I call!"

Startled, they came running at a stiff trot. He looked them up and down with a sneer; then shot a string of vicious words at them. The two old men trotted off and, wheeling, marched stiffly back, trying to achieve the goose-step and salute in Prussian fashion. Again he bawled insultingly in their faces; again, with crestfallen expression, they repeated the manœuvre. It was ludicrous and pitiable to watch. . . .

"*Gott in Himmel!*" cried the instructor to the world in general, shaking his fists in the air, "were there ever such animals? Again! Again! *Tchabouk! Run, damn you!*"

Meanwhile, the other soldiers and the peasants had withdrawn from range, and stood in clusters at a distance, mildly inspecting this amazing human phenomenon. . . . Of a sudden a little Turkish corporal detached himself from the throng, marched up to the Prussian, saluted, and spoke. The other glared, flushed to his hair, the cords stood out on his neck, and he thrust his nose against the little man's nose, and screamed at him.

"Bey *effendi*—" began the corporal. And "Bey *effendi*—" he tried again to explain. But the Bey went brighter scarlet, grew more offensive, and finally drew back in good old Prussian fashion and slapped him in the face. The Turk winced and then stood quite still, while the red print of a hand sprang out on his cheek, staring without expression straight into the other's eyes. Undefinable, scarcely heard, a faint wind of sound swept over all those watching people. . . .

All afternoon we crawled southeast through a blasted land. The low, hot air was heavy, as if with the breath of unnumbered generations of dead; a sluggish haze softened the distance. Thin corn-fields, irregular melon patches, dusty willows around a country well were all the vegetation. Occasionally there was a rustic thrashing-floor, where slow oxen drew round and round over the yellow corn a heavy sledge full of laughing, shouting youngsters. Once a caravan of shambling dromedaries, roped together, crossed our vision, rocking along with great dusty bales slung from their humps—the three small boys who were drivers skylarking about them. No living thing for miles and miles, nor any human evidences except the ruins of old cities, abandoned as the ebbing population withdrew into the city or Asia Minor beyond. . . . Yet this land has always been empty and desolate as it is to-day; even at the height of the Byzantine Empire, it was good policy to keep a barren waste between the City and the countries of the restless barbarians. . . .

Now we began to pass troop-trains. English submarines in the Sea of Marmora had paralyzed water transport to Gallipoli, and the soldiers went by railroad to Kouleli Bourgas, and then marched overland to Bulair. The freight-car doors were crowded with dark, simple faces; there came to us incessant quavering nasal singing to the syncopated accompaniment of shrill pipes and drums. One was full of savage-eyed Arabs from the desert east of Aleppo, dressed still in sweeping gray and brown burnooses, their thin, intense faces more startling for the encircling folds.

Tchataldja was feverishly active; narrow-gauge little trains loaded with guns, steel trench roofs, piles of tools, puffed off along the folds of the hills, and the naked brown slopes swarmed with a multitude of tiny figures working on trenches against the eventuality of Bulgarian invasion. . . .

The sun set behind, warming for an instant with a wash of gold the desolate leagues on leagues of waste. Night came suddenly, a moonless night of overwhelming stars. We moved slower and slower, waiting interminably on switches while the whining, singing troop-trains flashed by. . . . Toward midnight I fell asleep, and woke hours later to find one of the Germans shaking me.

"Constantinople," said he.

I could make out the dim shape of a gigantic wall rushing up as we roared through a jagged breach in it. On the right crumbling half-battlements—the Byzantine sea-wall—fell suddenly away, and showed the sea lapping with tiny waves at the railway embankment; the other side was a rank of tall, unpainted wooden houses leaning crazily against each other, over mouths of gloom which were narrow streets, and piling back up the rising hill of the city in chaotic masses of jumbled roofs. Over these suddenly sprang out against the stars the mighty dome of an imperial mosque, minarets that soared immeasurably into the sky like great lances, broken masses of trees on Seraglio Point, with a glimpse of the steep black wall that had buttressed the Acropolis of the Greeks upon its mountain, the vague forms of kiosks, spiked chimneys of the imperial kitchens in a row, and the wide, flat roof of the Old Seraglio palace—Istamboul, the prize of the world.

At four hours precisely, Turkish time (or three minutes past nine *à la fraqnue*), on the morning of *chiharshenbi, yigirmi utch* of the month of *Temoos*, year of the Hegira *bin utch yuze otouz utch*, I woke to an immense lazy roar, woven of incredibly varied noises—the indistinct shuffling of a million slippers, shouts, bellows, high, raucous peddler voices, the nasal wail of a *muezzin* strangely calling to prayer at this unusual hour, dogs howling, a donkey braying, and, I suppose, a thousand schools in mosque courtyards droning the Koran. From my balcony I looked down on the roofs of tall Greek apartments which clung timorously to the steep skirts of Pera and broke into a dark foam of myriad Turkish houses that rushed across the valley of Kassim Pasha, swirling around the clean white mosque and two minarets, and the wave of close trees they sprang from. The little houses were all wood—rarely with a roof of old red tiles—unpainted, weathered to a dull violet, clustered where the builder's caprice had set them, threaded with a maze of wriggling streets, and spotted with little windows that caught the sun—golden. Beyond the valley they crowded up the hillside, jumbled at every conceivable angle, like a pile of children's blocks—and all of the windows ablaze. Piale Pasha Mosque started up northward, dazzling, its minaret leaping from the very dome—built to look like the mast of a ship by the great Kaptan Pasha, who broke the sea power of Venice in the sixteenth century. Down this valley Mohammed the Conqueror dragged his ships after hauling them over the high ridge where Pera stands, and launched them in the Golden Horn. Shabby Greek San Dimitri to the right; a dark pageant of cypresses along the crest over Kassim Pasha, that bounds the barren field of the *Ok-Meidan*, whose white stones mark the record shots of great Sultans who were masters of the bow and arrow; the heights of Haskeui, sombre with spacious wooden houses weathered black, where the great Armenian money princes lived in the dangerous days, and where now the Jews spawn in indescribable filth; northward again, over the mighty shoulder of a bald hill, the treeless, thick-clustered field of the Hebrew cemetery, as terrible as a razed city.

Bounding all to the west, the Golden Horn curved, narrowing east, around to north, a sheet of molten brass on which were etched black the Sultan's yacht and the yacht of the Khedive of Egypt—with the blue sphinxes painted on her stern—and the steamer *General*, sleeping quarters of German officers; dismantled second-rate cruisers, the pride of the Turkish navy, long gathering barnacles in the Golden Horn; the little cruiser *Hamedieh*, swarming with tiny dots, which were German sailors in fezzes; and countless swarms of darting *caïks*, like water-beetles.

Up from that bath of gold swept Stamboul from her clustering tangle of shanties on piles, rising in a pattern of huddling little roofs too intricate for any eye to follow, to the jagged crest lifting like music along her seven hills, where the great domes of the imperial mosques soared against the sky and flung aloft their spear-like minarets.

I could see the Stamboul end of the Inner Bridge and a little corner of the Port of Commerce, with the tangled jam of ships which were caught there when the war broke out. Above the bridge lay Phanar, where the Patriarch, who still signs himself "Bishop of New Rome," has his palace, for centuries the powerful fountain of life and death for all the millions of *"Roum-mileti"*; Phanar, refuge of imperial Byzantine families after the fall of the city, home of those merchant princes who astounded Renaissance Europe with their wealth and bad taste; Phanar, for five hundred years centre of the Greek race under the Turk. Farther along Balata—the Palatium of the Romans—and Aïvan Serai about it, shadowed in the immense sprawling ruins of Byzantine palaces, where the walls of Manuel Commenus stagger up from the water and are lost in the city. Beyond, Eyoub, the sacred village of tombs around that dazzling mosque which no Christian may enter, and the interminable mass of cypresses of that holiest of all cemeteries, climbing the steep hill behind. Greek and Roman walls; the spikes of four hundred minarets; mosques that were built with a king's treasure in a burst of vanity by the old magnificent Sultans, others that were Christian churches under the Empress Irene, whose walls are porphyry and alabaster, and whose mosaics, white-washed over, blaze through in gold and purple splendor; fragments of arches and columns of semiprecious stones, where once the golden statues of emperors stood—and marching splendidly across the sky-line of the city the double-arches of the tree-crowned aqueduct.

* * *

The hotel porter was a clever Italian with a nose for tips. He bent over me deferentially as I breakfasted, rubbing his hands.

"Excellency," he said in French, "the secret police have been here to inquire about your Excellency. Would your Excellency like me to tell them any particular thing . . . ?"

Daoud Bey was waiting for me, and together we went out into Tramway Street, where the electric cars clang past, newsboys shout the late editions of the newspapers, written in French—and apartment-houses, curiosity-shops, cafés, banks, and embassies look like a shabby quarter in an Italian city. Here every one, men and women, wore European clothes, just a trifle off in fashion, fit, and cloth—like "store clothes" bought on Third Avenue. It was a crowd of no nations and of all bloods, clever, facile, unscrupulous, shallow—Levantine. At the gates of the few open embassies sat the conventional Montenegrin doorkeepers, in savage panoply of wide trousers and little jackets, and enormous sashes stuck full of pistols; *kavases* of consulates and legations slouched around the doors of diplomats, in uniforms covered with gold lace, fezzes with arms blazing on them, and swords. An occasional smart carriage went by, with driver and footmen wearing the barbaric livery of the diplomatic service. Yet turn into any street off the Grand Rue or the Rue des Tramways, and the tall overhanging buildings echoed with appeals of half-naked ladies leaning callously from windows all the way up to the fourth floor. In those narrow, twisting alleys the fakers and the thieves and the vicious and unfit of the Christian Orient crowded and shouted and passed; filth was underfoot, pots of ambiguous liquids rained carelessly down, and the smells were varied and interesting. Miles and miles of such streets, whole quarters given over to a kind of weak debauch; and fronting the cultivated gentlemen and delicate ladies of the European colony only the bold front of the shell of hotels and clubs and embassies.

It was the day after Warsaw fell into German hands. Yesterday the German places had hoisted the German and Turkish flags to celebrate the event.

As we walked down the steep street, that with the mercilessness of modern civilization cuts an ancient Turkish cemetery in half so the street-cars may pass, Daoud Bey related interesting details of what followed.

"The Turkish police went around," said he with some gusto, "and ordered the German flags pulled down. We had the devil of a row, for the German embassy made a strong complaint."

"Why did you do that? Aren't you allies?"

He looked at me sideways and smiled mockingly. "No one is more fond than I of our Teutonic brothers (for you know the Germans let our people think they are Mohammedans). According to the German idea, perhaps the taking of Warsaw was also a Turkish victory. But we are getting touchy about the spread of German flags in the city."

I noticed that many shops and hotels had signs newly painted in French, but that on most of them the European languages had been eliminated.

"You will be amused by that," said Daoud Bey. "You see, when the war broke out, the government issued an order that no one in Turkey should use the language of a hostile nation. The French newspapers were suppressed, the French and English signs ordered removed; people were forbidden to speak French, English, or Russian; and letters written in the three languages were simply burned. But they soon found out that the greater part of the population on this side of the Golden Horn speak only French, and no Turkish at all; so they had to let up. As for letters, that was simple. The American consul protested; so just a week ago the papers printed a solemn order of the government that, although French, English, and Russian were still barred, you might write letters in American!"

Daoud Bey was a Turk of wealthy, prominent family—which is extraordinary in Turkey, where families rise and fall in one generation, and there is no family tradition because there is no family name. Daoud, son of Hamid, was all we knew him by; just as I, to the Turkish police, was knows as John, son of Charles. In that splendid idle way Turks have, Daoud had been made an admiral in the navy at the age of nineteen. Some years later a British naval commission, by invitation, reorganized the Turkish fleet. Now, it is difficult to pry wealthy young Turks loose from their jobs. The commission therefore asked Daoud Bey very politely if he would like to continue being an admiral. He answered: "I should like to very much, provided I never have to set foot on a ship. I can't bear the sea." So he is no longer in the navy.

I asked him why he was not bleeding and dying with his compatriots in the trenches at Gallipoli.

"Of course," he said, "you Westerners cannot be expected to understand. Here you buy out of military service by paying forty liras. If you don't buy out it amounts to the admission that you haven't forty liras—which is very humiliating. No Turk of any prominence could afford to be seen in the army, unless, of course, he entered the upper official grades as a career. Why, my dear fellow, if I were to serve in this war the disgrace would kill my father. It is quite different from your country. Here the recruiting sergeants beg you to pay your exemption fee—and they jeer at you if you haven't got it!"

At the foot of the hill there is a tangle of meeting streets—Step Street, that used to be the only way to clamber up to Pera; the wriggling narrow alleys that squirm through a Greek quarter of tall, dirty houses to infamous Five-Piastre and Ten-Piastre Streets in the vicious sailor town of Galata; the one street that leads to the cable tunnel, where the cars climb underground to the top of the hill—all opening into the square of Kara-keuy before the *Valideh Sultan Keuprisi*, the far-famed Outer Bridge that leads to Stamboul. White-frocked toll-collectors stood there in rippling rank, closing and parting before the throng, to the rattling chink of ten-para pieces falling into their outstretched hands. And flowing between them like an unending torrent between swaying piles, poured that bubbling ferment of all races and all religions—from Pera to Stamboul, and from Stamboul to Pera. Floating silk Arab head-dresses, helmets, turbans of yellow and red, smart fezzes, fezzes with green turbans around them to mark the relative of the Prophet, fezzes with white turbans around them—priests and teachers—Persian *tarbouches*, French hats, panamas. Veiled women in whose faces no man looked, hurrying along in little groups, robed in *tcharchafs* of black and gray and light brown, wearing extravagantly high-heeled French slippers too big for their feet, and followed by an old black female slave; Arabs from the Syrian desert in floating white cloaks; a saint from the country, bearded to the eyes, with squares of flesh showing through his colored rags, striding along, muttering prayers, with turban all agog, while a little crowd of disciples pressed after to kiss his hand and whine a blessing; bare-legged Armenian porters staggering at a smooth trot, bent under great packing-cases and shouting *"Destour!"* to clear the way; four soldiers on foot with new rifles; helmeted police on horseback; shambling eunuchs in frock coats; a Bulgarian bishop; three Albanians in blue broadcloth trousers and jackets embroidered with silver; two Catholic Sisters of Charity walking at the head of their little donkey-cart, presented to them by the Mohammedan merchants of the Great Bazaar; a *mevlevi*, or dancing dervish, in tall conical felt hat and gray robes; a bunch of German tourists in Tyrolean hats, equipped with open Baedekers, and led by a plausible Armenian guide; and representatives of five hundred fragments of strange races, left behind by the great invasions of antiquity in the holes and corners of Asia Minor. Pera is European—Greek, Armenian, Italian—anything but Turkish. Where goes this exotic crowd that pours into Pera? You never see them there.

A thousand venders of the most extraordinary merchandise—Angora honey, *helva*, *loukoum* of roses, *kaymak* (made from the milk of buffaloes shut in a dark stable), obscene postal cards, cigarette-holders of German glass, Adrianople melons, safety-pins, carpets manufactured in Newark, New Jersey, celluloid beads—moved among the crowd shouting their wares, bellowing, whining, screaming: "Only a cent, two cents—*On paras, bech paraya.*"

To the right lay the Port of Commerce, crowded with ships, and the Inner Bridge beyond, all up the splendid sweep of Golden Horn. Outside the bridge was a row of pontoons placed there to guard the port from English submarines, and against the barrier the *chirket hariés*—Bosphorus steamboats—backing precipitously out with screaming whistles into the thick flock of *caïks* that scatter like a shoal of fish. Beyond, across the bright-blue dancing water, the coast of Asia rising faintly into mountains, with Scutari dotted white along the shore. Stamboul, plunging from that magnificent point, crowned with palaces and trees, into the sea. . . . From left to right the prodigious sweep of the city, and the great mosques: Agia Sophia, built by the Emperor Justinian a thousand years ago, all clumsy great buttresses of faded red and yellow; the Mosque of Sultan Selim, who conquered Mecca; the Mosque of Sultan Achmet; Yeni Valideh Djami, at the end of the bridge; Sultan Suleyman the Magnificent—he who was a friend of François Premier; Sultan Bayazid. . . .

The floating drawbridge swung slowly open with much confused shouting and the tugging of cables by sputtering launches to allow the passage of a German submarine coming up from the Dardanelles. She was awash, her conning-tower painted a vivid blue with white streaks—the color most disguising in these bright seas; but a momentary cloud passed over the sun, and she stood out startling against the suddenly gray water.

"It takes them about an hour to close the bridge," said Daoud Bey, and drew me into an alley between stone buildings, where little tables and stools hugged the shade of the wall, and a shabby old Turk in flapping slippers and a spotted fez served ices. Outside all roar and clamor, and hot sun beating on the pavement—here cool, quiet peace.

"Daoud Pasha!" said a laughing voice. It was a slender girl in a faded green *feridjé*, with bare brown feet, and a shawl pinned under her chin, in the manner of the very poor, who cannot afford a veil. She could not have been more than fifteen; her skin was golden, and her black eyes flashed mischievously.

"Eli!" cried Daoud, seizing her hand.

"Give me some money!" said Eli imperiously.

"I have no small money."

"All right, then, give me big money."

Daoud laughed and handed her a *medjidieh*—and she gave a scream of pleasure, clapped her hands, and was gone.

"Gypsy," said Daoud, "and the most beautiful girl in all Constantinople. Hamdi, a friend of mine, fell in love with her, and asked her into his harem. So she went to live at Eyoub. But two weeks later I came down here one day, and as I was taking my sherbet I heard a little voice at my elbow: 'Daoud Pasha, some money please.' It was Eli. She said she had tried to be a respectable married lady for fourteen days, because she really loved Hamdi. He was very kind to her—gave her clothes and jewels, and courted her like a lover. But she couldn't stand it any longer; begging on the streets was more fun—she loved the crowd so. So one night she let herself out of the harem door and swam across the Golden Horn!" He laughed and shrugged his shoulders: "You can't tame a *chingani*."

We paid. "May God favor you!" the proprietor said gently, and a Turk sitting at our table bowed and mumbled: "*Afiet-olsoun!* May what you have eaten do you good!"

Outside on the wharf where the *caïks* were ranked, each boatman yelling as loud as he could, a blind old woman in rusty black crouched against the wall and held out her hand. Daoud dropped a copper in it. She raised her sightless eyes to us and said in a sweet voice: "Depart smiling."

"*Kach parava?* How much?" said Daoud. A deafening clamor of voices shouted indistinguishable things.

"Let us take the old man," said my friend, pointing to a figure with a long white beard, burnt-orange skull-cap, red sash, and pink shirt open at the throat to show his hairy old chest. "How much, *effendim?*" He used the term of respect which all Turks use toward each other, no matter what the difference in their ranks.

"Five piastres," said the old man hopefully.

"I pay one piastres and a half," answered Daoud, climbing into the *caïk*. Without reply the *caïkji* pushed off.

"What is your name, my father?" asked Daoud. "My name is Abdul, my son," said the old man, rowing and sweating in the sun. "I am born of Mohammed the Short-legged in the city of Trebizond on the sea. For fifty-two years I have been rowing my *caïk* across the Stamboul Limani."

I told Daoud to ask him what he thought of the war.

"It is a good war," said Abdul. "All wars against the *giaour* are good, for does not the Koran say that he who dies slaying the infidel will enter paradise?"

"You are learned in the Koran?" exclaimed Daoud. "Perhaps, you are a *sheikh* and lead prayers in the mosque."

"Do I wear the white turban?" said the old man. "I am no priest; but in my youth I was a *muezzin*, and called to prayers from the minaret."

"What should he know of the war?" I said. "It doesn't touch him personally."

Daoud translated.

"I have four sons and two grandsons in the war," said Abdul, with dignity. Then to me: "Are you an *Aleman*—a German—one of our brothers who do not know our language and do not wear the fez? Tell me, of what shape and build are your mosques? Is your Sultan as great as our Sultan?"

I replied evasively that he was very great.

"We shall win this war, *inshallah*—God willing," said Abdul.

"*Mashallah!*" responded Daoud gravely, and I saw that his light European cynicism was a thin veneer over eight centuries of deep religious belief.

Lawrence the Train-Wrecker

LOWELL THOMAS

From *With Lawrence in Arabia*, 1924 (reprinted with permission)

American journalist Lowell Thomas was the man who made T. E. Lawrence an international celebrity in the 1920s. Hundreds of thousands saw Thomas's photograph-illustrated lectures in London after WWI. Thomas celebrated Lawrence as the leader of an Arab revolt against the Ottoman Empire, and as "the uncrowned prince of Arabia"—the liberator of Arab nations. Despite controversy and debate, Lawrence still retains that mantle today.

Thomas's brand of entertainment journalism and storytelling was a sensation. People were starved for heroes during the Great War. Thomas's version of Lawrence proclaimed that in the Middle East magnificent and hopeful things had been accomplished. Nothing could have contrasted more with the grinding, stalemated war of the Western Front than Thomas's thrilling stories of Bedouin riders and desert warfare.

Nonetheless, Lawrence shied away from his celebrity status. The final version of his book, *Seven Pillars of Wisdom*, did not appear until 1935, the year he died. Thomas had ignited Lawrence-mania fifteen years before that, publishing *With Lawrence in Arabia* in 1924. His vagueness about how much time he spent with Lawrence (and how much information he actually gleaned from other witnesses and official reports) led to some controversy about his account. Lawrence and Thomas both promoted romantic notions of war in the desert, spinning tales of how a few heroic Westerners had led Arabs to free the Middle East from the Ottomans. Neither author was inclined to discuss the overwhelmingly decisive British military victories that were achieved with the use of large, conventional armies.

Recent debate on U.S. policy in the Middle East in the twenty-first century regularly includes mention of T. E. Lawrence. Former Deputy Secretary of Defense Paul Wolfowitz was even dubbed "Wolfowitz of Arabia"—not as a compliment—by today's media. To what extent the architects of American strategies in Iraq believed their own miscalculations and myths of how little force would be necessary to "liberate" Iraq and Afghanistan remains a matter of debate—as does the entire legacy of T. E. Lawrence.

—J. H.

F ate never played a stranger prank than when she transformed this shy young Oxford graduate from a studious archæologist into the leader of a hundred thrilling raids, creator of kings, commander of an army, and world's champion train-wrecker.

One day Lawrence's column was trekking along the Wadi Ithm. Behind him rode a thousand Bedouins mounted on the fleetest racing-camels ever brought down the Negb. The Bedouins were improvising strange war-songs describing the deeds of the blond shereef whom General Storrs had introduced to me as "the uncrowned king of Arabia." Lawrence headed the column. He paid no attention to the song lauding him as a modern Abu Bekr. We were discussing the possibility of ancient Hittite civilization forming the connecting link between the civilizations of Babylon and Nineveh and ancient Crete. But his mind was on other things and suddenly he broke off to remark:

"Do you know, one of the most glorious sights I have ever seen is a trainload of Turkish soldiers ascending skyward after the explosion of a tulip!"

Three days later the column started off at night in the direction of the Pilgrim Railway. In support of Lawrence were two hundred Howeitat. After two days' hard riding across a country more barren than the mountains of the moon, and through valleys reminiscent of Death Valley, California, the raiding column reached a ridge of hills near the important Turkish railway-center and garrisoned town of Maan. At a signal from Lawrence all dismounted, left the camels, walked up to the summit of the nearest hill, and from between sandstone cliffs looked down across the railway track.

This was the same railway that had been built some years before to enable the Turkish Government to keep a closer hand on Arabia through transport of troops. It also simplified the problem of transportation for pilgrims to Medina and Mecca. Medina was garrisoned by an army of over twenty thousand Turks and was strongly fortified. Lawrence and his Arabs could have severed this line completely at any time, but they chose a shrewder policy. Train-load after train-load of supplies and ammunition must be sent down to Medina over that railway. So whenever Lawrence and his followers ran out of food or ammunition they had a quaint little habit of slipping over, blowing up a train or two, looting it, and disappearing into the blue with everything that had been so thoughtfully sent down from Constantinople.

As a result of the experience he gained on these raids, Lawrence's knowledge of the handling of high explosives was as extensive as his knowledge of archæology, and he took great pride in his unique ability as a devastator of railways. The Bedouins, on the other hand, were entirely ignorant of the use of dynamite; so Lawrence nearly always planted all of his own mines and took the Bedouins along merely for company and to help carry off the loot.

He had blown up so many trains that he was as familiar with the Turkish system of transportation and patrols as were the Turks themselves. In fact he had dynamited Turkish trains passing along the Hedjaz Railway with such regularity that in Damascus seats in the rear carriage sold for five and six times their normal value. Invariably there was a wild scramble for seats at the rear of a train; because Lawrence nearly always touched off his tulips, as he playfully called his mines, under the engine, with the result that the only carriages damaged were those in front.

There were two important reasons why Lawrence preferred not to instruct the Arabs in the use of high explosives. First of all, he was afraid that the Bedouins would keep on playfully blowing up trains even after the termination of the war. They looked upon it merely as an ideal form of sport,

one that was both amusing and lucrative. Secondly, it was extremely dangerous to leave footmarks along the railway line, and he preferred not to delegate tulip planting to men who might be careless.

The column crouched behind great chunks of sandstone for eight hours
until a number of patrols had passed by. Lawrence satisfied himself that they
were going at intervals of two hours. At midday, while the Turks were having
their siesta, Lawrence slipped down to the railway line, and, walking a short
distance on the sleepers in his bare feet in order not to leave impressions on
the ground which might be seen by the Turks, he picked out what he considered a proper spot for planting a charge. Whenever he merely wanted to
derail the engine of a train he would use only a pound of blasting gelatin;
when he wanted to blow it up he would use from forty to fifty pounds. On
this occasion, in order that no one might be disappointed, he used slightly
more than fifty pounds. It took him a little more than an hour to dig a hole
between the sleepers, bury the explosive, and run a fine wire underneath the
rail, over the embankment, and up the hillside.

Laying a mine is rather a long and tedious task. Lawrence first took off a
top layer of railway ballast, which he placed in a bag that he carried under his
cloak for that purpose. He next took out enough earth and rock to fill two five-
gallon petrol tins. This he carried off to a distance of some fifty yards from the
track and scattered along so that it would not be noticed by the Turkish patrols. After filling the cavity with his fifty-pound tulip-seed of dynamite, he put
the surface layer of ballast back in place and leveled it off with his hand. As a
last precaution he took a camel's-hair brush, swept the ground smooth, and
then, in order not to leave a footprint, walked backward down the bank for
twenty yards and with the brush carefully removed all trace of his tracks. He
buried the wire for a distance of two hundreds yards up the side of the hill and
then calmly sat down under a bush, right out in the open, and waited as non-
chalantly as though tending a flock of sheep. When the first train came along
the guards stationed on top of the cars and in front of the engine, with their rifles loaded, saw nothing more extraordinary than a lone Bedouin sitting on the
hillside with a shepherd's staff in his hand. Lawrence allowed the front wheels

of the engine to pass over the mine, and then, as his column lay there half paralyzed behind the boulders, he sent the current into the gelatin. It exploded with a roar like the falling of a six-story building. An enormous black cloud of smoke and dust went up. With a clanking and clattering of iron the engine rose from the track. It broke squarely in two. The boiler exploded, and chunks of iron and steel showered the country for a radius of three hundred yards. Numerous bits of boiler-plate missed Lawrence by inches.

Instead of provisions, this train carried some four hundred Turkish soldiers on their way to the relief of Medina. They swarmed out of the coaches and started in a menacing manner toward Lawrence. All this time the Bedouins, lining the tops of the hills, were popping at the Turks. Evidently one Turkish officer suspected that the lone Arab was the mysterious Englishman for whom rewards up to fifty thousand pounds had been offered. He shouted something, and the men, instead of shooting, ran toward Lawrence with the evident intention of taking him prisoner; but before they had advanced six paces Lawrence whipped out his long-barreled Colt from the folds of his aba and used it so effectively that they turned and fled. He always carried a heavy American frontier-model weapon. Although very few persons ever actually saw him, it was well known among the British officers that he spent many hours at target-practice, with the result that he had made himself an expert shot.

Many of the Turks dodged behind the embankment and began shooting through the carriage-wheels; but Lawrence, in anticipation of this, had posted two Lewis machine-guns just around a curve in the track, where they covered the opposite side of the railway embankment behind which the Turks had taken refuge. The gun-crews opened fire, and before the Turks knew what had happened their line was raked from end to end and every man behind the embankment either killed or wounded. The rest of the Turks who had remained on the train fled panic-stricken in all directions.

The Arabs, who were crouching behind the rocks popping away with their rifles, charged down, tore open the carriages, and tossed out everything on board that was not nailed down. The loot consisted of sacks of Turkish silver coin and paper currency and many beautiful draperies which the Turks had taken from the private houses of wealthy Arabs in Medina. The Bedouins piled all the loot along the embankment, and with shouts of glee commenced dividing it among themselves, while Lawrence signed the duplicate way-bills and playfully returned one copy to a wounded Turkish guard whom he intended to leave behind. They were just like children around a Christmas tree. Occasionally two men would want the same silk Kermani rug and begin fighting over it. When that happened Lawrence would step between them and turn the rug over to some third man.

Early in September, accompanied by two sheiks of the Ageilat Beni Atiyah from Mudowarrah, Lawrence left Akaba and trekked up to the multicolored sandstone cliff country which the tribesmen called Rum. In less than a week he had been joined by a force of 116 Toweiha, Zuwida, Darausha, Dhumaniyah, Togatga, Zelebani, and Howeitat.

The appointed rendezvous was a small railway bridge near Kilo 587 south of Damascus. Here Lawrence buried his usual bit of tulip-seed between the rails, and stationed Stokes and Lewis guns at vantage-points three hundred yards or so distant. The following afternoon a Turk patrol spotted them. An hour later a party of forty mounted Turks put out from the fort at Haret Ammar to attack the mine-laying party from the south. Another party of over a hundred set forth to outflank Lawrence from the north, but he decided to take a chance and hold his ground. A little later a train with two engines and two box-cars moved slowly up from Haret Ammar, machine-guns and rifles spitting lead from the roofs and from loopholes in the cars as the train advanced. As it passed, Lawrence touched his electric switch and exploded a mine directly under the second engine. The jar was sufficient to derail the first, demolish the boiler, as well as smash the cab and tender of the second, up-end the first box-car, and derail the second. While the Arabs swarmed around looting the wrecked train, Lawrence fired a box of guncotton under the front engine, completing its destruction. The boxcars were full of valuable baggage, and the Arabs went wild with joy. In all, seventy Turks were killed, ninety taken prisoner, and an Austrian lieutenant and thirteen Austrian and German sergeants blown up.

Every fourth or fifth man of the famous fighting Howeitat tribe is a sheik. Naturally the head sheik has but little power. Frequently these men would accompany Lawrence on a raid. On one such expedition to the railway near Biresh-Shediyah he had to adjudicate for them in twelve cases of assault with weapons, four camel-thefts, one marriage settlement, fourteen feuds, a bewitchment, and two cases of evil eye. He settled the bewitchment affair by counter-bewitching the hapless defendant. The evil eye cases he cleverly adjusted by sending the culprits away.

On still another occasion, during the first week of the following October, Lawrence was sitting out in the open near Kilo 500. His Bedouin followers were concealed behind him in the broom-brush. Along came a heavy train with twelve coaches. The explosion following the turning on of the electric current shattered the fire-box of the locomotive, burst many of the tubes, hurled the cylinders into the air, completely cleaned out the cab, including the engineer and fireman, warped the frame of the engine, bent the two rear driving-wheels, and broke their axles. When Lawrence put in his official report on this raid he humorously added a postscript to the effect that the locomotive was "beyond repair." The tender and first coach were also demolished. Mazmi Bey, a general of the Turkish General Staff who happened to be on board, fired two shots out of the window of his private car with his Mauser pistol, which then evidently jammed. Although it appeared advisable for him to take to the camels and the distant hills, Lawrence and his band swooped down on the train, captured eight coaches, killed twenty Turks, and carried off seventy tons of food-stuffs without suffering any losses.

His only European companion on some of his wildest train-blowing parties was a daring Australian machine-gunner, Sergeant Yells by name. He was a glutton for excitement and a tiger in a fight. On one occasion, when out with a raiding-party of Abu Tayi, Yells accounted for between thirty and forty Turks with his Lewis gun. When the loot was divided among the Bedouins, Yells, in true Australian fashion, insisted on having his share. So Lawrence handed him a Persian carpet and a fancy Turkish cavalry sword.

Shereefs Ali and Abdullah also played an important part in the raids on the Hedjaz Railway and in the capture of great convoys of Turkish camels near Medina. In 1917 Lawrence and his associates, in coöperation with Feisal, Ali, Abdullah, and Zeid, blew up twenty-five Turkish trains, tore up fifteen thousand rails, and destroyed fifty-seven bridges and culverts. During the eighteen months that he led the Arabs, they dynamited seventy-nine trains and bridges! It is a remarkable fact that he participated in only one such expedition that turned out unsatisfactorily. General Allenby, in one of his reports, said that Colonel Lawrence had made train-wrecking the national sport of Arabia!

Later in the campaign, near Deraa, the most important railway-junction south of Damascus, Lawrence touched off one of his tulips under the driving-wheels of a particularly long and heavily armed train. It turned out that Djemal Pasha, the commander-in-chief of the Turkish armies, was on board with nearly a thousand troops. Djemal hopped out of his saloon and, followed by all his staff, jumped into a ditch.

Lawrence had less than sixty Bedouins with him, but all were members of his personal body-guard and famous fighters. In spite of the overwhelming odds, the young Englishman and his Arabs fought a pitched battle in which 125 Turks were killed and Lawrence lost a third of his own force. The remainder of the Turks finally rallied around their commander-in-chief, and Lawrence and his Arabs had to show their heels.

At every station along the Hedjaz-Pilgrim Railway were one or two bells which the Turkish officials rang as a warning to passengers when the train was ready to start. Nearly all of them now decorate the homes of Lawrence's friends. Along with them are a dozen or more Turkish mile-posts and the number-plates from half the engines which formerly hauled trains over the line from Damascus to Medina. Lawrence and his associates collected these in order to confirm their victories. While in Arabia, I often heard the half-jocular, half-serious remark that Lawrence would capture a Turkish post merely for the sake of adding another bell to his collection; and it was no uncommon thing to see Lawrence, or one of his officers, walking stealthily along the railway embankment, between patrols, searching for the iron post marking Kilo 1000 south of Damascus. Once found, they would cut it off with a tulip-bud—a stick of dynamite. When not engaged in a major movement against the Turks or in mobilizing the Bedouins, Lawrence usually spent his time blowing up trains and demolishing track.

So famous did this young archæologist become throughout the Near East as a dynamiter of bridges and trains that after the final defeat of the Turkish armies, when word reached Cairo that Lawrence would soon be passing through Egypt en route to Paris, General Watson, G.O.C. of troops, jocularly announced that he was going to detail a special detachment to guard Kasr el Nil, the Brooklyn Bridge of Egypt, which crosses the Nile from Cairo to the residential suburb of Gazireh.

It had been rumored that Lawrence was dissatisfied at having finished up the campaign with the odd number of seventy-nine mine-laying parties to his credit. So the story spread up and down along the route of the Milk and Honey Railway between Egypt and Palestine that he proposed to make it an even eighty and wind up his career as a dynamiter in an appropriate manner by planting a few farewell tulips under the Kasr el Nil, just outside the door of the British military headquarters.

The Defense of Kotur-Dagh

RAFAEL DE NOGALES

From *Memoirs of a Soldier of Fortune,* 1932

Armenia: 1915. Dogs and crows skirmished over the corpses of Turks and Armenians in the streets of Yerevan. From a hilltop fortification, General Rafael de Nogales panned the city, the burning, siege-shattered capital of Armenia, and thought it "Dante-esque."

Rafael de Nogales was part soldier-adventurer and inevitably, part Baron von Munchausen. The core of his *Memoirs of a Soldier of Fortune* is true, though embellished. By his own account, he was an idealistic young Venezuelan army officer, exiled after a failed coup. He had an extraordinary career, first as a mercenary in China; then, as a gold seeker in Alaska, the Klondike, and Nevada; and as a bon vivant, always. After near bankruptcy in 1915, he went to Europe and attempted to join the Belgian army, but through German connections in Bulgaria, found it easier to enlist with the Ottomans.

At this time, Turkey was an ally of Germany and Austria, and Russia was allied with France and Britain. Armenian nationalists had rebelled against the Ottoman Empire, and Russian forces were pushing south to assist the rebels. The Turkish army sent de Nogales to lead Turkish troops into Yerevan in 1915, to stop Russia from linking up with the Armenians. Although de Nogales failed in this mission, he never suggested it was something to regret. De Nogales expressed horror at the Turkish persecutions of Armenians, which he clearly believed went beyond military necessity and were atrocities on a massive scale. The Russian advance offered some hope of protection for the Armenians.

The battle for Yerevan—or Van, as it was better known—appalled de Nogales, a veteran of jungle warfare and other sieges in his native Venezuela. According to de Nogales, he watched the inferno from a terrace with the

Turkish commander. He realized that the commander had sighted artillery on the American Mission, which he meant to destroy. De Nogales broached the matter diplomatically by suggesting to the Turk that he did not want to break international law by killing neutrals. For that, de Nogales wrote, the Turk decided to assassinate him. For the next three years, as long as he served in the Turkish army, a "sword of Damocles" hung over his head.

Absurdly effusive about his own bravery and soldierly skill, de Nogales was nevertheless a humane man, at least in his own retrospectives. He was heartbroken by the suffering of the Armenians and the horrendous spectacle of Ottoman collapse.

"Who remembers the extermination of the Armenians?" Hitler said famously in 1939. Details of the persecution, massacres, and mass deportations of Armenians in 1915 remain controversial. Only willful ignorance could prevent anyone from believing widespread, deliberate killing took place. Hundreds of thousands of Armenian civilians died as a result of famine, disease, forced marches, and outright killing. De Nogales was sickened by the indifference of his fellow officers to the killings, and was glad to leave the eastern frontiers for Syria, and finally, the Sinai.

Passages from his *Memoirs* describe warfare on the fringes of the Islamic world, where Moslem Central Asia meets the frontiers of Europe, in the area known as the Caucasus. The region of de Nogales's escapades, which now holds the independent countries of Georgia, Armenia, Azerbaijan, northern Iraq, Iran, and eastern Turkey, is at best still foggy geography to most Westerners.

This region still festers with ethnic and religious violence. When U.S. president George Bush visited Georgia in 2005, a grenade (which failed to explode) was thrown at him. Kurdish nationalist guerrillas and the Turkish army clashed. Russia carried out brutal reprisals against those it branded as Muslim "terrorists" in the adjoining regions. Today's violence and instability is rooted in the turmoil and genocide de Nogales witnessed so many decades ago.

—J. H.

After leaving Governor Djevded Bey in charge of the siege of the ill-fated city of Van, I hastened to the Persian frontier with only an armed escort, in an attempt to halt about thirty thousand Russians who were speeding to the relief of that city.

In the defile of Varak we ran into a band of Armenian *comitadchis* who put up a stiff fight at first, but finally withdrew into the shadows of a nearby cañon, hotly pursued by some of our men.

Next morning we crossed the snow-capped range of Kurd-Dagh, where Ibrahim Effendi, commander of the forces holding that pass, gave me a letter from Tchefik Bey, the sub-governor of Bash-Kale, in which Tchefik begged me to take charge of the defense of Kotur-Dagh, on the Persian border, where a handful of Turks were trying to stop the Muscovite advance, which grew stronger and more threatening every day.

That Turkish force consisted only of about a thousand Turkish and Kurdish volunteers, commanded by regular army and gendarmery officers. As the object of my mission was precisely that—to try to stop the advance of the Russians who were hastening to the relief of Van—I dashed across the dusty plain of Bash-Kale.

About three o'clock of that same afternoon I assumed the command of our handful of veterans, whom the Russian vanguard was already attacking. The Kotur-Dagh was a narrow defile across the Kurdistan range which forms the Turco-Persian border line.

Our men had taken up advantageous positions all along that pass and were already giving good account of several *sotnias* of Siberian Cossacks who had initiated a frontal attack. Those Cossacks were certainly a picturesque lot, with their sheepskin *kalpaks* perched in a cocky angle over their sun-burned, bearded faces, and the loose ends of their crimson or blue *kaftans* flapping wildly around in the air. They were whipping and spurring their shaggy little ponies mercilessly, while they howled and waved their broad, flashing sabers frantically over their heads.

Each of those Cossacks was carrying an infantryman behind, on the horse's haunches, who would jump off wherever he chose and, taking cover behind a rock, protect the advance of the charging cavalry with his rifle fire; a unique but rather useful combination of ancient and modern warfare which rendered the attacks of those Cossacks quite formidable.

It was extremely interesting to see them maneuver around like a swarm of angry wasps; now staging a frontal attack under the protection of their sharpshooters, or disappearing among the neighboring hills, to reappear suddenly in our flanks, where our machine-guns were waiting for them, making them retire headlong with scores of empty saddles.

By means of a counter-offensive which we launched that afternoon we succeeded in checking the second attack of the Russians, which had caused me considerable anxiety at first; but our Kurds stood their ground and the victory was ours. During the melée my A. D. C., Ahmed Effendi, a former student of the University of Heidelberg, came within an inch of being captured.

While trying to thwart off a vicious sword-thrust which a Cossack was aiming at me, he grappled with the man, and in their struggle both rolled over a steep cliff and down an inclined slope, where a party of Kurdish volunteers picked up Ahmed and carried him back to the top of the cliff before the oncoming, thundering mass of enemy cavalry could catch up with them.

It was a narrow escape for Ahmed Effendi, and a valiant deed on the part of those Kurdish boys, which made us feel proud of them. However, to judge by the way they climbed up that cliff, none of them seemed to be anxious to enjoy the delights of Paradise!

As soon as the Cossack blades had sparkled for the last time in the purple rays of a brick-red sunset, night settled over the mountains and the moon started climbing slowly into the starlit sky. Far away, in the distance, the Russian camp fires kept smoking and glowing mysteriously, while the gruesome silence of the night was rent, occasionally, by the mournful howl of a lone jackal or the strident scream of a wandering leopard which seemed to descend from the shadowy peaks that surrounded us almost in every direction.

After a frugal supper, consisting of a piece of stale bread and a drink of water, I disposed the defense for the following day and, shortly before midnight, set out with my escort toward the city of Bash-Kale where I intended

The Defense of Kotur-Dagh   193

to await the arrival of Kiasim and Khalil Beys. They were due on the following day with their two mixed divisions and three brigades of Turkish, Kurdish,
and Circassian volunteers. After Khalil's defeat near Shehir-Salamés they had
given the Russians the slip by crossing an unknown mountain-pass in the
neighborhood of Tocarague, south of Bash-Kale.

Unfortunately, after we were already well under way, I had to retrace my
steps in order to give Captain Fuad Effendi some additional orders in regard
to the defense of the defile. Owing to that delay we did not resume our journey until four in the morning. Dawn surprised us at the mouth of a cañon
which emptied into the plain of Tchoug.

While we trotted along, dreaming about a square meal, I could not help
admiring the beautiful tableland of the wild Kurdish range, encircled by silver mountains which sparkled like diamonds in the rising sun. There could
hardly be a lovelier landscape than that which surrounded us, especially toward the east. In a diaphanous world tinged with ivory and gold, the Djebel-
Tour rose distinct, snow-white, while on the north the Ararat flared and lifted
into the sunlight the glittering peaks whereon tradition says the ark of Noah
came to rest in the dawn of time.

I was riding some two hundred paces ahead of my escort; I had forgotten
all about the Russians, my whole attention being concentrated on the magnificent landscape which surrounded us, when, while trotting around a bend
of the steep cañon wall my horse collided with that of a Cossack officer who
was turning that bend also at a lively gait.

Our surprise was mutual, and rather disconcerting so far as I was concerned, at least, for I noticed that Captain Shmilinsky, or whatever his name
was, was also a few hundred paces ahead of an escort, a *sotnia* of vicious-looking
Cossacks who stopped short in their tracks and stared at me in a way that made
me feel everything but comfortable. And, to make matters worse, the captain's
A. D. C., a smart-looking, cross-eyed young fellow, was galloping up at forty
miles an hour with a nasty cheese-knife dangling in a loop from his wrist.

It did not take me long to size up the situation—perhaps less than a quarter of a second—while my Mohammedan horse pawed at the Gentile steed of

the Cossack officer in a fashion that made it impossible for me to raise my hand to salute. The captain of the Cossacks seemed to share my opinion that under those circumstances the customary salute might be dispensed with, for, holding on to the mane of his rearing horse with one hand, he drew with the other a Mauser pistol and fired it point-blank at me. Rather impolite, I should say!

Fortunately, before he could fire again, I knocked the gun out of his hand with a well-aimed saber cut, while his A. D. C., the cross-eyed young fellow, hit me over the head with his sword with so much enthusiasm that he made me see all the stars and nebulæ of the Milky Way.

If it had not been for my military *kalpak*, which caused the blade to slant off, I should not be telling the story now. To speak the truth, I don't really remember what happened after that, except that a few moments later I was galloping the shoes off my pony back toward my *gendarmes*.

When these had taken me under their protective wings and I turned around, holding my head with both hands, I saw my gallant foe, the captain of Cossacks, grinning back at me in a sheepish way, though from a safe distance, while nursing his right hand which my blow had nearly severed from his arm. In other words, we had each run away from the other at the sight of our escorts, without even the excuse of a blush!

After nodding at each other in a friendly way, and exchanging a few shots as a matter of courtesy, we withdrew in opposite directions, though looking over our shoulders carefully every now and then to make sure that the other fellow had not changed his mind in the meantime; for one's epidermis does not grow but once, and it's always better to be sure than to be sorry!

Escape

ALBERT BARTELS

From *Fighting the French in Morocco,* 1932

Albert Bartels was a German agent. His exploits took place in the Riff Mountains of northern Morocco during WWI, where his mission was to incite a
tribal revolt against the French. The German strategy was to snag French
troops fighting a Muslim insurgency in Morocco to prevent them from join-
ing the French Army in Europe, where they were fighting the Germans.

Bartels's mission ultimately failed. His sideshow war has long since been
forgotten, and rumors of German agents in the Riff Mountains are included
in only a few postwar histories. Bartels is virtually the only source for his adventures, recounted in *Fighting the French in Morocco.* His account shows
how Germany attempted to use Muslim hostility in Morocco against the
French. At the same time, the British had sent T. E. Lawrence into Arabia to
organize an Arab revolt against the Ottoman Empire—Germany's ally. So
how much of his fantastic story is true?

Bartels's credibility is somewhat diminished because he manages to celebrate himself while disparaging practically everyone else in the cast. Then
again, most of the cast was a pretty shady lot. Weeding out the exaggerations,
the gist of the truth resembles this: Bartels cobbled together a tiny alliance
of Berber tribesmen, German deserters from the French Foreign Legion, ex-
Algerian Saphis, outcasts, and other assorted riffraff. The titular head of this
group was a conniving opportunist named Abdel Malik.

Malik played a double game. For German money and arms, he agreed
to incite rebellion against the French. According to Bartels, he also under-
mined the campaign by indiscreetly dealing with the French. Bartels's book

is as much about his rearguard combat with Abdel Malik as it is about his guerrilla operations against the French.

By 1914, Morocco was theoretically divided into protectorates governed by Spain and France. The Riff was a confused tribal zone, completely beyond the pale of European control. Spain claimed it as part of their Protectorate of Northern Morocco. French Morocco ended along a ragged line on the southern foothills of the Riff. Bartels used the Riff, where Spanish authority was illusory, as a base for military operations against the French. By the time the war ended in 1918, he claimed to have a small army of over 3,000 ready for a campaign, but said that he was ordered to stand down by the defeated German government.

Bartels's story is sad and thrilling. He went to Morocco in 1905, earned his spurs working for a German trading firm, and then went out on his own. By 1912, his trading business was based in Rabat, capital of French Morocco. He had traveled widely, and spoke Arabic and some Berber dialects. During this era, Morocco was in the throes of a cosmopolitan, boomtown frenzy. European firms ventured into the countryside from the recently opened ports. Bartels socialized with French and British expats sand married a British diplomat's daughter.

All of this was suddenly snatched away in 1914 when German and Austrian residents in Morocco were rounded up and shipped to a prison camp in Sebdou, Algeria. Bartels was outraged, because the French had promised to send them to neutral Spain; instead, thousands were incarcerated, abused, and humiliated. Determined not to spend the war behind French barbed wire, Bartels and two companions escaped from Sebdou. Dodging Arab and French patrols, they made it across the border between French Algeria and Spanish Morocco. It was there, in Melilla, that the German consul offered them the chance to stir up rebellion against the French.

It's hard not to root for Bartels, even knowing that his view of the world—and the government he served—was wrong. He did not believe in Moroccan freedom as much as he did in punishing the French. Hazy and improbable notions of liberating Moroccans were secondary to his personal craving for vengeance.

—J. H.

Scarcely had I returned from solitary confinement to the general quarters than I proceeded with the execution of the plan which was to liberate me from this hell.

One night I secretly left the camp and supped in a neighbouring village with an Arab, who informed me of recent political happenings and, among other things, told me about suppressed revolts in Algeria.

After remaining with him a few hours I crept back to the camp unnoticed.

I spent every free moment upon gymnastic exercises in order to train my body for the coming fatigues.

I had discussed escaping with ten other German prisoners, but they were irresolute and wanted to keep postponing the attempt. I clearly perceived the danger of delay, for it was quite on the cards that our guards might become even stricter in supervision, or that we might be transferred to another camp.

On the 2nd October, 1915, I invited the men to flee with me at once. An Austrian possessed a compass and maps, which were most valuable articles for a flight in a foreign country. I begged him for them, but in vain. He feared that I should be captured during my flight and that he would get into serious trouble as the owner of the instruments.

Only two men, Gustav Fock and Thilo Müller, declared their readiness to flee with me in the coming night, with the intention of reaching Spanish territory. Sun, moon and stars must show us the way.

I was again down with fever and so weak that I could hardly stand.

When evening came I was sitting in front of my quarters. The outlines of the distant mountains were enticing; the Great Bear shone clear in the firmament. I roused myself, went into the quarters of a fellow prisoner, and asked him for a glass of wine, which I gulped down and for which I felt better. My resolve to escape was not taken seriously and I was credited with crazy ideas about breaking through. Only four prisoners knew that I intended to carry out my resolution.

At nine o'clock in the evening the bugle blew for parade. I slipped back to my quarters. We stood rigid. The sergeant passed us and called to me: "Attention, Bartels!"

When he was gone I went into my room, which was partitioned by canvas, and stepped to the window. Little more than four yards away were the barracks of the Zouaves. I threw out of the window a prepared sack, in which I had stowed some clothes, two loaves of bread and a bottle of wine mixed with water.

The Zouaves, who were standing in front of their barracks, laughed at me, because they thought the sack had fallen out of the window through negligence, and allowed me to go out to retrieve it.

Instead of returning through the door into the barracks, I ran straight across the camp ground, and in the darkness luckily passed one of the sentries stationed in the corner.

I threw myself on the ground as two guards passed the spot only a few yards away.

Their footfalls had scarcely died away before I began feeling my way along the fence which surrounded the camp, and after a short time I crept through a previously cut hole in the abbatis into the open.

At this place there was an old trench. I crept, again on all fours, into the bottom of the trench, where it was arranged I should wait for my two travel companions, Fock and Müller.

Half an hour went by and nothing stirred, except the sentries, whom I saw pass me several times darkly outlined. At last I heard a noise in the trench and saw what looked like a man lying down close beside me. A hand pressure. It was my ally Müller. We had been lying down about ten minutes when a man appeared above the trench, who ran off in hot haste after he had seen us.

We thought we were discovered and that all was lost; it was with difficulty that I restrained Müller from creeping back into the camp, especially as "lights out" was just sounded in the fort, which in his excitement he thought was an alarm, just as he mistook for a rocket a marvellous meteor which illuminated the whole place.

Then we heard a soft call and a whistle.

I pulled Müller up. We ran along the trench; Fock appeared, and our fear of betrayal was past.

A short hurried, whispered consultation, and we were off! At first, we made straight across a field towards a house which we had not seen, but from which we were chased by the dogs roaming around.

We cross the brook by the house and reached a highway, along which we hurried as quickly as we could.

After a little time a short halt was made. We put on our canvas shoes. Fock changed his linen, in order to make a good impression on the Spaniards, for whose zone we were making in a north-westerly direction.

Having run for another half hour, Fock discovered to his horror that he had left his shirt lying in the middle of the road: a misfortune which might frustrate our designs right at the very start, as we were forced to assume that our flight and its direction would soon be discovered, and that the French would pursue us as quickly as possible.

The road led to the river Tafna; to the right and left were high mountains; the road was quite smooth, as if constructed for running. Just then the moon rose over the mountains. Our spirits soared and kept whispering the word: Freedom! Free above all from the French yoke! Dreams of a great future for our fatherland filled my mind.

The fever had abated. Boldly we pressed forward, but soon we encountered the first obstacle. The road came to an end. It had not been built any farther. We found ourselves standing on the edge of an abyss in the midst of the mountains. Far below us on the left we heard the roar of the river; gigantic rocks barred our way in front; to the right were almost inaccessible mountain walls.

We sat down and refreshed ourselves from our scanty stock of provisions. We discussed our further flight and did not hide from ourselves the great difficulties and dangers which lay in our path. On the shortest calculation, we should have a five days journey, before we could reach Muluya, the dividing river between Algeria and the Spanish zone. Could we hold out? One of my companions became fainthearted and thought it would be better to return to Sebdou; perhaps if we returned our escape might remain unnoticed.

Away with such timorous thoughts! Forward!

I scrambled down to the Tafna, in order to ascertain whether one could proceed along its banks, but found it was impossible to make any further progress. I therefore climbed up again, where at length I found a shepherd's path.

I called my two travelling companions to the spot, but they had first of all to return to our resting place, as the field glasses had been left lying there.

Soon we found ourselves like pathfinders on the narrow way. The moon disappeared and it became pitch dark. One after another we scrambled down a ridge, and unexpectedly burst into an Arab garden.

We pushed our way through ditches and thickets, and suddenly saw a man running away from us.

In the darkness he probably took us for brigands from our dishevelled appearance. We ran after him and came to a path, which led us back to the Tafna.

Müller remained behind on the high river bank as a guard. Fock and I scrambled down, filled our bottles with water, and upon our return, after groping about in the dark, found our sentry, Müller, asleep like a bear.

After a short rest we proceeded on our way. Towards three o'clock in the morning we found a shallow part of the river, which was, however, completely covered with vegetation. We clambered down the bank, threw leaves into the water, to ascertain from the current of the river the direction of our flight, and after crossing the stream found on the other bank a well preserved forest track, along which we hastened.

The first day of freedom had dawned.

Through thick bushes we pushed our way up a mountain side, and laid down under the tangled bushes of thick trees, to rest and inspect the country.

Suddenly to our horror we discovered about 200 yards in front of us a village, from the neighbourhood of which it was imperative that we should vanish with all possible speed. Sleep was now out of the question. While we were still considering what was to be done, we observed below us at the foot of the mountain the first Goumier—country policeman—accompanied by two dogs, who was peering right and left. Luckily he soon took another way, and we were able to prepare our breakfast in peace.

Now, however, another danger approached in the shape of a buck, which invaded our ambush. We thought of killing the beast, but more and more goats came along, and the voices of goatherds, attempting to drive their animals by stones, re-echoed among the rocks. Everything passed off well; the goats scampered away, without our being discovered.

Just as I was about to utter El hamdulila—(thank God)—we were barked at by a watchdog, which despite all the cries of "Lei nal Buck" (God curse thy father) with which it was bombarded, would not stir from our vicinity. Not until he had been pelted with a number of stones by his master, who was, of course, unaware of the reason why he was barking at the bushes, did the dog run off.

The devil continued to play with us. Not far from our spot two ass-drivers sat down to pray and eat their breakfast. Then one of the asses remarked our comrade Müller; she had probably never seen a man with glasses, for suddenly the beast started kicking and ran braying down the hillside, dragging the driver after her.

No longer feeling secure in this spot, we plunged deeper into the thicket, and at length at the end of the day found the rest we needed so badly.

After sunset we resumed our march in a north-westerly direction through hilly country. It was pitch dark. As we were descending the flank of a mountain we saw a light coming towards us, in the neighbourhood of which we could hear whispering voices. It was two hours after midnight. The voices came nearer, and so did the light; which was for us the signal for instant flight. We scrambled down the mountain, until on reaching the foot we heard and saw nothing more. In front of us lay a deep ditch, completely covered with vegetation, which would have proved a very convenient resting place during the day, but owing to the danger from snakes and scorpions we dared not venture into it in the darkness.

I shivered in the frost; the fever had gripped me again. When dawn came, we sought out the above-mentioned ditch, and found in it a suitable, concealed camping place for the coming day.

The third night of our flight proved one of the hardest ordeals we had to go through. In the course of our wandering we suddenly stumbled on a thicket of thorns which imprisoned us like barbed-wire. We emerged from one spiky labyrinth nearly ten feet high only to pass into another. It cost us three hours of desperate exertion to fight our way through. We lost our bearings completely. At length, close on midnight, we escaped from the maze of torture. Almost fainting from thirst we found ourselves on a table-land. The cry now was: water, water.

In front of us was a second valley, surrounded by high mountains. The Great Bear shone in the north-west above a high mountain peak, which we took as our objective. Suddenly we came across a well-beaten track, which led under high trees. While we were still considering where we should find water the next day, I saw something silvery gleaming on the ground, and bent down—a murmur of joy! It was a spring bubbling out of the ground! We drank and drank, filled our bottles and thanked Providence for this mercy!

After barely escaping the danger of falling into a deep pit on our further march, we laid down on a projecting rock to rest and take counsel.

For hours we lay prone on the ground, when suddenly in the pitch dark night we saw ourselves encircled by twenty to thirty lights. The lights, however, we recognized as the glowing eyes of hyænas and jackals, staring at us from a distance of nine yards. We sprang to our feet and scared the cowardly band away within a short time by well-aimed stones. We continued to hear in the distance their sinister, raucous howls.

The morning of the third day of our flight dawned. Before us lay the whole valley in its savage beauty. We packed up and to our unspeakable delight discovered near a spring a tree bearing the Arab "Sassnu," a kind of strawberry, which indeed tasted mealy, but was for us priceless, as we had scarcely any food left.

After this precious refreshment we climbed a mountain. What a wide, splendid view opened out before us when we had reached its summit! Immediately opposite us, but in the distance, was the town of La Marnia, and on the left the town of Udshda, both lying on the great Oran-Fez railway line. In front of us the great plain and behind the two above-named towns a high mountain.

On the mountain we sought protection from the sun's rays and protection from our enemies under the low brushwood. Looking around us again we discovered the road that led to Udshda. It can be imagined with what trepidation we observed that it was patrolled by French Goumiers, who probably wanted to secure the reward offered for the apprehension of the fugitives. As I had already been before a court martial, my capture would have meant my death. We crept back to our bushes, and alternately remained on guard. The sun was scorching. Dismal thoughts stole into our minds. Would the flight succeed? We had already got so far that we could see salvation beckoning to us from the Spanish zone.

Müller was particularly downcast: He wondered if it would not be better to make for the French town of La Marnia and surrender to the local authorities. We managed to console him. The day drew to a close. Our watch showed half past five when Fock discovered at the foot of the mountain directly under us four horsemen staring steadily at us. That we had been discovered admitted of no doubt whatever, and the hunt might now begin.

Through our glass we saw two horsemen bearing to the right in order to come up to us by an easier slope of the mountain, while the other two remained where they were, apparently so as to keep us continually in view. We did not stir and resolved to await the onset of darkness.

With its coming we felt reprieved and whistled "All hail gladdening night!" Then we ran into the all-enveloping darkness. It was stiff going downwards, along the side of the road, as we had to keep as far away as possible from the vicinity of the observers. Every stone and every noise must be avoided. We hurried, we slid, we felt as if devils were after us.

Occasionally we had to stop in order not to lose the short-sighted Müller.

We landed suddenly in a dry bed, completely covered by vegetation, into which we stumbled as if into a pit. There we lay, but how were we going to get out! As the steep sides of the bank were covered with a network of bushes, climbing up was out of the question. An oleander tree came to our assistance; we swarmed up it, and, safe although somewhat shaken, we managed to get out of the pit.

After tramping for another two hours we came to a river, whose bed we only reached, after an unspeakable struggle with thick thorn bushes, with tattered clothes and completely torn shoes. Parched with thirst we drank the precious liquid and refreshed ourselves with a bathe which invigorated both body and mind. Then we were seized by overpowering fatigue; under a thick bush we laid down to divine sleep.

On the fourth day, just before three o'clock, we again broke camp and after about two hours reached a forest track, along which horses must have recently passed. Close in front of us ran a highway, along which Arabs were moving on horseback and on foot.

It now behoved us to be doubly cautious. We ascended some rising ground, in order to ascertain the position of the sun, which had already disappeared behind a mountain ridge, and settle the course of our further march, as well as to inspect the landscape more closely.

In front of us to the right we perceived the town of La Marnia. Consequently, our dangerous obstacle, the Oran-Fez railway, could not be so far away.

At nightfall we were on the march again and after passing European houses, arrived at a low-lying meadow, in which about one hundred oxen were rounded up. Then a motor car whizzed past us on the road, with our greatest enemy—men.

We hurried towards the railway line, which now glittered distinctly ahead with its lights. The station of La Marnia was brilliantly lighted up and seemed to us like a great palace. The night became quite dark; the railway, however, was no longer coming closer, and eventually we lost sight of it altogether; we must have missed our way in the elusive landscape. Differences of opinion arose as to the direction to be taken. We stretched ourselves on the ground for a rest; the second and last time that I was exhausted during this flight.

Fock and I had a raging thirst, but no water, as we had shared our last drop with Müller. But it was no use lying thirsty: we must go on and shake off our fatigue. We crossed two river beds, but in neither was there any water. We were nearing the point of collapse when, uttering a shriek of joy, we stumbled upon the railway track, which we so much desired and yet so feared. On all fours we crossed over, without being discovered, thank God!

Now the route lay forward across the plain towards the still distant mountain. Two roads must still be negotiated. Luckily, we got clear of them also. Then we stopped suddenly: close in front of us loomed a well-tended copse of oak trees with a house, from which a lamp was shining full on us, and from the steps of which a Frenchman was descending and whistling for his dog. We turned right about face, zigzagged in various directions, evaded discovery and hurried on our way.

After an hour we reached one of the canals which the French had constructed, and here we found water at last. We drank and drank as if we could never stop, re-filled our bottles, and then pressed onward with renewed strength.

All at once we heard quite close to us the cry "Mohammed," "By Scheib" the trampling of horses, the barking of dogs, and we bounded off to a hedge. One after another we jumped over. A watch dog ran off howling. Men and horses thundered past us. We ran back to the canal, skirted a village, and fell into a river; Fock and Müller both taking an involuntary bath.

Then forward once more. At half-past four it was light, but the mountain was still far away. There was no cover in the wide, open plain, but our luck did not desert us. Fock discovered ten yards in front of us an empty "Matmora," a hole for storing grain, wherein we hid ourselves without much hesitation. We then ate a piece of bread and the contents of our last box of preserves.

Fock cautiously pushed his head out of the hole, in order to survey the prospect.

About nine o'clock in the morning we were disturbed by a goat, which gazed down at us through the hole in the Matmora, and on discovering our presence bounded away with long leaps.

We had been sitting in the hole until nearly three o'clock in the afternoon, when our granary suddenly darkened. We looked up startled and observed an Arab, who was staring at us flabbergasted, his long nose thrusting deep into the hole; then, as if stung by a hornet, he withdrew and ran away shrieking.

Now, however, it was incumbent on us to get out of the hole with all celerity. We climbed out upon one another's shoulders; the last man being hauled out by the other two. We ran towards the north until we found a river bed which offered some cover, and then we turned south.

A band of old and young Arabs were running in pursuit of us; we on the other hand, proceeded farther and farther south, and when we lost sight of them, we made for a road, on which we met three women, who made astonished remarks about us. The impression we made in our tattered clothes could not have been of a confidence-inspiring character.

Towards five o'clock we became aware that we were being observed by a French patrol on our right, but we did not let this disturb us. We continued our course calmly, and in his full view sat down on the open edge of the ditch, as though the patrol did not concern us in the least.

Soon afterwards we pushed through a small cavity in the hedge and made for a thicket lying westward, where we remained concealed until darkness.

Came the sixth night. Towards seven o'clock in the evening we broke up the camp, followed a dry river bed, and then turned towards the mountain. Meanwhile it had become so dark that we could scarcely see our hands before our eyes. Suddenly a light appeared in front of us, and soon afterwards we heard whispers. We at once threw ourselves on the ground; then we heard an Arab say that the Hacking (the officer) had ordered them for three o'clock in the morning. It was now two o'clock and we knew immediately that the French patrol, enlightened by the shepherd, was on our track.

We crept back softly and, taking wide curves, raced towards the mountain. Passing various villages, at the threshold of which we were warned off by the barking of dogs, we reached a mountain slope unmolested, laid down between rocks and immediately went to sleep. We were all three completely exhausted.

When the sixth day of our flight dawned, we promptly broke up camp, as the vicinity of men spelt danger for us. Suddenly we came across a house, on the flat roof of which the owner appeared. Goats and oxen were led out of the farm, and then the owner disappeared into the interior of his habitation.

Observing great caution we attempted to creep past, but immediately came up against a second house and were discovered.

A man with a gun barred our road and asked whither we wanted to go. "To the French post of Sidi Berkan," we told him. He was joined by two more Arabs. The gang did not believe us and refused to let us pass.

A young, well-dressed Arab asked the time of Müller, who as a courteous man immediately drew out his watch. The rascal snatched it away from him and thrust it into his pocket. Then he pointed out to us the Kasba, the house of a kaid, which lay about two miles away on the mountain side, and added that he was going to deliver us up. I retorted that we also wanted to be taken to the kaid, so that the latter should make him return the watches and the thousand duro which we had given him. He knew quite well that if he did not restore the watches and the money, the kaid would have him thrashed within an inch of his life.

The Arab did not notice that we were superior to him in diplomatic art, for Müller had given him only ten duro and one watch. The other Arabs had in the meantime disappeared.

The elegant robber also vanished, but returned in a short time with another Arab, with whom he carried on a whispered discussion in our vicinity, so that we did not feel too comfortable.

Meanwhile we had sought shelter behind stones, in order the better to defend ourselves. Our presence of mind, as well as our humour, helped to extricate us from this awkward situation. After a private discussion, we arose very deliberately, and laughingly began a conversation with them. I was very thankful to Müller for not parting with all his money, as we were likely to have urgent need of it on our further flight.

After the Arabs had pondered the matter sufficiently, they decided to help, and after some bargaining even brought us bread and tea. This was the first time since we fled that we had something warm in our stomachs.

We took a special fancy to an Arab as tall as a tree, and tried to persuade him to conduct us for fifty francs to the Muluya, the boundary river between Algeria and the Spanish zone. He considered the proposal for a long time, but eventually he consented. It was arranged that we should wait for him in front of his house when it was dark.

In the meantime he brought me a dirty Arab Rusa—turban—and wound it around me, or, stuck it on my head. I recovered my humour and sang "When the lice are softly running," whereat he mended my tattered garment.

As it was getting dark his daughter, Chadiya, came and brought us coffee and barley-bread. Shortly afterwards appeared the tall Arab, accompanied by a nephew with an enormous cudgel, and henceforward the impression he made on us was anything but reassuring. His face was completely wrapped up and only his eyes darted restlessly around. To Chadiya, the darling, we presented a duro, and proceeded along smugglers' paths, between chalk mountains, towards a river.

Thus the seventh day of our flight approached. I insisted that the old man should go in front, behind him his nephew, and then came Fock and Müller.

Suddenly we saw men darting about on the other side of the river. I seized the old man's shoulder, and asked him what this meant. He shook his head to convey that he did not know. All of a sudden he wheeled round, seized me by the breast and hissed "Nkiddlick" (I'll kill you). I gave him a push and told him I was not afraid of a decrepit old man, and he had better hurry along. Whereupon he tried to laugh it off as a joke.

We continued to scramble along bad paths over rocks and stones, when, suddenly the old man was pitched to the ground with such violence that I thought he was seriously injured. However, his bones must have been made of iron, for, merely muttering a curse, he got on his feet again.

We came to a motor road; the river on the left, and on the right telegraph poles, sighing in the night wind. We made a brief halt, then I assisted Fock, who had a bad foot, also taking charge of his rücksack, and arm in arm we swept, in the literal sense of the word, along the street, for the rags which we had wound about his wounded foot were completely torn, and threw up thick clouds of dust at every step.

Towards eleven o'clock in the evening we were startled by the blast of a trumpet in our immediate vicinity. We thought at first of treachery, but perceived it came from a motor car filled with officers. In front of us was a French patrol. We crept right past him. The Arab and his nephew had vanished into the darkness; but it was only fright that had impelled them to run away, and they quickly rejoined us. We hurried on in a westerly direction and reached a river, which the old Arab asserted was the Muluya. This we did not in the least believe. The stream seemed to us too narrow, although it could have been the boundary river. The fifty francs conduct money was paid. After thanking us, the old man said he must take his departure and advised us to penetrate as far as possible into the wood, in order to get away from the dangerous frontier. Then, making us another Arab salutation, he disappeared with his nephew.

By this time we were on the other side of the river, and although tired to death we dragged ourselves another two and a half miles and reached the outskirts of a village, where we laid down to enjoy a refreshing sleep until dawn. This was the eighth day.

We arose reinvigorated and sang joyously "There sounds a call like Donnerhall," as we thought we were already traversing Spanish territory. After a two-hours tramp we reached two farms. I asked a Berber coming from one of these farms about its owner, who he told me was a Frenchman, while the other farm belonged to a Spaniard. He took us to be Jewish pedlars, on account of the bags in which we carried our belongings. Not until we were quite close to him did he recognise us as Christians. It was now full daylight.

A Frenchwoman drove away from the farm in a one-horse trap, while a second Arab, who came from the other farm, crossed our path. We turned aside; but after five minutes two huge fellows stood in front of us. They greeted us with the words "Salem ualikum," (Peace be with you) and then asked whither we were going. I replied that we were making for the French post of Sidi Berkam. Thereupon they felt my rücksack and inquired whether I had any slippers to sell. While they were thus engaged, they made a peculiar grimace and looked at me sideways, and at length intimated that we ought to tell them the truth, that we wanted to cross the Muluya. I regarded them intently and said in a serious tone: "If you betray us, may God punish you! Yes, we want to cross the Muluya." My knowledge of humanity had not deceived me in this instance. They invited us to accompany them to the farm and told us that the owner, a French officer, was at the front, and the wife did not bother about her affairs. When I declined to do so, they found shelter for us between thorn bushes, and called some swineherds, whom they instructed to guard us. They brought us tea and bread several times.

Evening was again approaching. We then proceeded, in the company of this Arab, who had armed himself with a long gun, across the densely populated plain of Beni Ssnassen to the house of the kaid, where we were told to wait in front of the door. We did not yet trust them and moved away from the spot where they had left us standing.

After some minutes they came back, accompanied by a number of people. When we heard what they were telling each other, we emerged from our hiding place. The Arabs, so they said, had not been able to meet their friend, the kaid, and had resolved to go with us through the midst of the forest which at this point was very extensive.

We then proceeded with them further. Around every tree trunk, around every hedge we raced like Indians on the war-path, bounding and creeping, suspecting patrols everywhere.

Suddenly the Arabs stood still in front of me, levelled their guns and whispered to me: "Here comes someone." I too suddenly saw a man in front of me standing by a thorn hedge. A glance and I had recognised him. Quickly I grasped the other's rifle and exclaimed: "For God's sake don't shoot." It was our fellow-traveller Müller, who had gone astray. They both muttered irritably into their beards, and then ran forward like weasels.

All at once a number of patrols emerged several hundred yards in front of us. They must also have observed us, for they turned their lanterns on us. Our leaders immediately threw themselves on the ground. Noiselessly we followed their example and waited, concealed behind stones, until the beams of light had passed us. Then we ran this way and that for half an hour and came to a house. Again we concealed ourselves, while the old man went inside. Shortly afterwards he came out, with eight natives. On this occasion also we did not show ourselves until after we had understood what they were whispering to each other. But oh horrors: they intended to deliver us up!

The last wild chase. We ran as fast as we could downhill, although we were frequently obliged to stop in order not to lose Fock, who could not follow so quickly on account of his bad foot. The chase lasted a good half hour. At last we reached the river. The Muluya flowed in front of us, shallow and peaceful, but very broad. As we ran along the river bank, suddenly a naked, brown giant emerged from the water. Like men possessed we raced along the bank; a shot was fired and we plunged into the river. A second, a third shot splashed in the water. We struggled against the current, which threatened to engulf us. Our clothes stuck to us and dragged us, but we touched bottom and reached the other bank, intoxicated with joy we threw ourselves among the ferns—we were saved! When we had clambered up the river bank, what an amazing spectacle met our eyes: close in front of us lay the sea, which we had imagined to be so very far away.

On the ninth day of our flight, completely dishevelled, we reached the coastal district of Cabo de Agua where we were sympathetically received by the Spaniards, and especially by the family of the Commandant.

We had achieved what had been regarded as quite impossible in the Sebdou internment camp. We had traversed two hundred and twenty miles of unknown country. Through valleys and across mountains, without map or compass, the stars as our guide. The news of our arrival rapidly spread in the little port. A French captain came in order to convince himself of our break through, and the Spanish Commandant found it incredible that we had been able to cross the strictly guarded frontier. From all sides the inhabitants flocked to us; they fêted us as heroes and offered the most cordial invitations. Even if we had possessed the means, it would have been quite impossible for us to buy anything; we received everything that we needed, clothes and food, as presents. The Commandant even provided us with mules, on which we rode along the coast to Nador, whence we took the train to Melilla. Melilla, dear old town how lovely we found you! How often we drank to your prosperity, inspired by the thought that you had become our salvation and refuge.

In Melilla I received one day through Mr. Salama, a letter from Mr. Ashfield, the captain of an English ship which lay in the harbour who was on terms of friendship with my English relatives and myself. The letter most cordially invited me to go on board, to receive news of my wife and little son in London. I had already decided to accept this invitation and was on my way to the ship when the thought suddenly occurred to me that I was walking into a trap. I wrote the Captain a letter and begged him to come ashore and lunch with me. I also thanked him for his cordial invitation and assured him that it would give me infinite pleasure to see him and hear from him about my family. The steamer remained in harbour for two more days; I heard nothing more from the Captain, who was doubtless sorry to have to proceed to Gibralter without me.

On one of the following days Fock and I went on a climbing expedition among the almost vertical cliffs of the coast. We were almost at the top, only about twelve yards of high rock-wall remained to climb. There were only small fissures, from which one could cling with fingers and toes. Without much reflexion I climbed up the steep wall. When I was half way up, I suddenly found that I could neither go forward nor backward. Then I said to myself: "So far you have luckily come through all dangers, and, without any reason, you must incur the foolhardy risk of falling headlong several hundred yards." For a moment a feeling of dizziness came over me. My entire past life flashed before my eyes like a vision. Already my strength was failing me, but the will to live conquered. I looked up, groped with my right hand, while I pressed hard against the rock—then with the left and drew up my leg. After groping above again I encountered loose stones, which fell on my head; I groped farther to the right, gripped firm stone, and was saved.

My companions, Fock and Müller happily reached Spain.

Intelligence in Transcaucasia

COLONEL ALFRED RAWLINSON

From *Adventures in the Near East 1918–1922*, 1924

Colonel Alfred Rawlinson arrived in Iraq in 1918 with two machine guns and two Colt .45s in his kit. He had been sent to join Dunsterforce, a secret—or "hush-hush"—army, as he called it. Rawlinson would lead seventy troops to help the city of Baku, which was under assault by a huge Turkish army. He would escape with only ten other survivors, and would later record his experiences in *Adventures in the Near East 1918–1922*.

Under the command of General Dunsterville, Dunsterforce consisted of around 1,000 elite Canadian, British, and Australian troops. This unconventional army was secretly assembled and dispatched to the region to catch the Ottoman army off guard—which suited Rawlinson's penchant for special ops. Within this seething cauldron, Turkish and German forces battled Armenian rebels, Bolsheviks, and the British for control of Persian oil fields. This confusing war zone was located on the southern coast of the Caspian Sea. Ottoman frontier provinces butted against southern Russia and the northern region of Persia, which is now modern Iran. Britain was concerned that a Turkish-German force, once in control of the region, would drive southward to the Persian oil fields.

The "Great War" strategies between empires were further complicated by local conflicts. WWI ignited long-stifled ethnic, religious, and political hatred. Armenians, both in the Ottoman Empire and in Russia, revolted. Their nationalist cause sometimes viewed the Bolsheviks as enemies, sometimes as allies. The Turks wanted nothing less than to crush them.

The Russian civil war after the Revolution further complicated matters. Russian factions—Bolshevik Reds and Czarist Whites—fought for control of the region. An enormous Ottoman army assaulted Baku in the autumn of 1918, in an attempt to crush Armenian nationalists who had seized the city, capital of Russian Azerbaijan.

The purpose of Dunsterforce was to covertly enter northern Persia from Iraq and prevent the enemy from taking the city of Baku. Ultimately, this was to protect the Persian oil fields (oil that was critical to the Allied war effort). To do this, the troops were equipped with cars and trucks with specially mounted machine guns. It was hoped that Dunsterforce's maneuverability, speed, and secrecy would compensate for being outrageously outnumbered.

Unfortunately, this was not the case. Undermanned and ill equipped, Dunsterforce was doomed to fail.

Baku was under the control of Armenians, a minority in a city mainly populated by Azeris, known to Rawlinson as Tartars. Armenian nationalists had a shaky truce with the Bolsheviks during the siege. Thus, Baku harbor was guarded by Bolshevik gunboats while the city's land defenses were manned by Armenians. Part of the reason Rawlinson was sent to Baku was to destroy the vast stores of weapons and munitions in the city, so that the Bolsheviks could not capture and use them against the Whites. As complicated as all this sounds, Rawlinson's "can-do" attitude never flagged.

In 1919 Rawlinson entered nearly inaccessible regions to investigate the disarmament of the Turkish army after WWI. He discovered they had other plans.

Rawlinson operated in a region that will undoubtedly become better known to Westerners in the future. Today, Baku is capital of Azerbaijan. Iran, no longer Persia, has an unhappy relationship with the West. Both Iran and Iraq are governed (Iraq in theory) by Shias. Iran's government brawls diplomatically with the Americans over its nuclear program. Tehran appears closer to having weapons of mass destruction than Saddam Hussein ever did. Abutting these Muslim countries is Armenia and Georgia, two countries that emerged as independent states briefly after WWI, and again, after submersion in the Soviet Union, in 1989. All have had territorial spats with their neighbors.

Curiously enough, the map of Central Asia looks remarkably like it did in Rawlinson's day—even down to the presence of Western troops and bases. What would the colonel say?

—◆ ◆ ◆—

The only road passable for vehicles, which crosses this range for at least 200 miles, is one that rises from Trebizond and crosses the Zigana Pass, at 6,500 feet above the sea about 50 miles inland. In our innocence we supposed that we should easily cross this pass the first day, as much of the snow had melted, and, our cars being in good condition, we anticipated no difficulty. Night was, however, coming on when we arrived at a Greek village, Hamsikeui by name, still 2,500 feet below, and 15 miles distant from, the summit.

As we were just on the edge of the snow, we there pitched the first of the many mountain camps and bivouacs we were destined to occupy in this wild mountain country. Our delay on this occasion proceeded from no defects on the part of our cars, but from the fact that the gradients were stiff and our loads heavy. However, the men were all well trained and full of "go," and we had the tent pitched and our meal prepared in less than half an hour, and after a very comfortable if somewhat cold night, were away again half an hour after daylight next day, to enter the forest belt which lies just below the snow, and after three hours' hard climb we reached the summit before ten o'clock.

Here, on the summit of the Zigana, looking south, we had our first view of the interior of Anatolia, and a very marvellous and beautiful one it was. In the bright morning sun, range after range of snow-capped mountains appeared on every side, except on the north, in which direction the great mountains on either side of the narrow valley we had been following obstructed our view. The impression produced by this remarkable scene was of an incredibly rocky and rugged country, of precipices and narrow, deep valleys, with absolutely no flat country in any direction, and the clearness of the atmosphere was also so deceptive that distances were impossible to estimate.

On many occasions since that first morning I have studied that view at my leisure, when, having become thoroughly familiar with the country for many miles, I have been able to pick out and identify prominent peaks of 11,000 feet and upwards, which I knew then to be over 100 miles away, but which on this first occasion, in our ignorance, we took to be not more than 30 or 40 miles distant.

The descent was steep at first, but after about 5 miles the road rose again, being there cut out of a sheer rocky cliff with a mountain of 11,000 feet rising perpendicularly on the left, and a deep, narrow valley on the right, at the bottom of which ran a roaring torrent at least 2,000 feet below the road. The rise continued for a mile or more, till a steep zigzag descent commenced which continued to the Kharshut River, 15 miles from the summit of the pass and 3,000 feet below it. Here we halted, took our midday meal, and, having closed up the column, continued on our way, ascending the narrow valley of the river to the eastwards.

This river, which is considerably the largest stream running into the Black Sea in the 300 miles which lie between the mouth of the Chorokh River, near Batoum, and that of the Kelkid Irmak (the Halys of ancient history), near Samsun, was at this time in full flood from the melting of the snows. During the last 30 miles of its course, below the point where the road enters the valley, the Kharshut runs through narrow gorges between perpendicular cliffs, where not even a mule-track is able to follow its course, though there would be no insuperable difficulty in constructing a railway from this point to its mouth at Tireboli. Above its junction with the road the valley becomes wider and receives three large tributaries in the next 20 miles.

Here, before entering the town of Gumush Khaneh (the Silver House), we halted and closed up our column again, as we heard the late Army Commander from Erzeroum was in the town, on his way to Constantinople, whither he had been called by order of the Sultan. We passed him in the main street with a polite salute, about five p.m., and made the best of our way up the valley beyond, without making any halt at all in the town.

The Kharshut Valley round Gumush Khaneh is far from spacious, being not more than a mile across at the widest point, with steep mountains everywhere rising to the snow on either side. The valley itself, however, is here well cultivated and the land rich and sheltered, there being many orchards which produce apples and cherries famous throughout all the upland country—a beautiful sight at this time in April, when the whole valley was a mass of apple-blossom. We kept on till dark, rising all the time, and were finally forced to bivouac at the roadside in the darkness, just under 100 miles from Trebizond, with the defile leading to the Vavok Pass just before us. Our bivouac was only 500 feet higher than our camp of the previous night, but was infinitely warmer, as, although the snow was all round us, yet the road-side where we had halted was well sheltered by the steep sides of the gorge.

Next morning at daylight we were quickly on the move, as we hoped we might be able to cross *two* passes during the day. Immediately on leaving, the gorge became so narrow as to barely leave room for a car beside the roaring torrent, but after not more than a quarter of a mile we came suddenly out on to the snow-field, with the ridge of the Vavok Pass (6,500 feet) 2 miles in front of us. Once over the ridge, on the southern slope the snow was less and the gradient favourable, and so we made good progress, passing through the outskirts of the town of Baiburt at 5,300 feet, 125 miles from Trebizond, before midday.

Baiburt, an ancient city, stands on the edge of an extensive and once well-cultivated plain on the banks of the Chorokh River. It was at this time the headquarters of a Turkish brigade of regular troops, and I instructed the Turkish Transport officer, who had been detailed at Trebizond to accompany us, to inquire at the military post outside the town what arrangements had been made by the Brigade Headquarters to help us over the dreaded Khop Pass, which lay some 25 miles ahead of us, and which we knew to be deeply covered with snow. The reply was "that a company of infantry had been sent out some days previously to endeavour to clear a passage for us, but no news of their success had yet come in." We therefore carried on in the hope that we might find the pass open.

Amongst the many difficult passes of Eastern Anatolia, very few can be passed by wheeled vehicles. The Khop is certainly the most difficult of these, as, although the road is well traced and constructed, not only is the actual upper pass unusually long (about 15 miles), but half of it is at over 8,000 feet, the road there is also much exposed, the wind being frequently very high and so cold as to have an absolutely paralysing effect on any one exposed to its full force.

The summit rises to 8,250 feet, and forms the actual watershed between the Black Sea and the Persian Gulf, the nearest point of which is 1,000 miles distant as the crow flies. No winter season ever passes without many lives being lost on this pass from exposure, as travellers who are caught on the upper pass in the dreaded *tépis*, or storms of snow and wind, which are frequent there, have very little chance in the deep drifts which rapidly form in the freshly fallen snow, and it is little wonder that the summit is often impassable for months on end. On this occasion fresh snow had fallen within the previous two days, and the troops who should have had a post at the commencement of the upper pass were, on our arrival there, nowhere to be seen, so that, in view of my appointment at Kars, still over 300 miles distant, it was hard to know what course to pursue, for more snow might fall at any moment and block the pass hopelessly for weeks. In the end, however, we decided to go on as far as we could before dark, and succeeded in getting more than 1,500 feet up the zigzag as night was coming on, before we reached fresh snow, where no sign of any road at all could be seen, and there we halted for the night.

Two tents were pitched in the snow, one for myself with two men and our machine-guns, and the other for the Turkish Transport officer and any men who might wish to join him there. The majority of the men, however, preferred to remain in the cars, which were fairly sheltered by the deep snow. I took the greatest care in pitching my own tent, as I was very doubtful of its ability to resist the icy gusts which were then increasing both in frequency and severity, and I went round every tent-peg myself before finally lying down, with my snow-boots and all my furs on, in the snow. It was indeed well that I did so, as during a more heavy squall than usual, about 2 A.M., we heard an outburst of yells which told us the other tent had "gone." It was impossible to give any assistance, as the men and myself had all our work cut out to save our own tent, and we could hear that the occupants of the other tent eventually reached the cars, where they got some kind of shelter till daylight.

Soon after daybreak some Turkish troops came into sight, coming in single file through the fresh-fallen snow. It appeared that they had sheltered the night before in a stone *khan*, or hovel, 3 or 4 miles farther on. They gave us a poor account of the state of the pass, as it appeared that the road on the slopes immediately above us had been entirely carried away by an avalanche within the last few days, and that higher up fresh snow lay deep, so that they had had oxen brought up from the other side of the pass to endeavour to get our cars over the summit if we could reach the place where the road still existed.

We therefore at once proceeded to carry out a survey of the ground immediately above us, and found that by keeping on up the extreme point of the spur on which we had halted we could get "up" on solid ground, from which the force of the wind had largely cleared the snow during the night. The slope, however, proved terribly steep, and it was necessary to unload the cars entirely, and then, having attached long ropes with cross-poles at intervals, we manned them with as many Turkish soldiers as possible, and with the greatest difficulty hauled the empty cars up, one by one, by main force. On reaching the road again, we found the Turks had collected about forty oxen, with their yokes and ropes, ready to tow the cars, and a start was promptly made with three pairs of oxen to each car. At frequent intervals it was necessary to double the oxen, putting twelve or more to one car, to get through some exceptional morass, and going back afterwards to bring on the others by the same means.

Some of these roads during the melting of the snows appear absolutely impassable, and it is only by the use of a long line of oxen that a passage can be effected. In places the mud and slush appear to be unfathomable, and two or even three yoke of oxen will at times absolutely disappear in the half-frozen mud. If, however, a start is made in the early morning, on the thin coating of ice which has formed during the night, the leading yokes who pass safely over may then succeed in dragging the following pairs, who break through the ice, safely across the morass, and last of all the cars may be made to slide over, with their floor-boards forming sleighs on the surface of the frozen slush and mud, into which, however, they must on no account be allowed time to sink.

It may be imagined that the rate of progress under these circumstances is not great. However, on this occasion, starting at daylight, we were able to cross the summit, about 3½ miles distant from our camp, by midday, and here enjoyed a view which is unsurpassable in any country. From the summit of the Khop, at 8,250 feet, the ground falls away steeply to the south and the main Euphrates Valley lies spread out far below, the foot-hills on either side of the river being about 25 miles apart, the crests of the main ranges beyond being from 30 to 35 miles distant. In every direction the scene is bounded by snow, with countless volcanic peaks and precipitous ridges rising everywhere to 12,000 feet or more.

In spite of the wild grandeur of this prospect, it is not advisable to waste any time in admiring it, for in winter the force of the wind on this exposed watershed is so great as to be dangerous, and the temperature falls so low that on several occasions the whole of my party have lost the skin off their faces from exposure to this truly "icy blast," not to mention other even more distressing effects resulting from the glare of sun on the snow which we have also experienced there.

On this occasion we were able to slide down off the main ridge without delay, as the force of the wind had done much to clear it of fresh snow. It was, however, long past nightfall ere we reached the last zigzags of the main pass, which we were able to descend in comparative shelter, and finally camped at 11 P.M., amongst deserted ruins, in a small village named Pirnikapan, which lies only 1,000 feet above the level of the great Euphrates River, 45 miles west of Erzeroum.

The sight afforded by our party of six cars descending the endless zigzags on the face of the perpendicular cliffs in the dark was truly remarkable, for looking back up the almost precipitous mountain the effect of the brilliant headlights of the cars on the rocks in all directions, as they followed each other, about 100 yards apart, down all the twists and turns on the face of the cliff was most effective, and was, in fact, the most striking incident of an eventful day.

Next morning all the party were suffering pretty severely from their exposure on the pass, and camp was not struck till 12 noon, when we started up the plain for Erzeroum. The road being good and fairly clear of snow, we reached the ramparts of the great Turkish fortress before 5 P.M., and were met at the carefully guarded gate by an officer sent by the military Headquarters to conduct us to the house placed at our disposal by the authorities. This proved to be a spacious mansion, originally an American school, and an officer and guard of twenty-five Turkish soldiers were quartered there, to assist us generally, or rather, as we well understood, to keep in touch with our operations. We reached Erzeroum on the 22nd, having taken five days to cover the 200 miles from Trebizond—not at all bad travelling, over that now familiar road, at that time of year, particularly as its peculiar difficulties were then all unknown to us.

Next day I called upon the Turkish civil Governor and on the temporary Commander of the Army Headquarters, as the late Army Commander (whom I had passed at Gumush Khaneh) had not yet been replaced. Presenting my credentials and the Sultan's "Firman," I was duly authorized to inspect all armament and military stores, as well as to examine the army muster-rolls and pay-sheets. The next two days were spent in a rapid survey of the arsenals and fortifications and an inspection of the army books, in order to obtain a rough idea of the progress of demobilization, and on the 26th, at daylight, I was able to start again, this time with only two lightly loaded cars, to cross still two more high ranges of snow-mountains and the old Russo-Turkish frontier, to report to the Commander-in-Chief at Kars, 130 miles away, on the 27th, as ordered.

Immediately on leaving Erzeroum the main road to the east crosses at over 7,000 feet the high Deveboyun Ridge, which here divides the valley of the Euphrates from that of the Aras, and so forms the main watershed between the Persian Gulf and the Caspian Sea. However, as the road was good and the snow hard in the early morning, we were soon over this comparatively easy pass, and descended into the wide valley of the Upper Aras River, known here as the Passim Plain. After travelling 25 miles across this plain, we reached Hassan Kalé, an old fortress now in ruins, but the site of many important battles dating back to the earliest times of which any historical records exist. The permanent Turkish barracks which stood here before the Great War were destroyed by the Russians under the Grand Duke Nicholas in their victorious advance on Erzeroum. Their ruins, however, still remain, and other signs are not wanting of the Russian occupation, especially the road over which we now travelled and the small Decauville Railway, extending to the frontier, which follows the same route and was constructed in six months, during the Russian advance to Erzeroum in 1916–17.

Beyond Hassan Kalé the great plain contained nothing of interest except its state of desolation, which, in view of its great natural fertility, was most remarkable. About 40 miles east of Erzeroum our road turned a little to the north and commenced to climb the foot-hills of the great Saganli Mountains, till 20 miles farther on we reached the Turkish military frontier position at Zivin, at the foot of the upper frontier pass. The latter part of the road was bad, as all roads become, in these parts of the country, when the snow first begins to melt, and we were bogged several times; so that night was coming on as we reached Zivin and bivouacked at the roadside for the night. The Turkish frontier post had been warned of our coming and were very friendly. We were able, therefore, to pass a good night, and early next morning we reached the actual frontier, and crossed the "No Man's Land" then existing between the last Turkish post and the first post of the new Armenian Republic, which the Allies were supporting in their occupation of Kars Province.

The road through the upper pass was good, but the pass itself was both long and difficult, as it extended for 30 miles with much deep snow, the summit being at an altitude of 7,500 feet. At Sarikamish, the old Russian military camp beyond the pass, 32 miles from Zivin, the snow had nearly gone; we were therefore able to average a good rate of speed across the plain, and to reach the fortress of Kars, 130 miles from Erzeroum, before 4 P.M. The Commander-in-Chief's train was in the siding there, where my own had been on the occasion of my previous visit, and though he himself had not yet returned from inspecting the Kars defences, we learned that he was not due to start back till late that night; there would therefore be all the time necessary to make my report. So we went straight on to the military Headquarters to arrange for a bed that night.

We received a very pleasant reception from the staff, and a good room with a fire and all the comforts of an English mess were duly appreciated; as also was an invitation to dine with the Chief on his train, which reached me whilst I was enjoying the unusual luxury of a good hot bath. The Chief was very kind at dinner, and I learned from him all the news, and in addition he gave me some invaluable English newspapers, to which I had long been a stranger.

My own orders were to return to Erzeroum to enumerate all the armaments in the hands of the Turkish IXth Army, and to take note of the measures being taken for demobilization, reporting the results of my inquires to Constantinople by cable. I was told officers would be sent to assist me in the work, and was instructed to examine and report on any means which might be available for getting out of the country all armament in excess of the limited amount which was allowed by the Armistice conditions. Ever thoughtful for our welfare and comfort, I found the Chief had even given instructions for two bottles of whisky to be put in my car, from his small private store on the train; these, of course, would have been otherwise unobtainable and would be worth their weight in gold in our freezing mountain camps after long days in the snow; and I feel sure that no man's health has ever been drunk with more enthusiasm than was his by my men when I served out this most welcome present to them from "Uncle George," under which familiar designation our Commander was universally known and loved throughout his army.

The Chief left for Batoum that night, and I was indeed fortunate to have reached such good quarters and a British doctor, as next day I had a bad "go" of fever, which, though it was nothing at all where I then found myself, would have been a very different experience had it caught me in camp in the snow. After the luxury of a long day in a good bed, with a blazing fire and English newspapers to read, I was all right next morning, the 29th, and we got away early on our return journey to Erzeroum, camping again at Zivin that night, and reaching our quarters before dark on the 30th.

The snow was now getting less daily, but the roads got worse, as the country becomes sodden at this time of year, and mud, of the depth it is found in those mountains, is an even worse obstacle to travelling on wheels than snow is, however deep the latter may be. The month of May in Erzeroum is always the most unhealthy of the year, as in May and June the snows are melting and all the evil smells and germs, which the arctic winter has hidden under its blanket of snow, begin then to come to light, causing us all to suffer from both malaria and dysentery. Our house was the only one still standing in the Armenian quarter, having been American property and therefore left untouched when the Armenian houses were destroyed. The ruins all round it, however, were to the last degree insanitary, so that even without reference to the peculiarly poisonous and persistent form of malaria which distinguishes the great marsh of Erzeroum, we soon found ourselves sadly in need of the medical stores and advice which we had been told were to be sent us from Constant on the first opportunity.

At Erzeroum both the fortress and town are full of interest, even though the former is quite out of date and the latter largely in ruins. The actual permanent fortifications round the city are elaborately constructed, with bastions, ravelins, curtains, sally-ports, etc., according to the old French system, and all these are well made and in fair repair, though quite out of date. The town, however, now depends for its military value on the defensive system of works which have been of late years constructed on the hills covering the fortress. The whole position is designed to cover the main road from the east, and is very elaborate, extending to a distance of 50 miles from flank to flank; the lines would thus require a force of 50,000 men to adequately garrison them, which is a greater force than the Turks would probably ever be in a position to produce for this purpose to resist an advance from the east (the Russian frontier). The works also have now little real military value, as the whole position is capable of being turned and passed on either flank. The fortress itself has always been the great military centre of the Turkish power in Eastern Anatolia, and the taking stock of its ancient and very miscellaneous military contents was therefore a somewhat arduous undertaking.

The town contains several most interesting old buildings, now mosques, which, however, before the advent of the Turks, were Christian churches, and previously were the seats of various much more ancient religions, some of them still bearing the device of the Sun-god fructifying the palm-tree, the sign of ancient Nineveh, which is easily decipherable on several of them to-day. The great plain of Erzeroum, which lies north of the city, is 25 miles broad at that spot, and is roughly 50 miles long, the greater portion of that large tract being occupied by the marsh which forms the true source of the great Euphrates River, although a mountain stream, one of several which feed the marsh from 50 miles or more beyond, is usually indicated as the parent stream. The town itself stands on the slope of the great Palenduken Mountains, at an altitude of just under 7,000 feet at it upper or southern ramparts, the hills immediately above the town reaching to 12,000 feet, and the marsh itself being 6,250 feet.

It is sufficient to remember that the great rivers of this part of Asia, which run to the Black Sea, the Persian Gulf, and the Caspian Sea, all rise within a few miles of this city, to realize at once that even in that bare and arctic country the city of Erzeroum, by reason of its great altitude and most exposed position, is a particularly uninviting spot, which no one who was familiar with that country would ever voluntarily select as his residence. The winds there blow with terrific force, and a piercing cold defies all furs, as it also does adequate description in conventional language. No tree or shrub of any sort can be found within over 50 miles, either to afford fuel when cut or shelter of any kind, and the words "dismal," "dreary," "desolate," and "damnable," suggest themselves irresistibly as a concise description of the whole locality. Our work in this delectable retreat was important, as on its result depended the estimate to be formed of the future intentions of the Turks. Though every facility was afforded to me in my inspections, I early understood and reported that no real progress towards disarmament was being made, or was, indeed, intended.

Mysterious Gorges

CAPTAIN L. V. S. BLACKER

From *On Secret Patrol in High Asia*, 1922

Captain Blacker and his band from the elite Indian Corps of Guides fought irregular warfare in some of the worst places on Earth. Blacker's book, *On Secret Patrol in High Asia* is a memoir of intense hardship endured for the paltriest of successes. Islamic Asia was being violently realigned by WWI and the Russian Revolution. For Blacker, a man seemingly adrift without combat and danger, opportunity beckoned.

After surviving the trenches on the Western Front, he was wounded and discharged from the Royal Flying Corps in 1918. Unfit for pilot duty, he rejoined his old unit, the Corps of Guides, in the Northwest Province in India. The Guides were one of the exotic formations of native troops and mostly British officers that protected the Raj. Blacker's troops were Pashtuns, a tribal people who are the majority ethnic group in Afghanistan and a sizable minority in Pakistan, which was part of British India in Blacker's day. With sometimes as few as sixteen Pashtuns—whom he greatly revered—Blacker went on implausible missions in China, Persia, Afghanistan, and the disintegrating Asian provinces of Russia.

In 1918, his enemies were German agents and anti-British Muslim forces. By 1919, he had stormed through chaotic regions where enemy Bolshevik forces clashed with friendly White Russians. Muslim warlords backed whoever suited them at the time. Blacker's vivid, fast-paced narrative churns factions, tribal and ethnic groups, regions, and physical geography into a compelling story set in the remotest of places.

Some of Blacker's narrative is tainted by offensive racist labels. If we edited all deplorable language from Western writings about Islam, our picture of it would become skewed. Blacker admired many Muslims. Perhaps, understandably, a battered professional killer like Blacker tended to judge people according to the fighting qualities they demonstrated. Nevertheless, at times his language is unsavory.

Absurdly outnumbered and far from friendly territory, Blacker's survival hinged on a detailed knowledge of the terrain and its people. Part mountaineer, cavalryman, cartographer, and explorer, he had no fewer skills than James Bond. The Pashtun guides he commanded were also a talented and lethal cast, including:

> . . . linguists of Russian, Persian, Turkish and Arabic . . . a bomber, a machine gunner, a signaller, graphic scouts, a "first aid" man, and a vegetarian . . . [E]very NCO carried . . . scars of the Western Front, and others had seen varied fighting in Africa, Persia, and the Afghan frontier.

Photographs of his troops show them humping through mountain ranges, such as Tien Shan and the Pamirs, over glaciers and deserts, all the while mapping, killing, and beating enemy after enemy. By the time his narrative ends in 1920, he fully expects another mission. From what Blacker tells of his men and their abilities, the other side was going to fare badly.

On Secret Patrol in High Asia is about warfare in a region of the Islamic world as incomprehensible to Westerners then as it is now. What will Blacker's successors, the Allied and American soldiers in Pakistan and Afghanistan, write after their tours are over? What will they have achieved?

—J. H.

In the morning there was an immense hullabaloo outside. The villagers were so excited at having seen two batches of strangers inside forty-eight hours that they all talked at once at the top of their voices. When we restored a little order out of the din, I found that the pursued were now less than forty-eight hours ahead. This was immense cause for congratulation; it meant that we had gained five or six days on them in the last eight. On the other hand, they seemed to have a straight run in down the Tiznaf Valley to Yarkand, and I was very anxious lest they should be lost to us in the maze of alleys of that hoary city. However, to our surprise, the villagers of Bulun insisted that they had not gone straight down the valley, but over the hills eastward to Ak Masjid.

This was startling, but the peasants' sheep and goats had smothered the trail, so there was nothing to do but to follow the villager who consented, for a price, to show us where the gang had gone.

He took us up a narrow side-valley of yellow sandstone, up which led a clear footpath which soon started to climb up pine-covered slopes.

The hills and scenery were remarkably like those on the Ambela (Umbeyla) Pass, which separates the Chamla Valley of Buner from the plain of Yusafzai.

The same firs and junipers propped up on the same sort of yellow rock let one imagine oneself beneath the Crag Picquet, on that famous pass, or on the slopes of Kutal Garh (the Place of Slaughter, so called from the heavy fighting there in 1864). It was on the climb up to here that we found that the men of Bulun had lied to us; it was clear from the absence of tracks that our gang had not passed this way.

This was desperately disheartening after our savage toil of the last few days, and the proposal was mooted of shooting the two liars then and there. A little reflection, however, showed that we should gain nothing by this, and might stand to lose. The liars, however, were green with fright by the time their fate had been decided: the cavalryman in whose charge they were was considerate enough to translate the proceedings for them into Turkish. It was too late to go back: it seemed better to push on to the Pokhpu Valley by what seemed from the map only a slightly longer route, trusting to be able to pick up the trail again by cutting across it from the eastward.

The pass that we were on seemed to be well over 15,000 feet, possibly 16,000, and we had climbed well over 4,000 feet up to it. The rough descent led down into a straight, narrow valley with steep, straightly sloping hillsides still dotted with pines. At about midday we came to a hut with as many fields around it as would total up in area to a suburban back-yard. There were no men here, only two women and three small children. They were of the little-known tribe of Pokhpu, who are supposed to be aborigines of pre-Uighur times, and to speak an unknown and lost language. They certainly were not Kirghiz, nor yet Sarikolis, and differed much in feature and bearing from the ordinary Altisharlik of the plains, of Uzbeg race. We had no time for scientific investigations, however, and asked them our questions in plain Turki, so that the solving of the mystery of the Pokhpu language did not receive any aid from us.

The tiny stream in the bottom of this valley was now dry, but a slightly brackish spring afforded a little water.

We made our midday halt here, and hastened on down along the steep, straight, pine-dotted slopes of the V-shaped valley. We soon came to the sizable Pokhpu flowing down a large valley at right angles to our course; that is to say, it ran north and south roughly. There was a tiny habitation here, and it seemed as though we should go downstream, to the northwards. However, no vestige of a trail could be found on the river-banks, and the sides of the valley lower down seemed to close in to form an impassable canyon, so we were, by fear of getting into a cul-de-sac, forced to follow the track across the main valley and up a steep, dry watercourse of yellow sandstone on the east side. It seemed from the map that the stream we had just crossed was the Pokhpu. The climb became more and more steep towards the summit, which was clear of snow and of a height that I judged to be over 15,000 feet; there was snow on the hillsides right and left of the crest.

The climb was exhausting and of over 3,000 feet. The pass seemed to be unknown and nameless, both to geographers and to the very few inhabitants of that region. The descent took us down a steep, winding valley in which grass-covered slopes of shale and loess replaced the yellow sandstone and straggling pines of the ascent. From the summit we had looked out over a dismal series of steep, almost vertical ranges unbroken by a single tree or any sign of life, and rendered the more uninviting by the deep shadows thrown by their dark wall-like spurs.

This descent, on the whole, is easy, and towards afternoon we came down by a side-valley on to a tributary of the Pokhpu River. This was about 10 yards wide by 2 feet deep here, flowing some five miles an hour in October. Again the question arose of following this stream to the north to meet the Shaksu, and again it was abandoned on account of the closing in of the vertical wall-like cliffs. Both banks of the river are desolate.

As soon as we had crossed we found ourselves again following a steep trail up to yet another pass, the third that day. However, there was nothing for it, so we toiled desperately upwards to the summit. This pass is the Sakrigu, which means Deaf (or Soundless), and when one stood on the crest in the awful solitude the name seemed well chosen.

The height of this appeared little short of 16,000 feet, and we were very weary by the time we had finished the climb and commenced the heartbreaking descent into another bare, deep gully of loess.

Soon the herbage disappeared from the slopes and the gully became a gorge. This became deeper and still deeper, and after a time we found ourselves toiling over huge smooth boulders where there was not the vestige of a track, along the narrow bottom of an abyss between walls of cliff that towered up to the very stars. The windings of this dreadful chasm seemed in the dark night to have no end, and we could well have believed that we were treading some path of Tartarus, or Inferno pictured by Dante. Weary to the very bone and crushed, as it seemed, by those titanic and ghostly cliffs, suddenly we came upon a giant excrescence of rock jutting out some hundreds of feet above, and, lit up by a single moonbeam, it showed like a perfectly formed ace of spades.

This we took for a good omen, and soon after, following a sudden turn, at midnight we came out upon the stony desolate valley of the Kalisthan

River (this signifies "the place where a robber was hanged"). The Sakrigu Pass seems from the map to be not more than 15,000 feet, but I should be inclined to estimate it at 1,000 feet more. The Kalisthan Valley is wide and level, and a sudden contrast to the chasm we had just come out of.

On the river-bank the map marks apparently as a village a place called Chiklik: nothing now exists, except a ruined stone hut. We could find neither grass, fuel, nor shelter, and though it was midnight and we had been on the move since eight that morning, decided to go on over what the man of Bulun called an easy pass, to Ak Masjid.

After the nightmare of this fourth pass we were numb and dizzy with fatigue, and it was in a sorry plight that at four in the morning we threw ourselves down in a deserted, but in a sandy, waterless valley called Jibrail (the Archangel Gabriel).

During that appalling single march I estimated that we climbed upwards, and toiled downwards, something like 30,000 feet, between seven of one morning and four o'clock of the next.

In the morning, just mounted, we surprised, coming round a corner, a very old Kirghiz with a small tail of armed men. He was a Haji by his green turban, and of some consequence, from his silver trappings, but we gave him no chance to ask us any questions. Instead we demanded to know what he was doing. He was rather taken aback by superior force, and we fell upon him with an insistent demand for his name, grade, and business; and as he did not like the look of the posse of savage-looking, hirsute, and ragged men that confronted him, he complied amicably. He explained that an important Chinese mandarin had sent him to meet a certain "guest." Now "guests" do not usually come into Chinese Turkistan via the Raskam, so here we smelt the Boche again. I informed him that I was the guest in question, and would be glad of his onward company. He had too much gumption to decline this polite invitation, and in due course we became great friends. The height of the hills lessened rapidly, the valleys opened out, and became level, thirsty, sandy stretches. In a hut in the valley of Ak Masjid a kindly old dame gave us all a drink of water out of a gourd that had come several miles on donkey-back. As we had drunk nothing for thirty-six hours, it was most welcome. Nightfall saw us in the big village of Kökyar, back again amongst human beings and reasonable food; we filled up on melons and corn-cobs, and replenished out many a corner that had been hungry for many days.

We were still behind in the chase; we had lost ground in spite of that last immense march, so we were off again at midnight, after five hours' sleep. We marched by compass north-eastwards over the low range of sandy hills that divides the Kökyar Valley from the Tiznaf. I hoped to cut back obliquely on to the trail we had lost; by the time the sun was well up, with good luck and careful steering we dropped down into the village of Arpat Bulung. Still no trace of the pursued. I told off one of the men to investigate a trail that led to the westwards. A reliable villager was sent into Karghalik town, three marches to the north, there to make certain unostentatious arrangements there, and the main body pushed on again. All that afternoon and night and next morning, fighting against sleep, we marched across the sand-dunes of the desert, dotted by a few infrequent hamlets, sprung from the attempts at irrigation made by some energetic mandarin towards Khan Langar, a big village of plains. Here we struck the trail again, halted for a very few hours' sleep, pushed on again at night, dodging about amongst the many channels and intricate irrigation ditches of the great Raskam River in its maturity.

It was in the evening of that strenuous day that, in a stone sheep-pen, lit by a blazing fire, I rode up to a tall, broad-shouldered shepherd. He seemed to understand little of our talk as we asked for news, and his aquiline features and fair hair, on which the firelight glinted, in contrast with those of the pudgy Yarkandis, remained long in my memory. It was not till long after that it struck me that he must have been one of that far-strayed Nordic tribe that science suspects still to lurk in the unmapped wilds of Pokhpu.

At midnight, in a labyrinth of water-cuts, I told the Haji to find an inhabitant who could show us the way without delay. Coming to a house, we hammered at the big locked courtyard gate with rifle-butts. Soon a harsh, croaking voice within told us to keep away. The Haji demanded admission in the name of the "Chinese Republic," whereupon the awful voice said that we might kill the inmates before they would allow our ingress. This seemed most suspicious; in a moment the gates were forced, and we rushed in to find a weird emptiness where we had expected a struggle with armed men. An N.C.O. ran up a ladder to the flat roof and there found a dreadful handful of lepers in the last stages of their mutilating disease. It was in silence that we marched on through the night. Posgam, a stage east of Yarkand, was reached in the early hours, and by the time the sun was well up the detachment had cantered the remaining dozen miles to the Chini Bagh, a walled garden, a few hundred yards outside the ramparts of ancient Yarkand. One of the men went in, disguised, to fetch out an acquaintance of 1914, who, as we hoped, was able to tell us that a party of suspicious strangers had come into the city some eighteen hours before, and was now probably in the Sarai of Badak-shan. Before the sleepy inhabitants of the narrow alleys of the depraved city knew what was happening, we had cantered inside the walls and thrown open the great iron-studded gates of the Badakshi Sarai.

Its hundred or so ruffianly Afghan denizens sprang to their feet, but their hands went up above their heads in a flash when they saw behind the bayonets gleaming in the morning sun the sixteen gaunt, wolfish faces of Pathan and Punjabi, Kanjuti, and Hazara.

A Faulty Guide on a Waterless Way

ROSITA FORBES

From *The Secret of the Sahara: Kufara*, 1921

It was 1920. A tall, beautiful Englishwoman and a handsome, Egyptian gentleman-scholar (who was also an Olympic Gold medallist fencer) were preparing to lead an expedition into the Sahara to reach the sacred Kufara oasis.

Photographs show a handsome pair, perfect for central casting. The ambitious Englishwoman was Rosita Forbes, age twenty-three. The dashing, Oxford-educated Egyptian was thirty-one-year-old Ahmed Mohamed Hassanein. They were attempting to cross the "Sea of Sand"—a region so hostile to outsiders that the last civilian expedition in 1879 had ended in disaster.

Kufara was deep in the interior desert of Libya, supposedly an Italian colony at the time. By 1920 Italian military forces had skirted Kufara, but had not entered it. Much of "Italian" Libya—the Kufara oasis included—belonged to local rulers. Kufara was inside a huge region controlled by an Islamic movement known as the Senussi Brotherhood.

Forbes's journey to Kufara proved to be a foolhardy one, with one debacle after another; everything from the selection of guides to provisioning went wrong. Forbes stepped outside the world familiar to Westerners and into the desert realm of the Senussi, where water runs short and guides prove unreliable. To reach Kufara, she was taking risks on many levels, and for uncertain rewards. At a minimum, Forbes and Hassanein deserve credit for surviving their own faulty leadership of the group.

That does not diminish the incredible tale of this journey, recounted in Forbes's *The Secret of the Sahara: Kufara*, a raw, no-bones-about-it narrative. This expedition ultimately made Forbes famous, even though she may have diluted how much she depended on Hassanein and how much the expedition was his initiative. She described him as her "co-explorer" and "friend," with whom she "laughed and fought . . . through all our difficulties together." Until a thorough study is done of Forbes's writing and travels, the Kufara story will remain incomplete.

During her career, Rosita Forbes traveled much more of the Islamic world than Freya Stark, Gertrude Bell, or Ella Sykes—all great pathfinders in their own right. Inexplicably, she is far less well known; no complete biography has ever been written. *Women of Discovery* by Milbry Polk and Mary Tiegreen (2001), a wonderful book about women explorers, includes brand-name adventurers like Stanhope, Montague, Digby, Stark, and Bell—but excludes Forbes.

Forbes's adventure writings are significant because she tried to reach a wide audience with books that combined adventure, history, politics, and culture in a fashion not unlike Robert Kaplan or Paul Theroux today. Forbes was always more journalist than explorer; part of what makes her so exceptional is that she was a *female* journalist entering unstable or hostile regions, which was a rare occurrence at the time.

—J. H.

N ew Year's Day dawned gloomily. We had two half-feeds for the camels and barely enough water for two days at less than a pint per day per person. We were, however, a little cheered up when, as we were loading the camels, Abdullah pointed out a faint blur to the east and said it was Mazeel, some hillocks he had hoped to see the previous day. On clear mornings, about an hour after dawn, when the desert is very flat, a mirage of the country about a day's journey distant appears on the horizon. For a few minutes one sees a picture of what is some 50 kilometres farther on. The Arabs call it "the country turning upside down." On January 1, the seventh day of our march, we saw this mirage for the first time—brushwood and hillocks quite clearly to the south, yet our guide turned deliberately west of it. My camel was ill after his unaccustomed date-feeding. Hassanein was in great pain from his blistered feet. A permanent north wind, warring for a week with a burning sun, had implanted rheumatism in my right shoulder. The firewood had given out, and there had been a sharp quarrel between the blacks and the Beduins on this account, each accusing the other of using more than their share.

Abdullah kept on his south-westerly course for a few hours, and then began to wander slightly. The blacks wanted to beat him. Even Mohammed was impatient with him. We steered almost due south. Hassanein had to ride all day and Mohammed's eyes were bloodshot with the pain of his feet, yet he struggled on. That night there were no fires in the camp, and I fully expected Abdullah would be murdered. However, when I woke before the dawn on January 2, I heard him laughing, so hoped he had recovered his head. We dared not start till "the country had turned upside down" and revealed to us what lay in front, so we occupied ourselves in finding our exact position. According to our map we were now within the borders of Taiserbo! This raised the problem of whether it were one consecutive oasis or whether it were possible to go between two groups of palms without seeing either!

At 8 A.M. the mirage showed us one sharp dune very much to the west. I wanted to go straight there, hoping by sunset to be able to climb it and have a good view of what lay beyond, but both Abdullah and Moraja insisted that no such dune lay anywhere near Taiserbo. "If we go as much west as that we go straight to Hell," said the guide decisively. With the ever-present danger of going beyond Taiserbo into the uninhabited western desert it was impossible to argue. With only one day's water and no fodder we dared not risk everything so boldly, but I there and then made up my mind that Taiserbo was smaller and much farther west than is generally supposed. I believe if we had gone to that dune we might have reached it. At that moment a thick, icy mist came down and blotted out everything, so I decided to go south for five hours, in which case, according to Jalo information and our map, we should have gone right through Taiserbo and possibly be able to recognize some landmarks near Buseima.

It was a terrible walk. Everyone knew that, humanly speaking, they were going to die of thirst within a day or two. Nearly everyone had blistered feet, and no one had had enough to eat, yet everyone laughed. "It is evidently the will of Allah that we die," said Farraj politely, "but no one will die before Sidi Abdullah." I doubt if the guide heard. He trailed along with a blank, dispirited stare, first edging west, then east. Mohammed was tottering on swollen feet. "I think that I would rather die beside my luggage," he said placidly. "Doubtless Abdullah and Yusuf would like to wander about to the end, but I do not know this country, Hamdulillah it will be quick!" Thereafter everyone spoke of death, and I was amazed at the way they calmly accepted its advent. The only thing that stimulated them was the demise of the guide. "By Allah, Sidi Abdullah shall go first and show us the way!" said the toothless one. "When I am certain of death I shall shoot him," said Shakri firmly. "But he called you a fool yesterday," reminded Farraj. This worried Shakri for a moment. Then he cheered up. "I will call him a fool first, and then I will shoot him," he said. Amidst this cheerful conversation the mist suddenly lifted and revealed nothing but the same flat, pale sand devoid of faintest shadow of grass or brushwood to give hope of an oasis.

It is amazing how desperation affects one. That morning Hassanein could not put his foot on the ground, but when he realized that his end was imminent he walked for eight hours without feeling pain. Mohammed also forgot his ills and I found myself wondering how soon I should awake from this realistic nightmare. When our southern course produced nothing but fanciful blue lakes and pools—for a burning sun now added to our woes—we took council and, ignoring Abdullah, decided to march east-south-east till water and camels gave out. There were several chances of salvation on this new bearing, we thought, for we might hit the most easterly end of Taiserbo if it were anywhere near its mapped position, or we might find ourselves in the recognizable country south of Zieghen or among the dunes near Buseima. We supposed these places to be too far away to reach with the camels, but if we could get anywhere near we could send a messenger for help and lie down to await his return. We knew there was a little water in the tins of vegetables, and hoped that if we kept very still this would keep us all alive for an extra day.

It was a terrible afternoon of mirage. I do not know whether weariness had affected our eyes, but on every side we saw hills, dunes, brushwood, and always they were the same dark patches of gravel. "It is a simple route to Taiserbo," had said the kaimakaan at Jalo, "but one mistake means destruction!" Had we really made the one mistake? Curiously enough, I felt no anger against Abdullah, even when he suddenly acknowledged he had not been to Taiserbo for twenty years. In fact, an odd fatalism had absorbed us all. The Beduins began discussing other disasters on these terrible southern routes.

One man had died within fifteen yards of the water he had failed to find in time. Another, whose water had gone bad on the Kufara route, had been found dead beside his camels, one of which he had killed for its blood. The blacks took an impersonal interest in these gruesome tales while they walked on with stolid calm. I gave them our last bag of dates, but warned them it would probably make them very thirsty. They replied with extreme cheerfulness that they did not want to drink in the least. They were really splendid that afternoon. They sang and laughed and cheered each other on. Little Abdul Rahim stalked on ahead with a grim smile, his rifle over his shoulder, his weakness forgotten. The only really dispirited member of the party was Abdullah, who trailed along at the heels of the caravan with downcast head. Once, when a low rise appeared to the south, he walked briskly towards it in hopes of a further view, but returned an hour later more gloomy than ever. The hot midday hours dragged along intolerably slowly. I did not feel very thirsty myself, but we had all drunk so little lately that our skins had become extraordinarily dry and parched. Our lips and gums were cracked and sore. The camels had had only a half-ration of dates the previous day and nothing that morning, so they were ravenous. They tried to eat the stuffing of the baggage saddles, and ran to every dark patch of stones in search of grass.

At 3 P.M. some faint dunes appeared on the south-east horizon. We expected Abdullah to recognize them, but his demoralization must have been complete, for he showed no interest in them. Yusuf and Moraja began speculating as to whether they could be the "hatia" which ran between Zieghen and Taiserbo. If so, there might be vegetation on the farther side and the mystery of our position be solved. Nearly everyone ran on ahead, and only Abdul Hafiz and Omar were left to drive the camels, who were stumbling badly. It was their ninth day without water, but this mattered less than the scarcity of food. For an exhausting hour everyone struggled along at their best pace, limping, wavering, with parched mouths and bloodshot eyes, before which danced the tantalizing sheets of water and cool, dark mirage hills. Suddenly Yusuf, who was on ahead, flung himself on his face and embraced the earth, afterwards executing a wild, bareheaded dance, during which he waved his long kufiya on the end of his stick. We rushed to join him and found him lovingly stroking a little mound covered with dry, brittle sticks. "It is brushwood-hattab," he said simply. "Inshallah! There is more beyond." Two other mounds appeared shortly with a little coarse, green shrub, over which the camels fought and struggled till the last scrap had disappeared. By this time sunset was near and we had to force our unsteady, aching limbs into a run to reach those elusive dunes in time to catch the clear, far view devoid of mirage that always comes at sunset. It was a pathetic race of the halt and the lame in which Hassanein and I were out-distanced. We saw the others clamber up the dune—we saw them stand gazing eastwards—and then we saw them sink motionless in silent groups. I think at that moment I felt our death warrant was sealed. I turned hopelessly to my plucky companion. "It is no good. They would have danced if it had been the 'hatia.'" "Yes, they would have made a noise," he said dully.

We crawled up to the top of the ridge, a series of wavy, curling dunes running north-west to south-east, expecting to see the same level, monotonous country that lay behind us. Instead, we were amazed to look down over a few lower dunes to an entirely changed tract. On every side were uneven mounds and hillocks covered with decayed scrub, leafless and brown, but a few hundred yards in front was a cluster of huge green bushes. We could not understand the apathy of the soldiers, who were dejectedly rolling pebbles down the slope. "Surely there is water there," I exclaimed impatiently. "Wallahi!

But that Abdullah does not know!" said Farraj. "He says only that it is not the Zeighen country." As I ran down the dune the camels literally rushed past me to the patch of green. But they did not eat. Apparently the great feathery bushes were not fodder, and the only other things among the mounds were a couple of skeletons to which the hooves and chest pads still clung. "This place is El Atash—the thirst," said Abdullah suddenly. "There is an old well here, but its water will kill you! It is salt and bad."

At the time we were obliged to rely on his statement, but since then I have discovered that he was entirely mistaken. The water at El Atash is brackish, but quite wholesome and the well can be dug out at any time. It is only filled up with sand because travellers never come there unless they have lost their way and are driven to the disused well by thirst—El Atash! There was plenty of brushwood, so we built enormous fires to cheer ourselves up, but we could cook nothing without water. The blacks ate macaroni dry and the Arabs tried flour, though we offered them our tinned meats. The soldiers had a cupful of water each, but the Beduins had none, so we had to share our last hoarded bottle with them. We dare not eat our meat ration because of the salt, so we sucked malted milk tablets and eagerly drank the water from some tinned carrots which were cool and damp. Then we tore up the baggage saddles to give the straw stuffing to the camels, for we thought we could manage one more day's march by riding.

The morning of January 3 was misty. Ripples of white fog blurred the landscape, while we silently loaded the camels, using blankets, tents, anything soft as pads to support the panniered luggage. We ate a tin of spinach because it was wet, but it was a hollow-eyed procession that started due east along the "hatia" in the hope of hitting one of the wells in the neighbourhood of Zieghen. Abdullah had held out many hopes the night before, but now all he would say was "Inshallah!" We left El Atash at 7.30 and toiled laboriously round the small mounds which looked so oddly like graves. Three green ones gave the camels a little respite, but there was no sign of the "gherds" (dunes) that generally mark the presence of water. The whole retinue spread out in a straggling line across the horizon, marching east, and every faint rise was passionately scanned and discussed. At last Mohammed said, "If you cut my throat now you will not find one drop of blood," referring to the Arab idea that when a man is in fear of death all the blood in his body rushes to his head. "It is time that Sidi Abdullah dies," said Farraj firmly, his finger on the trigger, and then, of course, the unexpected, the impossible, happened, and a faint dark blur appeared on the horizon.

I have no recollection at all of the next two hours. Whether I walked or rode or ran I do not know. What happened to the others I have no idea. My whole being was concentrated on those green mounds, which continually vanished and reappeared until at last they consolidated at 2.30 P.M. into a few clustered palms and some "gherds" covered with stubble. I remember tottering down a hollow and seeing some nude black figures madly scooping up sand, and then a silent little group crouched pitifully on the edge of the freshly-dug pit that meant life or death. The water came very slowly, for they had chosen a bad place in their hurry, but it came. Oozing through damp sand, the first muddy pool brought all the primitive emotions to our hearts — joy, relief, gratitude, too deep for words! An hour or two later life had become normal again and the deepening water brought us only the idea of a hearty meal and a bath in the biggest receptacle in the canteen.

I wonder how many readers will understand the tale of those three days, because being lost in Europe means merely an appeal to a map or a passer-by, but in Libya there is often no well for several hundred miles, and, per-chance, two caravans a year or none at all! A few, just a very few, will comprehend, quiet men with tired, keen eyes — an Italian after whom a Tripolitanian "gebel" is named, half a dozen Frenchmen scattered over the great white desert south of Insalah, any Australian who has been bushed without water and certainly one or two Englishmen in strange, sunburned corners of our ruthless Empire!

We camped near the largest clump of palms within sight of the blessed well, and all afternoon I lay on my camp bed with my "zemzimaya" beside me, drinking every few minutes and when I could not drink any more I would shake it now and then to hear the delicious clutter of the water inside.

In spite of all this joy we were not really out of wood yet, for the "hatia" contained practically no forage. The camels were all feeble after their long journey and the fast at the end of it. They had to be driven here and there, from small bush to smaller tuft. It was a laborious business for our tired men and I had to leave my water-bottle once or twice to see how matters were progressing. Abdullah and Abdul Hafiz were very anxious that night, for the camels would not drink properly, so we tore up some straw mats, soaked them, and gave them to the beasts. I wanted to try them with rice, but Abdul Hafiz said they would die if they ate it.

Our guide had recovered some of his calm when he realized that we were camping at El Atash in the Zieghen district, at least a day and a half to two days' journey east of the elusive Taiserbo. I was delighted when I understood this, for fate was obviously giving me a chance of accomplishing my old desire for travelling to Buseima by the uncharted route which had tempted me at Jalo.

I explained this to the retinue, and was met with blank dismay. They wanted to go to Zieghen and then safely by the caravan route to Kufara. They assured me that Buseima was most dangerous, that a particularly savage portion of the Zouia tribe dwelt there and attacked every strange caravan at sight. I gathered that while Kufara is a large and imposing group of oases round the belad of the holy qubba, a big desert market and the centre of the whole Sahara trade, besides being the headquarters of the Senussi Government and the sacred headquarters of its religion, Buseima, although very sparsely inhabited, is also to a minor extent a "business centre," for caravans from Wadai and Jalo visit it. There is no zawia there and no Government official. The Zouias fiercely assert their independence and refuse to admit the complete authority of the Sayeds in order to avoid paying taxes in money, although they pay great respect to the Senussi family and to their wishes. They have never seen a soldier within their boundaries, and on no account allow a stranger of any race or sect to enter their country.

"If they do not kill us in the oasis," said Yusuf dolefully, "they will lie in wait for us outside among the dunes and murder us on our way to Kufara." I said that I thought we could massacre a few Zouias first, but even Mo-hammed was frightened. "It is a bad country," he remarked. "Why did not Allah allow us to reach Taiserbo in safety? There is a zawia there and I have heard of the sheikh, Sidi Mohammed. His brother was with me at the Jaghabub zawia."

I asked about the tribes in Taiserbo and was told that it was the second largest oasis, but unimportant and sparsely inhabited, that many of the date-trees belonged to the people in Buseima, that there were a few Tebus and some Zouias, of whom the larger part were Senussi. "There are different par-ties there," said Moraja, "but they are all good people — nahs taibeen. Beyond Taiserbo is a country of fighting. No stranger may go there. There is much danger. If we escape the Buseima people we shall fall into the hands of the Tebus of Ribiana or of wandering Tuareg bands."

In spite of these gloomy prognostications I pointed out that the camels cer-tainly could not go five days to Kufara without food and that I had no intention whatsoever of trusting Abdullah's ideas as to the location of Taiserbo. Instead I made the guide and Moraja each draw his idea of the famous gebel at Buseima. They both outlined in the sand a long, low, square-topped ridge. "Very well," said I firmly. "At sunset we will climb to the top of the largest gherd here and see if we cannot locate that mountain!" Having once and for all put our deco-rative but useless map out of our heads, we were able to reason out that Tais-erbo lay to the west, ran north-east and south-west and could not be more than 25 to 40 kilometres in length, while I pinned my faith to due south for Buseima.

The desert had nearly killed us in her most ruthless mood, but when we mounted the sandy gherd and saw the red splendour fade into cold mauve and grey of the sand, while the evening star blazed as if it were a drop of liq-uid flame in a sapphire cup, we forgave her, especially as due south, just ex-actly where "instinct" had suggested to us, a faint black ridge rose, low and square, over the horizon. I took some bearings for fear of mirage and ordered an early start next morning in spite of wild protestations and appeals.

As a matter of fact everyone was so tired that we did not get off till 7.30. The camels groaned plaintively and continuously, refusing to rise from their knees. I had insisted on filling girbas enough for a four days' march, though Abdullah said it was only two, and, with no saddles it was difficult to balance the packs on rolled blankets and canvas. All that day was a weary succession of changing loads. When one camel sank wearily down and refused to move, we dragged off his load and placed it on another. No one rode, however blistered were his feet. Some of the blacks had raw toe joints, but we dared not risk the camels further. After about three hours we left the little mounds and sparse sticks of the "hatia" and the unbroken sands lay in great flat waves before us. We stopped at the last moment to pick the brittle wood for our evening fires, and then marched on steadily till 6 P.M.

The "gara" of Buseima appeared suddenly at 12.30. It looked like a solid, black ridge on the horizon, but we knew it was more than a day's journey away. The camels wandered and lagged and stumbled. I doubt if we did more than 2 miles an hour. In the afternoon the sand waves developed into hard dunes, low and round-backed. We could no longer make straight for the black mark in the distance, but had to swerve eastward to avoid the higher dunes. About four I thought the camels could not go another step. Several of them lay down at the same time, but somehow we got them to their feet again, chiefly by dint of song! The reiterated refrains of the Sudanese had a great effect on the weary beasts, but never had the barraking cry "Adaryayan!" "We have arrived at the house, oh sick ones!" sounded more welcome. It was the cool, pale hour that precedes night when we encamped in a great hollow among white dunes. The stars were triumphing over the last glowing rays of the sunset and the mysterious mountain that had fired my imagination for so long lay, violet-hued and sombre, to the south.

Next morning, January 5, we again started at 7.30 and plunged immediately into a maze of dunes, great, curved, hard-backed ones, with a few soft patches in the hollows into which the camels sank, protesting. They walked rather better than the previous day in spite of a continual series of ascents and descents. Perhaps it was the sight of the strange, sinister ridge in front, coalblack against the surrounding white sand. Perhaps it was the very cold south wind which blistered our faces as we moved into it. At any rate, at 12.30 we arrived at the mysterious gebel which had first appeared as a solid even ridge with a flat top, had then added to itself a sort of squarish, sugar-loaf hill at each end and now turned out not to be a ridge at all but a chain of cliffs, some square, some roundish, but all of sombre dull black stone with faint reddish patches. To my eyes, uninitiated into the by-ways of geology, it looked like a vast volcanic eruption, for passing east of the main body of the hills, we entered a veritable inferno of desolation. Right in the middle of the white, curly sand dunes lay a tract of about 8 kilometres of scattered black stones. Their brittle sheets of ebony matter stood up in lines—it looked as if all the old slates in the world had been flung in careless piles in this dreary region. Experts later informed me that the black stone was Nubian sandstone impregnated with iron and manganese, nothing volcanic at all. The other stones were sandstones of lighter colour, fossilized wood, and flints.

For two hours we stumbled and clattered over this blistered, black waste, picking up specimens of as many kinds of stone as possible and then, as we clambered up a rough bank between two of the sombre sheer-cut hills, the long line of Buseima palms spread before us with the thin silver strip of lake—real water, no mirage—that had seemed to be but a fable of Jedabia imagination! Till we reached the stony track by the gara we had marched in very businesslike formation—three soldiers ahead, the camels in the middle, and scouts flung out on the highest dunes, while everyone had rifle or revolver ready. Abdullah, himself a Zouia, had mocked the blacks with "Look out, you soldiers, for now you are coming to the land where men fight!" and therefore every slave was athirst for battle and revenge!

The Siege of the Qeshlah

ZETTON BUCHANAN

From *In the Hands of the Arabs*, 1921

Pistol in hand, Zetton Buchanan and her husband made a last stand against Iraqi tribesmen. Her husband was killed. She was captured and imprisoned in a harem.

In the Hands of the Arabs is Zetton's heartrending account of her ordeal as a prisoner. She accused the British government of not protecting people like her family, who were in Iraq to rebuild the country after WWI. They were part of T. E. Lawrence's legacy. After "liberating" the Arabs, Britain was granted the former provinces of the Ottoman Empire as League of Nations mandates. Britain hoped to develop political and economic institutions in these new countries to make them viable states. Guiding—and sometimes bullying—them to abide within the British sphere of influence was also a priority. Mandates were not colonies or protectorates, but temporary occupations. *Nation building* might be a comparable term.

Buchanan's story should resonate with us because it provides testimony about what happens when policies like the current U.S. intervention in Iraq go wrong. Her chief accusations against the British government were that it lied about the extent of anti-British sentiment, and that it was underprepared for the scale of resistance. She also regarded it as a pity that so much of what her husband had accomplished might be lost.

Buchanan had left her baby son in Scotland when she joined her husband in Shahraban, Iraq, in 1920. Their post was northeast of Baghdad, near the Iraq-Iran border. Captain "Billy" Buchanan supervised the Shahraban Canal, which used the Diyala River to irrigate local Arab farms. Currently, American troops garrison Shahraban.

The couple lived in a two-story house across from an Arab café and brothel. Unveiled prostitutes cavorted freely with coffee drinkers. Buchanan loved the other view from the house, overlooking the mountains across the border in Iran. Her household included "Cook," a houseboy, and an Armenian maid. The Armenian was from the nearby Ba'qubah, a camp for refugees from the disintegrating Ottoman Empire.

Life at Shahraban suited Buchanan. Billy went to great lengths to comfortably furnish the house in native style, each room plush with divans, cushions, and layered carpets. She approved, except when it came to the dining room, which had to maintain the more formal British style required for entertaining. In time she had a pet gazelle called Gazooka, a dog called Scut, and a horse. She socialized with locals, even participating in a kind of baby shower.

Besides her husband, who was the official in charge of irrigation, there were four other soldiers and a civilian official. These unmarried men lived at the Qeshlah, a two-story building with a central courtyard, gardens, and a tennis court. Pictures of it suggest a fort wrapped in arcaded verandas. From time to time, Billy and Zetton went to a place they called "Table Mountain" where they rode, hiked, and lived a little rough while Billy inspected the canal works.

In August of 1920, central and southern Iraq exploded in an insurrection. Tribesmen attacked British outposts and their allied militia. British retaliation was massive, and in a few months the revolt was suppressed.

Buchanan's ordeal began when rumors reached Shahraban of raids by tribesmen on Table Mountain. She noted how the town braced itself; shops closed up, and the local Arab postmaster asked for a gun to defend himself. For two nights, Zetton and Billy joined the four other British soldiers and the civilian, Baines, at the Qeshlah. On the third night, while the British brought food and other supplies from their homes, the attack started. "As we got to the Qeshlah, bullets were whistling overhead," she wrote.

Within hours, the Qeshlah was surrounded by hundreds of townsmen and tribesmen firing rifles. The Arab militiamen were wounded or killed, or they deserted. Billy came into their room and asked his wife to get their pistols from under the beds. Side by side, they made a stand.

Billy was killed before her eyes, and Buchanan was held captive for more than a month in a local harem before a British force saved her. She departed Iraq for Britain alone in October 1920.

—J. H.

B efore I begin the story of the siege, I may as well give a list of the little garrison which went through it. There were Captain Bradfield, Commandant of the Levies; Captain Wrigley, Assistant Political Officer of Shahraban; my husband, Assistant Irrigation Officer of Shahraban; Sergeant-Major Newton; Sergeant-Inspector Nisbett; Mr. Baines (though I was not at first aware of his presence at the Qeshlah); myself; our Armenian boy Gosdan, and Cook; some Baboos of the political staffs; and fifty Arab levies.

This was the force—including non-combatants—on which it fell to defend the Qeshlah against the attack of the tribesmen. With regard to the latter's numbers, we had only seen some thirty in the street, but when I asked Captain Wrigley how many they were who were attacking us, he estimated them at between five and eight hundred. The odds, therefore, were not quite so overwhelmingly against us as the first reports of the affair made out. But, on the other hand, the native levies were new and untried—and, as will appear, their conduct was *not* what these same reports represented it to be.

We had with us at the Qeshlah a few Arab prisoners who had been sentenced for various offences. They were locked in a room at the back of the building, with a guard over them.

As soon as we had arrived safely at the Qeshlah, the gates were shut and bolted. I have mentioned that Captain Wrigley had gone over that morning to help to barricade them. There were only two doors to the building, gates at the front, and one in the stable-yard at the back. The gates in front were of iron bars. That at the back was of wood, and only had one wooden bolt upon it. Against it the Ford car had been pushed close up, as an extra security; but, apart from the bolts, this was all the barricading which it was possible to do.

Nevertheless, I somehow felt safe now that we had reached the Qeshlah, and thought it was all over and finished, and that we had won a great victory.

I was so sure that if my husband was with me nothing could happen. Perhaps it was the reaction after that terrible journey through the street and the open road. When we got in, Billy took me to a little room which Captain Wrigley used as his office, and made me sit down upon a mattress on the floor. I could hear the bullets buzzing round outside. The heat was terrific.

I sat here until Billy came back a little later and took me to a large barn-like room at the back of the building, facing the yard where the horses were tethered, the windows of which had thin iron bars to them. This had been used by the sergeants as their living-room; its furniture comprised two camp-beds, a table, and a coffee-bench. There was one wooden door in the middle wall of the room. Bullets were occasionally coming in through the windows, so Billy put down a mattress on the floor for me. I lay down, suddenly feeling very tired. Billy and the two captains came in from time to time to reassure me and tell me not to be afraid—which at that time I was not.

At about 2.30—I could keep count of the time, for I had my wrist-watch on me—Captain Wrigley came in, saying, 'My billet's gone West!'

'How do you know?' I asked.

'I've been watching the townspeople carrying my stuff away.'

Not long after, the three came in together and sat down to talk matters over. Things were not going well. The levies had been placed mostly in the front of the building, where they could shoot from behind the pillars of the verandah and from the low wall, and some on the roof. But half an hour ago two of them had deserted, and others had been running off in twos and threes since. Moreover, they could not be stopped from firing all the time and without taking aim. This was most important, as each levy was equipped with only 200 rounds of ammunition, while a reserve supply of 4000 rounds was taken, thus making 280 rounds for each levy, and it was essential that every shot should be made to tell. The levies, in fact, were quite out of hand, and would not obey their orders.

On the other hand, the shooting of the tribesmen at times was very good. Captain Bradfield had a star shot clean off his shoulder. Sergeant Nisbett's topee was knocked off by a bullet, and Mr. Baines's topee was pierced right through the crown.

Captain Bradfield was terribly worried about the deserters and about the growing shortage of ammunition. 'If only we had a couple of machine-guns!' he said. 'And I've asked for more ammunition, but it never arrived!'

About three o'clock our hopes were raised, only to be cruelly disappointed. An aeroplane was sighted, and the three officers came in for sheets to spread on the roof as distress-signals. I heard the machine coming, and went out into the yard to see it. It came straight over the Qeshlah, at a height of about 500 feet. It then turned and circled over our little fortress twice. The sheets were now on the roof, and the men were up there waving hard. Whoever were in the plane must have seen in what a plight we were, how few were the garrison and how many the tribesmen.

The plane turned away and went off. The men came down from the roof, however, full of hope. The signals had been seen, and the plane would come back, bringing Lewis guns and ammunition. If we could only hold out till they came!

The plane never returned. No Lewis guns or ammunition came to save us. What was the explanation? I have never been able to make out. Afterwards when I got to Baghdad I tried to find out; but all the answer I got was that I was too ill and must not worry about these things.

Now followed a lull in the firing. We thought that this was probably because the tribesmen had collected in the bazaar, out of sight of the Qeshlah, and were discussing the situation and the best method of attack.

Then the men came in and said that a strange Arab had somehow managed to get into the Qeshlah. Not knowing his face, Captain Bradfield had taken him for a spy and put him under arrest. It did not seem to me at the time that the tribesmen had any need of a spy, as they were well aware what our strength was. Tribesmen are not in the habit of tackling anything stronger than themselves. Still, the man may have been a spy. Anyhow, later he escaped, and with him went his guards.

About 3.45 the firing was renewed heavily from all quarters, especially from the neighbourhood of the gardens by the tennis-court, which was quite close to the Qeshlah.

So far, since my arrival here I had felt quite brave. But now something occurred to destroy my courage. I heard Sergeant Newton's voice on the roof calling out for a rope. The body of one of the levies was lying at his feet, and when the rope was thrown up to him he tied it round the body and let it down the wall into the yard. Try as I would, I could not help watching what was going on. As the body slid down, a trail of blood was left all down the wall. It was a sickening sight and thoroughly unnerved me. I think it was only at this moment that I fully realised that the tribesmen were out to kill all of us as soon as they got their chance.

At about 4.15 Cook brought in tea, and Billy and the two captains came in. They were still quite calm, but had come to a decision to send an urgent message to Baqubah—not knowing, of course, that the day before Baqubah had been captured by the Arabs, with no British casualties.

As far as I can remember, the message ran something like this:

'Qeshlah heavily surrounded. Ammunition, water running short. If no help sent, propose getting away on horse 3 A.M. to Deltawah.'

The water question was a serious one, and the men were very troubled over it. There was only one well at the Qeshlah, and at this time of year it was not very full. As far as provisions were concerned, we had an abundant supply. But if the defence was to continue, water would be as great an anxiety as ammunition. There were the horses to water in addition to ourselves, it must be remembered.

The message was sent off immediately by an Arab on horseback; and now we thought for certain that help would come to us in the shape of either aeroplanes or light armoured cars.

Then we discussed our plan of escape. It was arranged that at 3 A.M., if help had not arrived, we should leave with the remaining levies, and if necessary fight our way out through the tribesmen to Deltawah. This was indeed a forlorn hope. It seemed to me utterly desparate. But what was the alternative—to be reduced to surrender by lack of water and ammunition and end with a horrible death?

The three now went back to their posts and relieved the sergeants, who came in for tea. With Newton and Nisbett came Mr. Baines, commonly known as 'Sergeant Baines,' but as a matter of fact Assistant Grass Farm Manager of Shahraban. He lived in a house near out billet, but I did not happen to have seen him before this moment.

They did not stay long over their tea. As they left, I said to Sergeant Newton, who had been walking about on the roof, regardless of shots, as though the siege were an everyday occurrence: 'Sergeant Newton, do take care. You are asking for trouble on that roof. Do at least bend down as you cross, or I know you'll get hurt.'

He laughed. 'I've got a charmed life,' he answered. 'Don't worry, I'm all right!'

He was always like this—brave, cheerful, and full of life, seeming to enjoy everything that came.

'But you have forgotten that to-day is Friday and the 13th,' I cried; for that thought had been running in my head.

They went out, and I lay down on the floor again. The firing was growing much stronger, and I felt thoroughly panic-stricken.

It was at this point Captain Bradfield thought it was advisable to make an attempt at terms. We could at least test the disposition of the enemy.

We did not take long to find out. Two of our levies were sent through the gates and along the road on the way to the bazaar, which the tribesmen had made their headquarters. With them they carried a piece of white material tied to a stick. There could be no doubt that we were ready to discuss matters with the tribesmen.

The two men were shot down.

After this Captain Wrigley burnt all the papers and paper money, locked up the chest of rupees, and threw the key down the well.

The firing still increased, and now the noise was terrific.

It was about a quarter to six when Billy came into the room and said: 'Zett, you must be very brave. The tribesmen are scaling the walls. The gates are down. We must put up as good a fight as we can.'

He turned to go.

'Oh! don't leave me alone,' I cried.

'I must go now, but I shall come back again.'

He went out. I took my suit-case, which had my jewellery and money in it, and I struggled to get the locks undone. I was in such a state that I fumbled in vain. One came undone, but the other resisted all my efforts. I had thought of taking the best pieces of jewellery out and putting them on, in the hopes of getting them away. It was the one small mercy Providence showed me in not letting me carry out my intention. I should probably have lost my hands for the sake of my rings.

Giving up my attempt on the suit-case, I pulled my mattress over into the corner of the room farthest from the door, and put two revolvers—Billy's Colt and a little Browning—just underneath it, where they could be easily got at when they were wanted. We might indeed want them—very soon—to end it all.

The sound of firing was not continual, and mingled with it were the shouting of men and stamping of horses, a deafening noise. Then Billy, Bradfield, and Wrigley all came hurriedly into the room together.

I looked at them.

'Where are your rifles?' I screamed.

Billy said one word: 'Gone!'

Very briefly they told me how, after they had fired their last shots, they had been surrounded and their arms snatched away. The levies had practically all deserted and given up their weapons without a struggle, only a few standing firm to the end. The few prisoners whom we had at the Qeshlah had been set free by the tribesmen. Nisbett had been shot at the gate. Newton was on the roof— they did not know that he had been killed. They had fought their way into the room, unarmed as they were, to gain a breathing-space for the final struggle.

What struck me then at the moment, as it does now with much greater force when I am able to think over the tragedy quietly, was the utmost calm and bravery that all the three men with me showed in this awful hour. It was this splendid behaviour if theirs which had led me to believe, up to the time when they told me of the loss of their rifles, that things were not looking quite so black.

But now what could I think? The end could not be far off.

A pathetic object, to add to our misery, was Captain Wrigley's black dog, Girlie, which followed her master about to the end. The last I saw of her was in a terrible state, all covered with mud and blood, as she wandered into the room looking for him.

Now that we were all together, and with us the Armenian boy and Cook, we took up our position in the corner of the room farthest from the door, in two lines of three each. I was nearest the angle of the room, next me Cook, and then Gosdan. In front of me stood Billy, then Bradfield, and the Wrigley.

We waited for what seemed like a minute, with an appalling din going on outside. Then Bradfield turned to Billy and said: 'I must try to stop this.'

He went out of the room, and we could hear his voice shouting in Arabic. Then came two distinct shots.

'Bradfield, Bradfield,' I screamed, 'come back!'

But there was no answer.

'I'll go out and see,' said Wrigley a moment later.

He went straight out.

I never saw either of them again alive.

The moment he had gone, a horde of tribesmen suddenly burst into the room. Seen at close quarters, they were short-built men, dirty, and repulsive looking. Their *abbas* were tucked in at the belt to keep them out of the way. They were armed with curved knives, daggers, and rifles. The noise of shouting increased in volume.

They were firing aimlessly. The flashes from the rifles showed up in the growing dusk. The heat of the room was terrific.

Billy turned to me and said, 'Come on, Zett, we must finish it. Got my revolver?'

I had taken the revolvers from where I had put them, under the mattress. I handed Billy the Colt and kept the Browning myself. He told me what I already knew, that all the ammunition there was for the Colt was five rounds. There was plenty for the Browning; but it was little more than a toy.

'Don't fire until I tell you,' said Billy.

They were now right on us, surging around us. Some were busy looting, dragging out whatever they could lay hands upon, shouting, yelling, and quarrelling among themselves. The whites of their eyes gleamed horribly.

Then one Arab got sideways, and I felt him catch hold of me. He tried to pull me out of the corner. Then I screamed.

My husband fired—the Arab fell.

Then we put up a fight on our own in the failing light.

I was out in the road, with a stinging pain in my side. In a dazed way I noticed a hole in the garden wall, through which I jumped, and ran on wildly across the garden until I came to a ditch. Then I lay down and hid, every nerve in my body throbbing.

I could not get my breath. My tongue was swollen, and my throat sore and dry from my continual screaming and the dust. I felt a mass of pain from head to foot.

The sound of firing was still going on. Presently I heard steps. Looking just over the edge of the ditch, I saw men coming towards me, hunting as they went in likely hiding-places; the first man was carrying a rifle. This was really the end, I thought. I stood up and called to them, trying to tell them where to shoot, and pointing frantically to my head and heart.

'Yawash, yawash!' (Gently, gently!) they said. So I knew that they were not going to kill me straight away, and at that moment I longed for death, my misery was so great.

They came up and took me by the arms and pulled me along. I tried in vain to pull back. I knew that Billy was lying dead, and I wanted them to fetch him too. They dragged me on. There were five of them in all, two of them awful-looking creatures in rags caked in dirt, the other three not quite so wild in appearance, but with most repulsive faces. They were obviously townspeople—had they been tribesmen they would have killed me then.

They brought me to a wall, which led to the roof of a *khan*, and this they made me climb with them. Here I had to sit down. Unutterably miserable in mind, and with every limb aching, it seemed another step was impossible.

From sheer force of habit I looked at my watch, which had been overlooked by the looters in the Qeshlah. It had been too dark in that barn-like room to see so small a thing. My hands had been felt many times, to see if I had any jewellery; but my wedding ring was so small and their hands so hard and horny that they had not noticed it.

The time, I saw, was 6.40 P.M. Immediately my hand was caught hold of, and the men started shouting all together. A dagger was drawn, and a thrill of terror ran through me. I did not want to die that way. I wrenched my arm free and got the watch off my wrist as quickly as I could, and threw it in their midst, and they settled among themselves the question of its possession.

Then followed a discussion, in very heated tones, where they should take me. All said different names. The easiest name to catch, and the one most often repeated, was that of Sheikh Majid. I caught at this and kept repeating, 'To the house of Sheikh Majid!' Not that I knew him, nor had I the slightest notion who he was; but I was in mortal dread lest any of my captors should take me to his own house.

At last we proceeded. We went across the roof, down some little steps, and through the *khan* for a little. Next we climbed over another broken-down wall and came to the back door of a house.

A man knocked. A woman's voice answered. Then a man came, and after a little delay the door was opened. We crossed a courtyard, through another door, and into a second courtyard. It was almost too dark to see anything clearly. But a man came up and put a lamp near my face and looked at me. He pointed to the blood-stains all over my frock. A long conversation followed. What it was about I had not the remotest idea; but I suppose that the man with the lamp was surprised that an Englishwoman should be in such a state as I was in.

I was indeed in a terrible plight. My topee had gone, and my hair was half down. My frock was, curiously, not much torn, though my petticoat was torn badly; but it was spattered with blood-stains everywhere.

The second door was at length opened, and we stepped through on to the path by the canal, along which so often Billy and I had walked our way to the tennis-court. What a ghastly mockery it all seemed!

When we came near the bridge, I could make out that a huge crowd of people was standing by it. As soon as I saw them, I began screaming again and tried to run back into the courtyard which we had just left. The men with me, however, prevented me and forced me on with them.

Then it dawned on me that the crowd was townspeople, not tribesmen. I pulled at the *abba* of the cleanest looking of my captors and made him take it off. I wrapped it round me, and after that I felt a little safer.

There was a great deal of murmuring as I passed through the crowd. They had obviously recognised me, in spite of the borrowed *abba*. But there was not a tribesman to be seen. All were still busy looting at the Qeshlah, I suppose.

The way led on to where our billet stood. It was now so dark that I could not make out much. But at least I could see that, as far as the outside was concerned, our old home was just as we had left it. The front door was open, it is true; but the curtains were still up at the windows, and the lamp had been lit in the entrance. Nobody appeared to be about.

We passed the billet, turned round the corner, and went down a narrow alley-way. This, I thought, could not lead to a sheikh's house, and I kept on repeating, 'This is not the way to Sheikh Majid's house; take me to Sheikh Majid's house!' But they made me understand that it was the way.

We arrived eventually at a door, at which they knocked. There was immediate silence within, until at last some one answered. This was the beginning of a long conversation through the door, of which I could not gather the purport.

All the while I went on saying, 'This is not Sheikh Majid's house.'

I still had, of course, no idea who the sheikh was, or where his house lay. And certainly, had I known of his identity, I should never have asked to be taken to him. As a matter of fact, as I afterwards learnt, he was a cousin of Sheikh Hamid, the head of those very tribesmen who had murdered our brave men. Apart from that, it will be seen that the house was an exceedingly poor one, and that the sheikh had not enough food to give even to his own women-folk.

Here I was, however, at Sheikh Majid's house, as I had begged to be brought. When the conversation had finished, a heavy wooden bolt was drawn back and the door opened a little way, then pulled wide open. I went through, followed by the others.

There was comparative quiet for a moment, and I looked round the sea of faces, all turned to the door through which we had entered.

I was, as may be imagined, in no state to take in details. There seemed about a hundred people there, perhaps more, all men. What stood out clearly to me above everything else was those cruel-looking curved daggers, of which nearly every one had one stuck in his belt.

The courtyard into which we had come was a square, with rooms leading off all round. There was a mud floor, beaten very hard by the constant passing of feet. Benches were set in a square in the middle. On these some sat, while others stood about. The yard was lit by hurricane lamps, hanging on the wooden beams which supported the roof.

When I realised that the door was shut and bolted, and that I was locked in, I turned and pulled hard at the bolt, but could not move it. I screamed.

Then suddenly I heard, in English, 'It is all right, Mem Sahib, don't be afraid.'

When I looked I saw some of the Indian subordinates who had worked under my husband. There were about eight of them, and with them was Mohammed Din, who had brought us the first news from Table Mountain.

'Are they going to kill me?' was my first question.

'No, no,' said Mohammed Din, 'they will not.'

I would not believe him, and exclaimed to the Indians that I was going to be killed, and probably they also. 'But, Mohammed Din,' I asked him, 'tell them to shoot me when they come. Then it will be soonest over.'

He assured me again that they would not kill me yet. 'You are in their house now, under their protection, and safe for a while.'

This did not convince me. I had seen too much killing in the past hour to believe that I was safe, even for a time.

Now an old man approached, and I heard some one say, 'Sheikh Majid.'

I turned and drew him nearer a lamp, where I could see his face. 'Are you Sheikh Majid?' I asked.

I looked well at him. It was not a pleasing face which I saw. The eyes were small and watery, close together and very shifty, set in a rather long, sallow face, with a white beard. Immediately I felt that I could not trust him.

I stared at him for a long while. Then he suddenly began talking. I tried in vain to understand what he was saying; but he went much too fast for my very limited knowledge of Arabic to grasp his meaning.

At length an Arab boy, who could speak English, came up and began to interpret for me. What the sheikh said was to the effect that I must not be frightened. He would protect me. So long as I was in his house I need have no fear.

Well as this sounded, I was very far from comforted. I felt sure that the sheikh's protestations were false, that he did not mean them at all.

I made my first request, however. My Sahib had been killed, I said, and I must have his body brought to the house.

It was impossible, replied Sheikh Majid.

I begged him desperately to grant my prayer. It was my one desire at the moment, and I implored him to send some one to bring his body to me.

The sheikh repeated that it was impossible; and he appeared disgusted at the idea.

I turned to the Arab boy, and asked why I could not have my Sahib's body.

The boy shook his head. No, he said, it would be very bad. Sheikh Majid could not have him brought to the house.

It was useless to say more, and I was told that I was to be sent to the women's quarters. I was taken to a door, and passed through it out of the courtyard.

Shooting Expeditions

GEORGE-MARIE HAARDT
AND LUCIEN AUDOUIN-DUBREUIL

From the *The Black Journey*, 1927

Killing exotic animals was irresistible sport for Haardt and his expedition. Arriving in Ubangi-Shari (then part of French Equatorial Africa) in February 1925, they had hardly crossed the border from Chad before they began stalking elephants and hippos. Big game was scarce in the Sahara. Having reached the northern edge of Africa's interior forests, carnage beckoned the French adventurers. Using Arab-speaking guides, the expedition left the Saharan region in pursuit of elephants.

George-Marie Haardt and his junior partner, Lucien Audouin-Dubreuil, were professional show-offs. Their first expedition crossed the Sahara from the Mediterranean to Timbuktu in 1921; the second, from French Algeria to Madagascar in 1924 and 1925; and the third began in Damascus in 1931 and ended in Tiensten, China, in 1932. Haardt died in China at the end of the third trip.

The Black Journey is the disturbingly racist account of Haardt's second expedition. Like many of the other writings in this collection, the Western attitudes depicted in Haardt's book make us wince. Haardt and Audouin-Dubreuil were ostentatious imperialists; their attitude toward black Africans is almost a caricature of the Great White Hunter syndrome. Nonetheless, their treks earned them international celebrity status—which was, after all, their objective.

Haardt led "caterpillars" of new Citroën half-track vehicles, each convoy carrying a battalion of scientists, mechanics, photographers, cooks, and even a taxidermist. Films of the expedition's exploits were shown in cinemas around the world, bringing international attention to Citroën, and promoting France's technology, colonization, and supremacy over "less civilized" people.

Ubangi-Shari no longer appears on maps. Today it is the Central African Republic. Gone too is the French Empire, which Haardt and his colleagues believed would be strengthened and expanded using new technologies.

—J. H.

The *tippoy*, a kind of sedan chair, is composed of two long litters on which is placed a cross-legged armchair covered by a little round roof like a gondola. One fares very well in it if the *tippoyeurs* are well trained and know how to step with the care necessary to carry a pitcher full of water without spilling a drop; but if it is a question of entire novices the pitcher has every chance of being empty after five hundred yards have been traversed.

One can imagine the condition of the traveler who is obliged to go for several hundred kilometers in a *tippoy*.

These contrivances require two gangs of four men accompanied by an overseer. It should not be considered that these *tippoyeurs* are mere beasts of burden; they are very proud of their calling, from which they derive both glory and profit; and so we do not fare so badly.

Moreover, several of us have been able to procure mounts, either mules or lean horses. Donkeys will carry the heavier baggage, for the rôle of porter is less distinguished than that of *tippoyeur*. As the load of each porter cannot exceed forty-five pounds, we require more than one hundred men to transport our camp equipment, provisions and cinema apparatus.

In addition, we shall be accompanied by eight Arabic-speaking elephant-hunters in the pay of a certain Malik, and commanded by Gadem.

Gadem and his men seem to correspond in every way to the idea we have formed of the famous Kresh. They are armed with a long lance of flat iron, the traces of which the unfortunate soldier of Ouadda bore in his body;

they prance about like Cossacks; as for Gadem, he is a type of the brigand of the time of Ali Baba.

Iacovleff cannot resist the pleasure of doing his portrait and that of the sultan. The sultan accedes to this with a very bad grace, for by the law of the Prophet it is forbidden to reproduce the features of the human face; after the sitting, Aïm-Gabo goes away furious, without even looking at the drawing, as all Iacovleff's other models are in the habit of doing. This exhibition of bad temper, together with some glances exchanged with Malik, and the conversation of the latter with the illustrious Gadem, causes us some perplexity,

The 135 men of the *safari*, or hunting caravan, are got together within forty-eight hours, and the rations are distributed; on the following morning the long file starts out from Birao toward the northeast, zigzagging through the brush.

The charm of traveling in *safari* fashion is great. It recalls memories of our ancestors. We give extracts of the cinematographic notes made by Léon Poirier on the impressions which we all experienced.

On the Am-Dafok track, Feb. 4, 1925.

Tippoy

The footsteps of eight flat feet are padding over the gray dust of the track through the brush.

We might call it a little house walking along on legs; I am seated in the little house; I watch the regular motion of a porter's back and the flat knife hanging to his elephant-hued loins.

A silent swaying to and fro. . . . Heat. . . . The smell of the negro. . . . Drowsiness. . . . The noise of branches catching. . . . The sound of grass being pushed aside. . . . The brush passes by.

The sun is sinking.

The long caravan under the light of the moon. . . . White in the open glades. . . . Night in the undergrowth. . . . Procession of shadows, shadows of the past: *Tippoys*, sedan chairs, horsemen with assagais, armed men, porters, rough peasants loaded with boxes and wearing apparel.

An owl is hooting as in the past. . . .

During the first day we kill a few antelopes of differing varieties, and numerous birds. At night we form a bivouac in an open space, in accordance with the practice of the brush, more often in a clearing that has been made by recent fires. The view opens out through the leafless bushes. In a huge circle, in the circumference of which fires are lighted every twenty paces, the natives are grouped; our beds are unfolded in the center, and our weapons propped up against a makeshift gun-rack made out of branches. A tree serves to hang our clothes upon; we have to suspend our boots on a branch in order not to find in the morning a snake concealed in them for warmth.

We rise with the sun. The departure of the caravan takes place in some turmoil. The porters are arguing about their loads. There are some laggards whom Maigret and Specht, who are riding behind, vigorously round up.

We see few wild animals; they have reason to hide themselves at the approach of a convoy of one hundred and fifty men.

Specht, whose enthusiasm for hunting has not been quenched by his mistake over the elephant, searches the savanna with a keen look, and frequently questions his companion in front of him:

"Maigret . . . Maigret . . . down there . . . look, a buffalo!"

"No, no, Specht! It is no different from yesterday and the day before; it is an ant-hill."

"Ah! but this time I'm sure of it; it really is one!"

"Well, then, go and see for yourself!"

Specht starts off at a gallop and comes back rather crestfallen, but all the same with the light of faith still in his eyes.

"Maigret, the buffalo . . ."

"What? . . . Was it an ant-hill?"

"No, it was the trunk of a tree . . ."

There is one person who persists in seeing animals where there are not any, and in refusing to look at them where they are: this is Gadem. With his riders he scouts ahead through the brush, or round our flanks, and comes back with a noble air to give us an account of the presence of elephants either more to the left or more to the right, and of how little hope there is of our being able to come up with them.

When he comes to see that this perpetual chapter of accidents rather surprises us, he returns from one of his reconnaissances holding in his hand triumphantly something brown which there is no mistaking.

"Dung, still fresh!" exclaims the experienced Maigret. "The troop cannot be far off."

Gadem remains impassive, and explains that he must go on beforehand and examine the traces of the elephants, rejoining us afterwards by the swamp at Koundouma, where we expect to make our midday halt. When we have received his report we can start off again with him and leave the rest of the caravan.

This seems a prudent course, and as Gadem appears confident of the result we agree to meet him at the swamp of Koundouma.

We settle ourselves under the shade of a huge green tree overhanging the marsh; we cannot see the water on account of the high grass. The prospect in front of us might be like the view over Sologne, or Brière, were it not for the sight of some Latania palms rising here and there.

After we have lunched we shoot some aquatic birds—herons and pelicans—while waiting for Gadem. He arrives at four o'clock, and in polished but roundabout phrases, explains to us the flight of the elephants eastward and his powerlessness to come up with them.

Maigret grumbles, declaring:

"This man is no poacher, he is a gamekeeper; he wishes to prevent us from diminishing the Kresh preserves.

"Gadem, the sultan spoke of you as being one of the greatest of hunters. He can't know you very well, for you are not capable of coming up to the animal after you have discovered its traces."

The blow strikes home; Gadem draws himself up with an offended air.

"Give me five days," he says, "and leave me alone with my men; if I do not bring back proof that I have killed the elephant you may then say that I am no real hunter."

Our minds are already made up, and not caring to utilize the services of Gadem any longer, we generously grant him the liberty he requests. Before taking his departure he dispatches two of his men to find water for his horses; they soon return and lay at our feet a fine python, thirteen feet in length, which they have killed with a blow from a lance just when it was going to dart upon them.

"This is an omen!" exclaims Maigret. "You will see that we shall now have greater luck."

And as if to prove him right, one of our number without having to disturb himself brings down, at a distance of two hundred yards, a big cat which was going toward the marsh in the evening mist. It looks like a panther, but is a tiger-cat of great size. A very rare find.

We camp at Koundouma, and next day in the afternoon at last reach Am-Dafok.

Groups of antelopes are grazing around the swamp, or rather on the swamp, for it gives the appearance of a vast meadow with muddy pools of water here and there.

"*Tetel!*" triumphantly shout the natives, pointing out flocks so numerous and so peaceful that we look mechanically for their invisible shepherds.

Tetel is the native name for the Jackson antelope, which is extremely abundant in this region. Relatively easy to approach, this game will form a valuable accessory for replenishing our *safari* with fresh meat.

A little group of palm trees (Borassus or Latania) from which we can see over the whole extent of the marsh, strikes us as an excellent observatory and an agreeable spot for our bivouac. Here we shall realize for a few days the inexpressible charm of life in the brush.

We each choose our tree and make ourselves comfortable in accordance with our tastes and occupations. Maigret builds for himself a shelter out of palm leaves; Iacovleff plants his easel in the shade, and soon all our interesting trophies of the chase will take their places successively before him. The cinema has its studio; Bergonier, his laboratory, where boxes of arsenical soap form an imposing line and cause much uneasiness by reason of its proximity to our kitchen. Our excellent taxidermist, whose devotion is inexhaustible, is good enough to concern himself with the kitchen, and his boys, with equal nonchalance, take up alternately boxes of arsenical soap and boxes of butter.

Nevertheless, we have a good appetite for dinner. Night falls; silence broods over the solitude, but it is of short duration; soon the yelping of the jackal breaks forth, then the cry of the screeching wildcat, which the hyena mocks with a burst of evil laughter; then, as if to call the world to order, a hoarse and deep note rings out; it is the roar of a lion! After this, all becomes silent once more, but on the outskirts of our camp the fires blaze up, projecting brilliant shafts of clear flame. The natives have understood the meaning this time; they will not all go to sleep again.

The following morning we approach without difficulty a herd of *tetel* while Specht turns the handle of his apparatus. Three antelopes remain stretched out on the grass.

Poirier, in concealment on the right, sees the whole herd go by him at a heavy gallop over a narrow little path, where the animals pass in Indian file under the fire of his lens. There are more than three hundred.

Whether by instinct or terror they follow each other exactly. The whole file stops if one of them slackens speed, without any seeking to get in front of another. Poirier then shows himself, and draws near; the pace of the procession grows quicker, but not an animal changes the direction of its course. This is not due to the ground, which is hard; in a few bounds they could disappear into the long grass. We soon become aware that this open prairie must have formerly been a hollow depression filled with mud; the elephants have left imprints two feet in diameter and three feet in depth; these are veritable pitfalls, very close to each other, in which an antelope would inevitably break its fetlocks. Their flight in Indian file was therefore a wise maneuver.

In order to explore the savanna it seems preferable that each of us should go off in a different direction. As we are passing round the marsh on horseback, before separating, we notice a gray stone standing in a rustic enclosure made of the trunks of palm trees; it is a tomb. We dismount and go inside the enclosure. There is a cross, and an English inscription graven on the stone:

> In ever abiding memory of
> Hugh Drummond Pearson
> D.S.O. R.E.
> President of the Wadaï Darfur Boundary Commission
> Died Dec. 28th, 1922.

Lieutenant-Colonel Pearson fell in the heart of the brush, when he was working in the interest of peace. There he reposes in silence, absolute silence disturbed only by the beasts of the wild. Our emotions are deeply stirred, and it is with slow footsteps and without uttering a word that we pass on, after a few moments of recollection beside this solitary tomb.

We continue our way separately, and meet again at the camp in the evening. We have each made an abundant bag; several kinds of antelope make up the picture: bubal antelopes with flat foreheads like the hinds we find in tapestries, koba antelopes (*adenola kob*), marsh antelopes (*katembourou*, our guides call them), reed antelopes, which the natives call *bouchmat*, springboks, impalas and a kalao, the bustard's bird friend and one of our former acquaintances.

But here comes Bettembourg with his trackers. At his side Bergonier is making eloquent signs from a distance; behind them is Kantou-Bama, who looks after our campfires at night, carrying in his arms an enormous bird with its wing broken; its plumage is black and yellow, it has a long red beak, a fierce eye and hooked claws; it is a stork, to whose foot Kantou-Bama has attached a long cord for safety, which Brahim-Nielli, the tracker, is complacently holding as if it were a handcuff fastened on the wrists of a criminal.

Kantou-Bama takes the stork to Iacovleff's studio, but the bird is decidedly a bad character, for it precipitates itself on our friend's box of water-colors. It would doubtless have made havoc among them if it had not suddenly found itself opposite to a small mirror before which it stopped dumbfounded.

After two days of shooting we have killed thirty large animals of all kinds; the laboratory of the taxidermist looks like a charnel-house. On the trees skins are hanging to dry, on the ground are lying pell-mell hoofs, horns and bones. Bergonier is exultant; all day Moussa has his hands plunged in the arsenical soap and spreads terror among the cooks.

All this dissecting causes an appalling smell, not the least discomfort of which is to attract the vultures, which incessantly hover about. Wild animals likewise keep roaming around us; lions even importune us during the day; a tracker saw two a few hundred yards away from the camp.

One morning, after having heard his roaring during the night quite close, we see the "King of Beasts" at a distance of not more than fifty yards from our protecting line of fires.

It would be interesting to secure a lion by day in order that the hunt might be filmed. Bélès, a tracker skilled in the pursuit of wild animals, successfully enables us to see a lion and a lioness gliding through the tall yellow grass, but the distance is too great. Following the tracks we discover their lair in a bushy thicket, from which a few palm trees stand out. A careful watch through one whole day proves fruitless.

We then try another method, and take up our position in a hiding-place at 3 A.M., in the hope that on their return from their nocturnal roaming they will stop at our bait, a dead antelope.

It is a long wait; dawn comes without any sound of their roar. Nevertheless, something is attracted by our bait; it is a magpie! Then birds of prey arrive from all quarters of the horizon, and soon the antelope is covered by a compact mass of vultures, falcons and marabous. In less than an hour only the carcass will be left. On the following night the hyenas will come and crush up the bones; insects will clear up the crumbs left over from the feast.

A fresh hiding-place is decided upon, but this time we shall pass the whole night in it. Everyone lies down on his bed fully dressed to take a few minutes' rest. We get up at midnight. The moon is still high; the porters take our rifles; the little column steals away in silence.

Our place of concealment is a platform built upon stakes and hidden by the reeds. The natives lay down the koba for the bait at a distance of ninety feet. Then they go back to the camp, and the long wait begins. The moon is sinking in the west. Suddenly we hear a roar coming from a distance of a mile; it approaches nearer; we judge the distance by the gradual crescendo of the deep note: three-quarters of a mile . . . one-half . . . but the beast halts. There is another roar in the direction of the camp. A second lion is roaming around the men and horses.

The moon is now touching the horizon. The pool of water which has been gleaming in the light, becomes gradually darker. A leopard passes by a few yards from our platform; we let him go away; it is not for him that we are on the watch tonight. Soon another roar rises to the south, much nearer this time. Then profound silence. We have the sensation that the lion is approaching; but will he be visible in the dark night? A shadow creeps forward. Should we fire? The shadow stops. It stands up uneasily; it is going to run away. At that moment two shots flash through the obscurity; there is a prolonged roar in reply, it goes away toward the south, grows fainter and ceases.

Next morning Bergonier finds the still warm body of a magnificent male lion stretched out on the dry grass. He has fallen with his face toward the camp whither he was making his way with a dying instinct for battle and vengeance.

The camp has now been at Am-Dafok for a whole week. Our food is beginning to run out. Antelope liver makes an excellent dish, the roots of the palm supply us with delectable hors-d'œuvre, but we have no more salt or sugar, or coffee or tea. We still have a few biscuits left, and a small supply of preserved food; for some time we have had no other drink than the marsh water rendered aseptic and filtered.

We decide to break up our camp tomorrow morning.

A last shot brings down a hippotragus, called *abourou* by the natives. Some of them absolutely refuse to eat the flesh of this animal; these are fetishists; their sorcerers teach them that the meat of the *abourou* is fatal to men. The black Mohammedans in mockery of the "savages"—for so they dub their fetishist brothers—have for their dinner an *abourou* as big as a mule.

Now next morning, just when we are about to start, some of those who partook of *abourou* are seized by strange uneasiness, and soon are writhing under an appalling attack of colic. Panic spreads, and the disorder becomes general in the twinkling of an eye. The porters leave their loads where they are and disappear with cries of dismay. In order to reestablish confidence Bergonier and Maigret rush forward. Maigret stumbles on a metallic object which has been left near the fire among the remnants of the feast. Picking it up, he exclaims:

"Parbleu! This was bound to happen! They have drunk out of the old tins of arsenical soap!"

It is quite true.

"Moussa! . . . Moussa! . . . Quick, the ipecac!" cries Bergonier.

A few seconds later the genuine sufferers are relieved, while the others are radically cured. Is not the fear of ipecac among the ignorant the beginning of wisdom from all antiquity?

After a delay of two hours the safari, burdened with all our hunting trophies, again takes the road to Birao. But we increase the pace and make only two bivouacs en route, one of them being near the Maï-Stour marsh, where we did not stop on our former journey. Specht arms himself with a string at the end of which is fixed a bent pin, and fishes for some silurians; these are doubtless without experience, for an adventure of this kind can never have happened to them before.

Then a personage we have forgotten reappears; it is the illustrious Gadem with his troop of horsemen! They arrive at a gallop through the brush, and Gadem, without uttering a word, detaches from his saddle-bow the tail of an elephant and the end of a trunk—trophies quite recently cut off.

Bibliography

Baker, Sir Samuel. *The Nile Tributaries of Abyssinia and the Sword Hunters of the Hamran Arabs*. London: MacMillan and Company, 1868.

Bartels, Albert. *Fighting the French in Morocco*. London: Alston River, 1932.

Barth, Heinrich. *Travels and Discoveries in North and Central Africa*. Philadelphia: J. W. Bradley, 1860.

Blacker, Captain L. V. S. *On Secret Patrol in High Asia*. London: John Murray, 1922.

Blunt, Lady Anne. *Bedouin Tribes of the Euphrates*. New York: Harper and Brothers, 1879.

Buchanan, Zetton. *In the Hands of the Arabs*. London: Hodder and Stoughton, 1921.

Burnaby, Lieutenant Colonel Frederick Gustavus. *A Ride to Khiva*. London: Cassell, Petter, Galpin and Company, 1878.

Burton, Sir Richard. *Personal Narrative of a Pilgrimage to Al-Madinah and Meccah*. London: George Bell and Sons, 1906.

De Nogales, Rafael. *Memoirs of a Soldier of Fortune*. New York: Garden City Publishing, 1932.

Etherton, Lieutenant P. T. *Across the Roof of the World*. London: Constable and Company, 1911.

Forbes, Rosita. *The Secret of the Sahara: Kufara*. London: Cassell and Company, 1921.

Griffin, Ernest H. *Adventures in Tripoli: A Doctor in the Desert*. London: Philip Allan and Company, 1924.

Haardt, George-Marie and Audouin-Dubreuil, Lucien. *The Black Journey*. New York: Cosmopolitan Book Company, 1927.

Harris, Walter B. *The Land of the African Sultan*. London: Sampson, Low, Marston, Searle and Rivington, 1889.

Haywood, Captain A. H. W. *Through Timbuctu and Across the Great Sahara*. London: Seeley, Service and Company, 1912.

Meakin, Budgett. *The Land of the Moors*. New York: MacMillan and Company, 1901.

Pellow, Thomas. *The Adventures of Thomas Pellow, of Penryn, Mariner*. London: T. Fisher Unwin, 1890.

Perdicaris, Ion "Morocco, 'the Land of the Extreme West' and the Story of My Captivity." *National Geographic*, vol. xvii, 3. Washington: March, 1906.

Rawlinson, Colonel Alfred. *Adventures in the Near East 1918–1922*. New York: Dodd, Mead and Company, 1924.

Reed, John. *The War in Eastern Europe*. New York, Charles Scribner's Sons, 1916.

Sykes, Ella and Sir Percy. *Through the Deserts and Oases of Central Asia*. London: MacMillan, 1920.

Thomas, Lowell. *With Lawrence in Arabia*. New York: Grosset and Dunlap, 1924.

Twain, Mark. *The Innocents Abroad; or, The New Pilgrim's Progress*. London: Chatto and Windus, 1906. (First published as a subscription book in the United States in 1869.)

Vambery, Arminius. *Arminius Vambery, His Life and Adventures*. London: Fisher Unwin, 1884.

The Explorers Club

History and Mission Statement

Founded in 1904, The Explorers Club is a multidisciplinary, professional society dedicated to the advancement of field research, scientific exploration, and the ideal that it is vital to preserve the instinct to explore. The overall mission of the Club is the encouragement of scientific exploration of land, sea, air, and space, with particular emphasis on the physical and biological sciences. The headquarters for the worldwide activities of The Explorers Club and its Chapters is the landmark Lowell Thomas Building on East 70th Street in New York City.

The Club is international in scope, with 3,500 members representing every continent and more than sixty countries. Over the years, membership has included polar explorers Roald Amundsen, Robert E. Peary, Matthew Henson, Ernest Shackleton and Richard C. Byrd; aviators James Doolittle, Charles Lindbergh and Chuck Yeager; underwater pioneers Sylvia Earle, Jacques Piccard, Don Walsh, and Robert Ballard; astronauts John Glenn, Buzz Aldrin, Neil Armstrong, Sally Ride, and Kathryn Sullivan, and cosmonaut Viktor Savinykh; anthropologists Louis Leakey, Richard Leakey, and Jane Goodall; mountaineers Sir Edmund Hillary and Tenzing Norgay; former U.S. Presidents Theodore Roosevelt and Herbert Hoover; and other notables, including journalist Lowell Thomas, explorer/anthropologist Thor Heyerdahl, and biologist Dr. James Watson.

The Explorers Club is a gathering place and unifying force for explorers and field scientists the world over, serving as a base for expedition planning, presentations, meetings, and events. The Club's library and archives holds an unparalleled collection of exploration-related literature, documents, and artifacts. Its unique grants programs provide funding to undergraduate and graduate students who are pursuing field research around the globe.

Today, the importance of The Explorers Club's mission remains as powerful as ever: to be a wellspring for the impulse to explore and to serve as a stimulus for the enduring spirit of exploration and scientific inquiry in human life.

For more information on The Explorers Club, go to www.explorers.org.